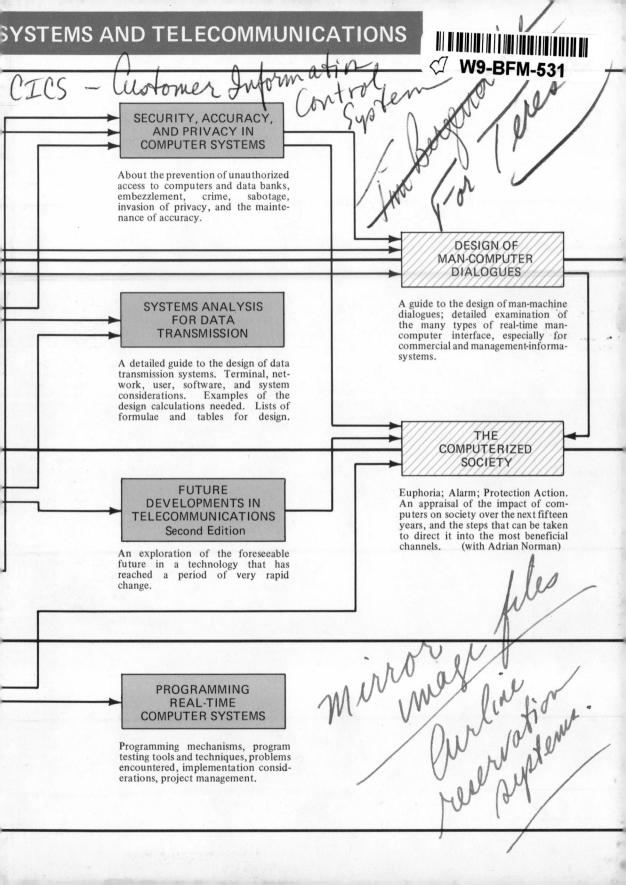

SECURITY, ACCURACY, AND PRIVACY IN COMPUTER SYSTEMS

About the prevention of unauthorized access to computers and data banks, embezzlement, crime, sabotage, invasion of privacy, and the maintenance of accuracy.

DESIGN OF MAN-COMPUTER DIALOGUES

A guide to the design of man-machine dialogues; detailed examination of the many types of real-time man-computer interface, especially for commercial and management-informa-systems.

SYSTEMS ANALYSIS FOR DATA TRANSMISSION

A detailed guide to the design of data transmission systems. Terminal, network, user, software, and system considerations. Examples of the design calculations needed. Lists of formulae and tables for design.

THE COMPUTERIZED SOCIETY

Euphoria; Alarm; Protection Action. An appraisal of the impact of computers on society over the next fifteen years, and the steps that can be taken to direct it into the most beneficial channels. (with Adrian Norman)

FUTURE DEVELOPMENTS IN TELECOMMUNICATIONS
Second Edition

An exploration of the foreseeable future in a technology that has reached a period of very rapid change.

PROGRAMMING REAL-TIME COMPUTER SYSTEMS

Programming mechanisms, program testing tools and techniques, problems encountered, implementation considerations, project management.

p. 211

query languages {
IQF – interactive query facility;
GIS – generalized information system.

PRINCIPLES OF DATA-BASE
MANAGEMENT

A *James Martin* BOOK

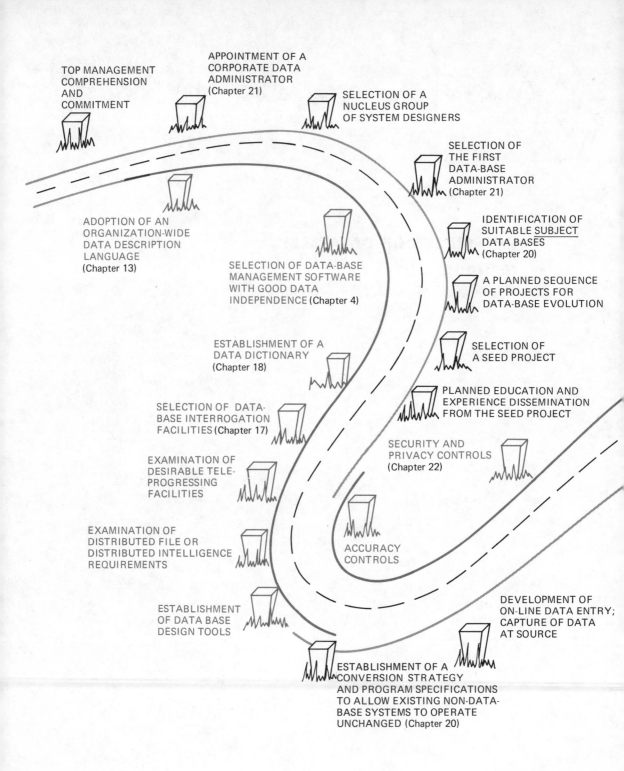

TOP MANAGEMENT COMPREHENSION AND COMMITMENT

APPOINTMENT OF A CORPORATE DATA ADMINISTRATOR (Chapter 21)

SELECTION OF A NUCLEUS GROUP OF SYSTEM DESIGNERS

SELECTION OF THE FIRST DATA-BASE ADMINISTRATOR (Chapter 21)

ADOPTION OF AN ORGANIZATION-WIDE DATA DESCRIPTION LANGUAGE (Chapter 13)

IDENTIFICATION OF SUITABLE SUBJECT DATA BASES (Chapter 20)

SELECTION OF DATA-BASE MANAGEMENT SOFTWARE WITH GOOD DATA INDEPENDENCE (Chapter 4)

A PLANNED SEQUENCE OF PROJECTS FOR DATA-BASE EVOLUTION

ESTABLISHMENT OF A DATA DICTIONARY (Chapter 18)

SELECTION OF A SEED PROJECT

SELECTION OF DATA-BASE INTERROGATION FACILITIES (Chapter 17)

PLANNED EDUCATION AND EXPERIENCE DISSEMINATION FROM THE SEED PROJECT

EXAMINATION OF DESIRABLE TELE-PROGRESSING FACILITIES

SECURITY AND PRIVACY CONTROLS (Chapter 22)

EXAMINATION OF DISTRIBUTED FILE OR DISTRIBUTED INTELLIGENCE REQUIREMENTS

ACCURACY CONTROLS

ESTABLISHMENT OF DATA BASE DESIGN TOOLS

DEVELOPMENT OF ON-LINE DATA ENTRY; CAPTURE OF DATA AT SOURCE

ESTABLISHMENT OF A CONVERSION STRATEGY AND PROGRAM SPECIFICATIONS TO ALLOW EXISTING NON-DATA-BASE SYSTEMS TO OPERATE UNCHANGED (Chapter 20)

MILESTONES ON THE ROAD TO A
COMPREHENSIVE INFORMATION SYSTEM

PLANNED INTERRELATION
OF GEOGRAPHICALLY
SEPARATE DATA BASES
(Chapter 12)

EXTENSION OF
DATA COMMUNICATIONS
NETWORK

INFORMATION
QUALITY
CONTROLS
(Chapter 23)

PLANNED USE OF
DISTRIBUTED
FACILITIES

ADOPTION BY USER GROUPS
OF DATA-BASE INTERROGATION
LANGUAGES (Chapter 17)

IMPROVEMENT
OF DATA
SEARCHING
CAPABILITIES
(Chapter 11)

DEVELOPMENT
OF FUNCTIONAL
INFORMATION
SYSTEMS
(Chapter 6)

DEVELOPMENT
OF ON-LINE
OPERATIONS
SYSTEMS
(Chapter 6)

ON-LINE FACILITIES PERMITTING
NON-PROGRAMMERS TO SEARCH
AND MANIPULATE THE DATA
(Chapter 17)

USE OF PROGRAM
AND DIALOGUE
GENERATORS TO
AVOID APPLICATION
PROGRAMMING

AIDS FOR DATA-
BASE MONITORING
AND PERFORMANCE
IMPROVEMENT

DEVELOPMENT OF A
SEARCH ENGINE

IMPLEMENTATION OF A
DISTRIBUTED DATA-BASE
NETWORK (Chapter 12)

AUTOMATED
DATA-BASE
ORGANIZATION

PRINCIPLES

OF DATA-BASE
MANAGEMENT

JAMES MARTIN

IBM Systems Research Institute

PRENTICE-HALL, INC., Englewood Cliffs, New Jersey

Library of Congress Cataloging in Publication Data

MARTIN, JAMES
 Principles of data-base management.

 Includes bibliographical references and index.
 1. Data base management.   I. Title.
QA76.9.D3M37   001.6'442   75-29054
ISBN 0-13-708917-1

Principles of Data-Base Management
James Martin

10

Printed in the United States of America

PRENTICE-HALL INTERNATIONAL, INC., *London*
PRENTICE-HALL OF AUSTRALIA, PTY. LTD., *Sydney*
PRENTICE-HALL OF CANADA, LTD., *Toronto*
PRENTICE-HALL OF INDIA PRIVATE LIMITED, *New Delhi*
PRENTICE-HALL OF JAPAN, INC., *Tokyo*
PRENTICE-HALL OF SOUTHEAST ASIA (PTE.) LTD., *Singapore*

TO CHARITY

CONTENTS

x

PART IV MANAGEMENT CONSIDERATIONS

PREFACE

INTENT   One of the most badly needed courses in universities, business schools, and other establishments which teach computing is a course on the realities of data-base technology. The 1970's is the decade of the data base. Probably the biggest difference between the next generation of computers and the present will be massive on-line storage and its software. By the end of the 1970's, much of the computing in industry and government will relate to the data bases which have been painfully constructed piece by piece, and management effectiveness will relate to the quality of their organization's data sources and the versatility with which they can be used.

At the time of writing, data base technology is widely misunderstood. Its role as the foundation stone of future data processing is often not appreciated. The techniques used in many organizations contain the seeds of immense future difficulties. Data independence is often thrown to the winds. Data organizations in use prevent the data being employed as it should be. And most educational establishments do not yet teach a data base course. This book is being used at the IBM Systems Research Institute as the text for such a course.

The book covers the topics of logical and physical data structures, data security, accuracy and privacy, and dialogues with a data-base system terminal, in what is considered sufficient detail for an introductory text. These topics are covered in more detail in some of the author's books listed on the front endpapers.

ACKNOWLEDGEMENTS   The author wishes to thank many students who have reviewed the text critically. He is very grateful for the detailed comments from Mr. R. M. Gale, Dr. E. F. Codd, Mr. R. W. Holliday, Mr. H. S. Meltzer and Mr. John Mahony of AT&T. The author is especially grateful to his wife for her assistance, and to Miss Cora Tangney who helped with the manuscript. Last, and most important, he would like to thank the late Dr. Kopley whose encouragement will bear fruit for decades.

JAMES MARTIN

INDEX OF BASIC CONCEPTS

The basic concepts, principles, and terms that are explained in this book are listed here along with the page on which an introductory explanation or definition of them is given. There is a complete index at the end of the book.

PART I WHY DATA BASE?

Knowledge is power.

Francis Bacon

He who runs the information runs the show.

Joseph Goebbels

1 CORPORATE DATA BASES

It is pleasant, now that the world of computers has become so complex, to let one's imagination drift back to the days of Dickens. In those days data processing was done by a clerk with a quill pen who was perched on a high stool and perhaps wearing a top hat. In front of him he had a set of thick and well-bound ledgers. If an order were made for a certain quantity of goods, a clerk would deal with this transaction in its entirety. He might look at his stock sheets to see whether the order could be fulfilled from stock or whether some of it had to be manufactured. He would update the order book, and if any goods were sent, he would modify the stock sheets to make out a bill for the customer and make an entry on the appropriate page of a customer ledger—a simple process which was easy to understand. If anyone had any query about the state of the business, about a certain item of stock, or about an outstanding debt of a customer, the clerk could turn to the appropriate pages of his ledgers and immediately produce the answer. One can imagine such a clerk today taking orders by telephone and answering queries over the telephone. He would balance his books at the end of each day, and if costing figures were required, he could maintain them so that they were as up-to-date as required.

However, admirable as the methods of the Dickensian clerk were, they could work only in a fairly small company. As the company grew, the size of the ledgers increased until several clerks were needed to maintain them. Division of labor made the job easier, and one clerk would maintain the stock sheets while another did the billing, and so forth. Earlier in this century various means for mechanization were introduced, and to make efficient use of them, the work was split up into batches. For example, several hundred transactions may have been grouped into a batch. One accounting function would be carried out on all the transactions by one clerk or one machine, and then the next function would be performed by another clerk or another machine. When punched-card accounting was introduced it became economical to have very large batches. Many trays of cards would be fed through one machine before the setup of that machine was changed for the next function it would perform. Similarly, with the use of magnetic tape on computers, large tape files would be processed with one program before the file was sorted and made ready for the next operation. In working this way the flexibility of the old clerical methods was lost. It was no longer possible to give one transaction individual treatment. It was no longer possible to give quick answers to inquiries about status of the account, or the credit worthiness of a customer, or the amount of an item in stock. Or, at least, if such an inquiry was made, the answer might be a week or more out-of-date. When items were to be posted it was necessary for the computer to read every item in the file as it scanned its way to the ones to be updated, and every item had often to be written out afresh on a new tape, whether it was updated or not.

Batch processing with data rigidly divided into separate files for each application was not the ideal way to operate. It would have been much more convenient for management to have all the information about running their organization up-to-date and at their fingertips. Because of the nature of data-processing techniques, management was living with a compromise. Today the compromise has been in existence for so long that it has become the accepted method of operation, and little thought is given to its desirability.

The use of a data base is like having a superbly fast and brilliant Dickensian clerk who keeps data for many applications. He organizes his books so that minimum writing is necessary and so that he can search the books quickly to answer any queries that may come along. Unlike his pedestrian predecessors who could write or read items in only one ledger, he rushes from one set of data to another collecting together separate items to respond to highly varied requests for information. He is a godsend to management.

Executives often need information which spans departments or spans traditional boundaries in the corporation such as the engineering, accounting, personnel, production, and marketing functions. They need information on personnel implications of marketing decisions, or the impact on production of a new distribution strategy, or the labor costs associated with higher sales. Where each department has its own batch processing operations, the computer is of little value in answering such questions. However with a data-base approach the Dickensian super-clerk rushes from one department's books to another, searching and correlating the data. The structure of the data that are stored is agreed upon centrally so that interdepartmental usage is possible.

The data within a corporation (or other organization) will increasingly be regarded as a basic resource needed to run the corporation. As with other basic resources, professional management and organization of the data are needed. The importance of efficient use of data for production control, marketing, accounting, planning, and other functions will become so great in a computerized corporation that it will have a major effect on the growth and survival of corporations in a competitive marketplace. In government departments and the massive data factories of modern man, the Dickensian super-clerks will make the difference between data being used efficiently, facilitating delicate control mechanisms, and data being a labor-consuming encumbrance of sluggish bureaucracy.

The value of data depends on the uses to which they are put. Often today, data needed in an important decision-making process exist somewhere in an organization in a machine-readable form but are not available to the decision makers when they need them. Furthermore, the cost of producing new computer programs and modifying old ones is often extraordinarily high because the data are not in the right form. To make data as useful as possible and to control system development cost, appropriate design of data systems is necessary. Decision makers can have far better information than they had before computers, and they can have it immediately when they need it. However, the task of building up the information sources is exceedingly complex, and many managers have underestimated the difficulties involved.

The data both for routine operations, such as invoicing and payroll, and for the support of decision making whether computerized or not will reside in computer storage units. A corporation will have various different collections of data for different purposes in different locations. They may be linked by telecommunications to the machines or people who employ them. They can differ widely in their structure.

A collection of data designed to be used by different programmers is called a *data base*. We will define it as *a collection of interrelated data stored together with controlled redundancy to serve one or more applications in an optimal fashion; the data are stored so that they are independent of programs which use the data; a common and controlled approach is used in adding new data and modifying and retrieving existing data within the data base.* One system is said to contain a collection of data bases if they are each entirely separate in structure.

In earlier data processing one or more "files" of records were kept for each application. The intention of a data base is to allow the same collection of data to serve as many applications as is useful. Hence, a data base is often conceived of as the repository of information needed for running certain functions in a body such as a corporation, factory, university, or government department. Such a data base permits not only the retrieval of data but also the continuous modification of data needed for the control of operations. It may be possible to "search" the data base to obtain answers to queries or information for planning purposes. The collection of data may serve several departments, often cutting across political boundaries.

In the much publicized dream of a data base a corporation, or other organization, keeps all of its data in a large reservoir in which a diversity of data users can go fishing. Such a data base would be highly complex, and in general the dream is far from being achieved in reality. It may remain a worthy goal of data processing decades hence. A complex data base has to be built up stage by stage. In reality today most data bases serve a varied, but limited, set of applications.

One computer may use many different data bases. Eventually the data bases for separate related functions may become combined where this integration can increase the efficiency or usefulness of the overall system.

A major task for most corporations over the ten years ahead is to decide what data bases they need, where they are best located, what data should be stored in them, and how they should be organized. Large progressive corporations already store a gigantic amount of information in their computer storage units yet realize it is only beginning. The amount of data stored will increase drastically, and the ways the data are organized will be fundamentally changed to increase their usefulness.

DATA ITEMS *The smallest unit of data that has meaning to its users* is called a *data item*. It has traditionally been called a *field* and is now also called a *data element* or *elementary item*. (Computer people change the names they use for concepts as capriciously as fashion designs.) We use the term *data item* throughout this book because it is the word used by the CODASYL committee [1].†

Data items are the molecules of the data base. There are atoms and sub-atomic particles composing each molecule (bits and bytes), but they do not convey meaning in their own right and so are of little concern to the users.

The data items are grouped together to form *records*, and a program usually reads or writes whole records. A set of data items can be grouped together in different ways to form different records for different purposes. A named group of data items within a record is referred to as a *data aggregate* in some structures, or *segment* in others.

The types of data items that are used in a corporation have to be given names and must be defined. Many corporations are in the process of building a *dictionary* specifying and standardizing the types of data items in their corporate data bases. In a payroll application the data items have names such as GROSS MONTHLY PAY, FEDERAL INCOME TAX DEDUCTION, EMPLOYEE NAME, and SOCIAL SECURITY NUMBER. In a purchasing application they have names such as SUPPLIER NUMBER, SUPPLIER NAME, INVOICE DATE, QUANTITY ORDERED, and so forth. As the desire to analyze the corporate activity develops—a natural by-product of computer usage—more elaborate data items are needed, such as QUANTITY OF DELIVERIES LATE YEAR-TO-DATE FROM THIS SUPPLIER. Large corporations have more than 10,000 data items, with the number still growing rapidly.

Different computer applications, serving different departments of the corporation, can share many of the same data items. An employee's name, a part number,

†Numbers in brackets refer to items in the section of references at the back of the book.

a customer order, and the details of these need not be separately recorded for each different application or department that uses them (as they often have been in the past). They can be recorded once in a standard fashion and the data organized in such a way that they can be used for many different purposes.

The standardization and definition of this large number of data items is a lengthy operation and is made longer because different departments often define the same item differently or disagree about its precise meaning. Many corporations have not yet reached the stage of standardizing the corporate data items, but this is an essential step toward building up the data bases they will eventually need.

One corporation which is spending considerable effort on standardizing the definitions of its data items writes as follows:

"Common records at each location will increase our effectiveness in. . .interpreting and assisting with another plant's problems. . .transferring or promoting personnel to other locations. . .transferring product responsibilities. . .exchanging product information. . .starting up new plants. . . . Will be of great significance to new people joining the company. . . . It will be easier for personnel to exchange information when that information has a common meaning. . . . Other areas of interplant communications will be substantially improved. . .faster, more accurate communications. . .faster response to changing conditions. . .shorter lead times. . . improved performance at lower cost. . .will result."[2]

The difficulties of linking together or integrating the data base, and of standardizing the data items, can be particularly acute in a corporation with several divisions or plants, which have each evolved their own ways of keeping accounting, engineering, sales, production, or other data. In some corporations the struggle for standardization of computer-processable data will go on for many years. It can be a Herculean task—data-processing-man's equivalent of the Augean stables.

DATA-BASE   For the man who presides over the task of developing a
ADMINISTRATOR   data base a new job title has been created: *data-base*
                       administrator.

The data-base administrator is the custodian of the data—or that part of them which his system relates to. He controls the overall structure of the data. It is a very important job that combines a heady mixture of technology and organizational politics.

Note that being *custodian* of the data is quite separate from being its *owner*. A bank manager is the custodian of what is in his bank vault but not its owner. A department or an individual may *own* the data. The data-base administrator is responsible for safekeeping and controlling the data. The data may be *used* by any persons who are given authority to use them.

Note further that controlling the data does not mean that the data-base administrator knows the contents of records. He knows that the PAYROLL record contains a SALARY data item, but he does not know the value recorded in this data item; indeed he is specifically locked out of that data item so that he cannot read it. However, if the SALARY data item must be expanded from six digits to seven digits, only the data-base administrator can accomplish this change.

The data-base administrator maintains the *overall* view of the data in his domain. He encourages standardization of data items and determines what data structures and layouts will be best for the data users *as a whole*. He attempts to referee the feuds that develop between departments or divisions about the nature of the data.

If an application programmer wants to create a new type of record, to modify an old record by including new data items, or to expand the size of a data item, he must apply to the data-base administrator for permission. The data-base administrator will make suitable arrangements to modify the data structures in whatever manner he thinks best for the system as a whole. An application programmer or a systems analyst working on one application is not permitted to change the overall data structures; only the data-base administrator or the staff with a global viewpoint can be familiar with the overall economics of the data.

There is a variety of other functions associated with being the keeper of a corporation's data. We will discuss those functions more fully in Chapter 21 after we have discussed the many aspects of data-base organization. Meanwhile, we will make references to the data-base administrator as having the global view of how a data-base is organized. In reality the data-base administrator is often a department or group rather than one man. A complete understanding of the data base, its organization, its economics, its design criteria, and requirements of its many users may be too much for one man.

HIGH-LEVEL DATA ADMINISTRATION   A large corporation has many data bases, many data processing centers, and often many data-base administrators. It is steadily becoming recognized that top-management involvement is needed in the planning of the overall information resources of the organization. One indivdual in the top ranks of the organization should be responsible for that organization's data—both computerized and non-computerized. This individual has become referred to with the title *data administrator*. The custodian of a data base is also sometimes called "data administrator". In this book we reserve the term *data administrator* for the top mangement job and recommend that this should be distinguished from the lower level more technical job of a *data-base administrator*.

Chapter 21 discusses data administration and data-base administration.

2 DATA BASICS

In this chapter we will describe some of the basic concepts of data storage. A reader knowledgeable in data processing may skip it, with a glance at the figures.

FILE HARDWARE   There is a fundamental difference between *on-line* and *off-line* storage. An *on-line* device, whether it is a terminal, a printer, a storage unit, or other machine, is one the computer can access without human intervention. *On-line storage* is storage readable by the computer without human intervention. Magnetic tape on the shelves of a tape library is not on-line; it must be loaded by an operator. Once loaded onto a tape unit the magnetic tape is "on-line."

Again, there is a fundamental difference between a *sequential-access* and a *direct-access* storage device. The direct-access device (also called *random-access*) can move its reading mechanism directly, at random, to any record that is to be read. The sequential-access device cannot go at random to any record but has to pass sequentially over the records until it finds the one that is needed. A machine for reading punched cards is a sequential-access device because it has to read the cards in sequence. If it could take a card out of the middle of the deck as a human being might, then it would be a random-access device.

Figure 2.1 summarizes these categories of storage device. Direct-access devices which do not have any mechanical moving parts can read any piece of data as soon as they are instructed to do so. The time taken to read the data might be a millionth of a second or so. Direct-access devices which store a substantial quantity of data are electromechanical rather than purely electronic—for example, disk units. When these are instructed to read data there is a time delay of a fraction of a second before the data are read. A reading mechanism may have to be moved into position in an operation called a *seek*.

8

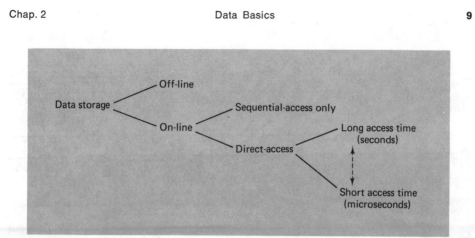

Figure 2.1   Categories of storage devices.

Decades hence, all data may be stored in electronic devices which will enable them to be read almost instantaneously and searched very rapidly. Until then, many constraints will be placed on the physical organization of data by the time lags associated with mechanical devices.

A tape unit (Fig. 2.2) is a sequential-access device; a disk unit is a direct-access device because it can move its access mechanism directly to the track on which a required record resides. Figure 2.3 shows some direct-access devices.

If we were storing music rather than data, we might refer to a jukebox as a random-access or direct-access device. It will go directly to a record of the Beatles when you instruct it from your "terminal" at a cafe table. On the other hand, an ordinary tape recorder is not random-access. You take a tape from the shelf if it is off-line (very much as in Fig. 2.2) and load it on your tape recorder; then because the tape contains many songs, you must scan sequentially through it to find the one you want. The jukebox could conceivably have been on the other end of a telephone line and you could have selected, and listened to, the Beatles over the telephone. The tape recorder could not, because there is no automatic mechanism for selecting and loading the tape. Similarly, data stored on magnetic tapes are not quickly accessible nor automatically accessible by telecommunication links.

A disk file is a random-access device for storing data, and one is shown in Fig. 2.3. It makes a large quantity of data quickly available to the computer. The computer can read, or update, any item on the files at random in a fraction of a second by moving its read/write mechanism to the track on which the data reside. A fast response cannot be given to a terminal inquiry if the data in question reside on a tape but can if they reside on a disk loaded onto the disk unit in Fig. 2.3. Some types of disks reside permanently on their disk unit and others can be removed so that they become off-line disks or stored in libraries along with tape.

The tape library of the Firestone Tire & Rubber Company's computer center at Akron, Ohio—a fireproof vault containing 18,000 tapes and documentation.

The UNISERVO 14 tape subsystem used on the Sperry UNIVAC 90/60 and 90/70 computer systems.

Figure 2.2 A tape library and tape units.

IBM 3410 tape units being loaded. These units are designed primarily for small computers such as the IBM System/3.

Figure 2.2—Continued.

The NCR 656 disk unit can have one removable disk, and optionally one fixed disk. Data from these is transferred at 312,000 characters per second.

A single disk (platter) storing over 4.8 million characters, used in the NCR 656 disk unit (above).

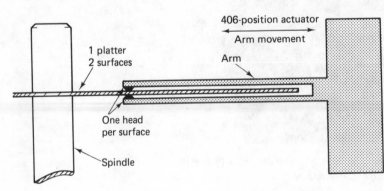

The access mechanism of the NCR 656 disk unit. The access arm can be moved to any of 406 tracks.

Figure 2.3 Direct-access storage devices.

A diskpack being loaded into the IBM 3330 Direct Access Storage Device. The diskpack contains up to 200 million characters.

Cartridges being loaded into the IBM 3850 Mass Storage System. Each cartridge contains up to 50 million characters.

The IBM 3330 disk unit—up to 1.6 billion characters stored.

The IBM 3850 mass storage system—up to 472 billion characters stored.

Figure 2.3—Continued.

Storage of data on magnetic tape has the advantage of economy. Storage of data on disks or other random-access devices has the advantage of permitting automatic access to any item of data *quickly*. Because of the long time it takes to scan tape files, requests for access to these files are normally grouped together, sorted into the same order as the tape records, and processed in a *batch*.

Although records on some of the storage devices in Fig. 2.3 can be read in a fraction of a second, this is still not fast enough for some potential applications. Some of the questions which managers or other staff would like answered at their terminals require an examination of a large number of records, sometimes hundreds or thousands. Sometimes a large number of operations is needed in order to find what a user is looking for. It would be desirable to have a file mechanism or "search engine" which could *search* through many items at very high speed looking for items with particular characteristics. This can be accomplished only if the computer can have very fast access to data and switch its attention from one data item to another at electronic speeds without having to move any mechanical device.

Generally, the faster the data can be accessed, the more expensive is the storage medium. Printed paper is cheap; machine-readable punched cards are more expensive; storage on disk is more expensive than storage on tape; and purely electronic storage is more expensive than storage on disk.

Table 2.1 shows some order-of-magnitude figures for cost per bit, size, and access time of today's storage devices. It will be seen that they spread over a very wide range. The systems designer has the job of selecting appropriate devices from this list and fitting them together to form a cost-effective system. He may use several levels of storage device, some being small and fast, others being large and slow. The relative costs are changing. The cost per item stored on disk has dropped drastically, and larger, slower electromechanical storage units give a much lower cost per bit than disk. New techniques promise to make electronic storage cost drop at a rate that would make my stockbroker run out of superlatives.

It will be seen in Table 2.1 that there is a large gap in access time between the storage devices with no moving parts (i.e., entirely electronic) and those with moving parts. As the costs drop and the technologies change, this access-time gap will nevertheless remain, and for many years in the future the electronic storage devices will be backed up by electromechanical devices with moving parts. Figure 2.4 illustrates the access mechanisms in use on direct-access storage units.

The rapidly changing hardware technology has an important implication for data-base design. The storage devices in most installations are going to change, and so data-base techniques must be used that permit the old application programs and their data to operate successfully with fundamentally changed hardware.

Table 2.1 Typical cost per bit, size, and access time of today's on-line storage technologies (order-of-magnitude figures); cost includes the transport mechanism cost

Type of Storage	Cost Per Bit	Size of Storage (*Millions of Bits*)	Access Time	
Register	$10	0.001	0.01 microsecond	
High-speed cache	$1	0.01	0.1 microsecond	
Main memory	10 cents	1; 10	0.5 microsecond	
Large core storage	1 cent	10; 100	5 microseconds	⎫ Access-time
Drum and fixed-head disk	0.1 cent	10; 100	0.01 second	⎬ gap
Movable-head disk	0.01 cent	100; 1000; 10,000	0.1 second	⎭
Magnetic strip	0.001 cent	1000 to 10,000	1 second	
Mass (archival) store	0.0001 cent	100,000 to 1,000,000	10 seconds	

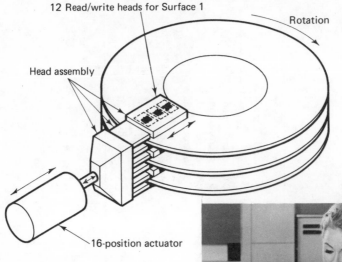

12 Read/write heads for Surface 1

Rotation

Head assembly

16-position actuator

The NCR 655 disk pack has six recording surfaces on its three disks. Each surface is served by 12 read/write heads which move in and out together on a single actuator (seek) arm. There are 16 positions for the actuator arm, enabling it to read or write 192 tracks per surface.

Left: A typical 10-surface disk and a seek arm with one read/write head per surface.

Figure 2.4 Access mechanisms on direct-access storage devices.

The cartridge selector in the Control Data mass storage system picking up or returning a stored cartridge. The selector transfers cartridges between *x-y* storage locations and a cartridge transport.

The cartridge accessor fetching or replacing a cartridge on the IBM 3850 mass storage system. The cartridge contents are staged to a 3330 disk storage.

Figure 2.4—Continued.

Entity: An employee.

Below is a schema. If the attribute values in the box were removed.

*— * When filled with data this is "an instance of the schema."*

Name of the attribute:	Employee-number	Name	Sex	Grade	Date	Department	Skill-code	Title	Salary
Form of representation:	N5	AV	B1	N2	N6	N3	N2	AV	N4
	53730	JONES BILL W	1	03	100335	044	73	ACCOUNTANT	2000
	28719	BLANAGAN JOE E	1	05	101019	172	43	PLUMBER	1800
	53550	LAWRENCE MARIGOLD	0	07	090932	044	02	CLERK	1100
	79632	ROCKEFELLER FRED	1	11	011132	090	11	CONSULTANT	5000
	15971	ROPLEY ED S	1	13	021242	172	43	PLUMBER	1700
	51883	SMITH TOM P W	1	03	091130	044	73	ACCOUNTANT	2000
	36453	RALNER WILLIAM C	1	08	110941	044	02	CLERK	1200
	41618	HORSERADISH FREDA	0	07	071235	172	07	ENGINEER	2500
	61903	HALL ALBERT JR	1	11	011030	172	21	ARCHITECT	3700
	72921	FAIR CAROLYN	0	03	020442	090	93	PROGRAMMER	2100

Name of the attribute:
Form of representation:
Value of the attribute:
Record or segment

Primary key

Secondary keys

Entity identifier

A set of values of one data-item type

Some attributes are themselves entity identifiers of another file.

Figure 2.5

18

ENTITIES
AND ATTRIBUTES

We will refer to items about which we store information as *entities*. An entity may be a tangible object such as an employee, a part, or a place. It may be nontangible, such as an event, a job title, a customer account, a profit center, or an abstract concept. An entity has various attributes which we may wish to record, such as color, monetary value, or name. Often in data processing we are concerned with a collection of similar entities such as employees, and we wish to record information about the same attributes of each of them. A programmer commonly maintains a *record* about each entity, and a data item in each record relates to each attribute. Similar records are grouped into *files*. The result, shown in Fig. 2.5, is a two-dimensional array.

Inside the box in Fig. 2.5 is a set of data items. The value of each data item is shown. Each row of data items relates to a particular entity. Each column contains a particular type of data item, relating to a particular type of attribute. At the top of the diagram, outside the box, the names of the attributes are written. The leftmost column in the box contains the data items which *identify* the entity. The entity in this example is a person, an employee. The attribute referred to as the entity identifier in this case is EMPLOYEE NUMBER.

Such a two-dimensional array is sometime referred to as a *flat file*. The use of flat files dates back to the earliest days of data processing when the file might have been on punched cards. Each card in a file or deck of cards such as that in Fig. 2.6 might contain one record, relating to one entity. Certain card columns were allocated to each data-item type, or attribute, and were called a *field*. When magnetic tapes replaced decks of cards and disks replaced magnetic tapes, many programmers retained their view of data as being organized into flat files. No matter how the data are stored in a data base, the software must present the data to the application program in flat-file if that is the way the program is written (glance ahead to Fig. 4.6).

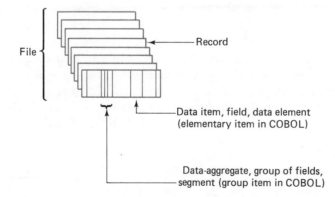

Figure 2.6   A flat file, showing the wording commonly used to describe the application programmer's view of data. Most decks of punched cards are flat files.

ATTRIBUTE   The collection of bits or characters representing a par-
VALUES   ticular data-item value must be associated with the
                       data item which has that value. The data item repre-
sents an attribute, and the attribute must be associated with the relevant entity.
One attribute has a special significance in that it identifies the entity. A collection
of bits or characters representing a single data-item value could exist *independently*
of any information that is stored. It takes on meaning only when it is associated
with the data items which assume that value. We could, for example, permanently
store the data-item values BLUE, ORANGE, and PURPLE WITH GREEN
STRIPES in a location separate from the records, and these values could be associated at a later time with specific data items.

Figure 2.5 shows below the name of the attribute, the form of encoding used
for representing the attribute value. The attribute values must be stored using
predetermined forms of encoding. Common types of representation are as follows:

Alphanumeric characters

Decimal, fixed-point numbers

Decimal, floating-point numbers

Binary, fixed-point numbers

Binary, floating-point numbers

Bit strings

The representation will indicate whether the data item is fixed length or variable
length, and if fixed length, how long.

In Fig. 2.5 the representations have meanings such as the following:

N6 = decimal, fixed-point, six digits

AV = alphanumeric, variable-length

B1 = binary, 1 bit

The attribute names and representations will not be recorded in the file,
although they should be recorded elsewhere, for example, in a data dictionary
which lists the names and types of all data items in the data base.

Note that some of the attribute values may themselves be the names or
identifiers of entities in another file. DEPARTMENT in Fig. 2.5 is an attribute
of the entity EMPLOYEE. Elsewhere there may be a DEPARTMENT file giving
the attribute values of each department.

LOGICAL AND   The form in which the data are actually stored does
PHYSICAL DATA   not necessarily resemble the form in which they are
                                              presented to the application program. The application
programmer's view of the data may be much simpler than the actual data and
tailored to his own application. The data structure which the application program
employs is referred to as a *logical* structure. The data structure, which is actually
stored on tape, disks, or other media, is called a *physical* structure. The words
logical and *physical* will be used to describe various aspects of data, *logical* always
referring to the way the programmer or end user sees it and *physical* always referring to the way the data are recorded on the storage medium.

   The difference between logical and physical records had a humble beginning.
When records were first stored on tape, the *interrecord gap* between records was
long compared with the records themselves. The gaps wasted much space, so it
was economical to have lengthy physical records. Many logical records were
therefore grouped into one physical record. The software separated them when
they were presented to an application program and combined them when they
were written on tape.

   Today the differences between logical and physical data can be much more
complex. The linkages among data are often different in the programmer's view
and in the physical organization (for example the linkage between a factory *part*
record and a record for the supplier who supplies that part) We use the terms
logical relationship and *logical data description* to describe the programmer's
view. *Physical relationship* and *physical data description* describe actual ways in
which data are stored. The reasons the logical and physical views of the data are
different will be discussed later in the book. It is a function of the software to
convert from the programmer's logical statements and descriptions to the physical
reality and back again.

   Figure 2.7 shows an example of different logical and physical structure.
Physical records on a disk contain logical records which are *chained* together;
i.e., a pointer in one logical record links it to another. The programmer requires a
file of logical records in the sequence of the chain. He does not necessarily know
about the chain. The software presents his program with logical records in the
required sequence. Other programs may be given records in a different sequence.
Many different types of data structures are possible.

   This capability of software to convert from one data structure to another is
the key to many of the advantages we will illustrate in using a data base rather
than the separate files that were used in earlier days.

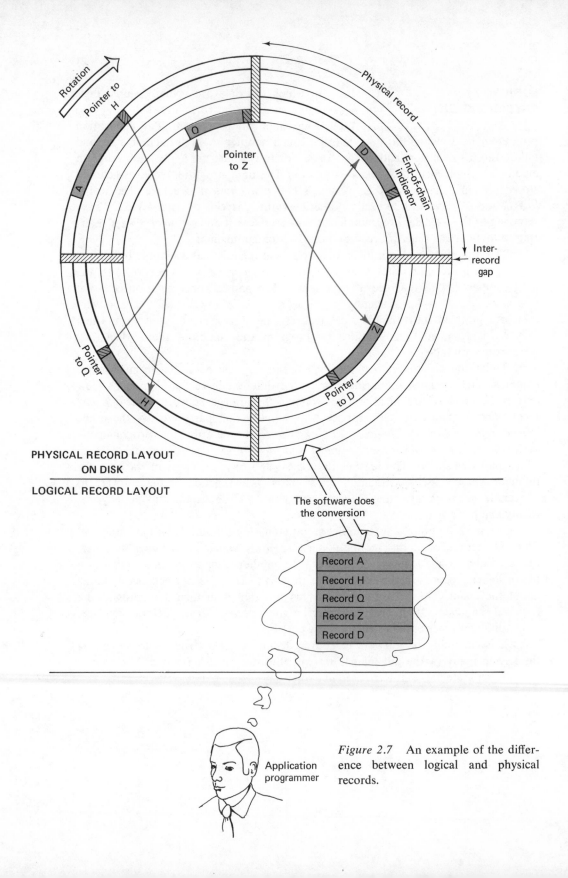

Rotation

Pointer to H

Physical record

Pointer to Z

End-of-chain indicator

Inter-record gap

Pointer to Q

Pointer to D

PHYSICAL RECORD LAYOUT ON DISK

LOGICAL RECORD LAYOUT

The software does the conversion

Record A
Record H
Record Q
Record Z
Record D

Application programmer

Figure 2.7 An example of the difference between logical and physical records.

3 CATEGORIES OF DATA USAGE

Data bases are built for a wide variety of purposes and differ accordingly in the way they function. Figure 3.1 summarizes the main types of data usage. The physical structuring of data bases will differ substantially with these different types of usage.

SCHEDULED OR ON-DEMAND USAGE The major division of Fig. 3.1 is between scheduled operation and on-demand operation. Scheduled operation means that the data usage is planned in detail when the system is designed (or redesigned). Files are updated on a preplanned schedule, and information is printed out at a preplanned time of the month. Scheduled operation usually refers to batch processing with files that are organized sequentially (i.e., traditional data processing). Figure 3.2 shows a typical batch-processing operation with punched-card input. The files can only be accessed sequentially and hence have to be sorted between one operation and another.

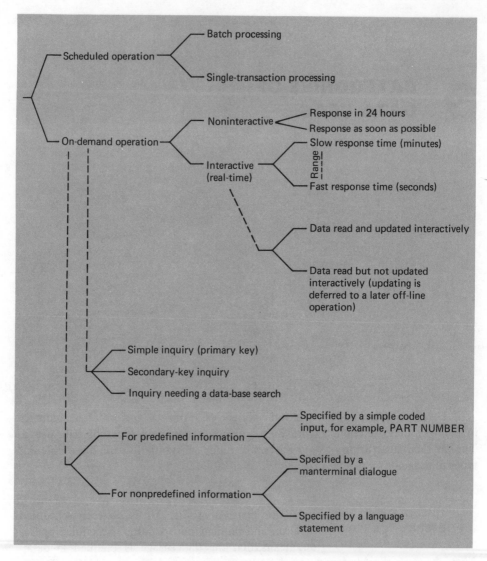

Figure 3.1 Categories of data-base usage.

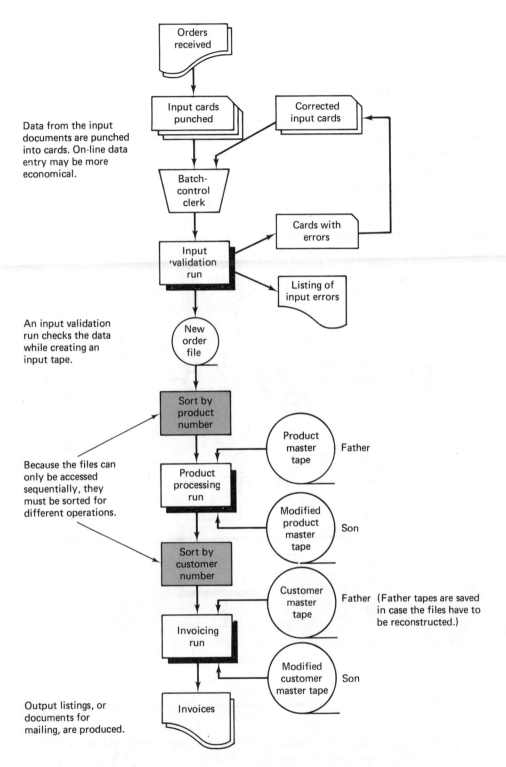

Orders received

Input cards punched

Corrected input cards

Data from the input documents are punched into cards. On-line data entry may be more economical.

Batch-control clerk

Input validation run

Cards with errors

Listing of input errors

An input validation run checks the data while creating an input tape.

New order file

Sort by product number

Product master tape Father

Because the files can only be accessed sequentially, they must be sorted for different operations.

Product processing run

Modified product master tape Son

Sort by customer number

Customer master tape Father (Father tapes are saved in case the files have to be reconstructed.)

Invoicing run

Modified customer master tape Son

Output listings, or documents for mailing, are produced.

Invoices

Figure 3.2   A typical example of traditional batch processing.

Scheduled operation could also apply to systems which use direct-access files and carry out *transaction-oriented processing*, sometimes called *in-line processing*, as in Fig. 3.3. With transaction-oriented processing each transaction is processed completely and the relevant files updated at one time. To achieve this, the files must *all* be on direct-access devices. No sorting of data is needed between the updating of one type of file and another. An advantage of transaction-oriented operation is that the transaction cycle time is cut to a low figure. With batch processing a transaction may have to wait a week or a month before the point in the batch cycle when it can be processed comes around. With transaction-oriented processing it can be handled immediately.

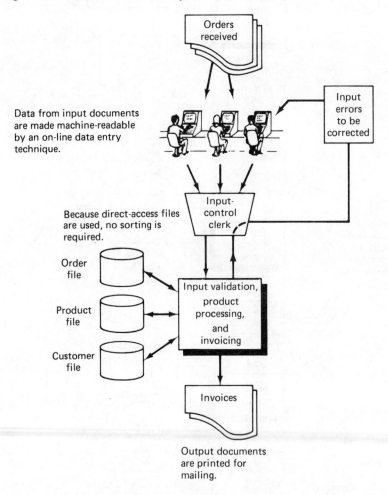

Figure 3.3 A transaction-oriented operation equivalent to the batch-processing operation shown in Fig. 3.2. The usage of data is still entirely prescheduled in this illustration, although on-line inquiry facilities could easily be added.

Although Fig. 3.3 does not describe the system, it shows itself as being an *on-demand* system; in fact its files must be organized so that records can be obtained as soon as they are required, and in any sequence. The systems analyst cannot predict the sequence in which the records will be accessed. Exception conditions, such as a stock level dropping below a recorder point, will trigger an unschedulable action. Terminals for inquiries concerning the contents of individual records can be added to the system in Fig. 3.3, thus introducing an *on-demand* use of the data without substantially changing the requirements of the file organization.

REAL-TIME AND NON-REAL-TIME SYSTEMS   The term *real-time* implies that the data are needed fast, usually in a few seconds. The most common real-time use of data is to give answers to inquiries from terminal users. The word *interactive* is used in Fig. 3.1 to refer to the use of data by terminal operators. The time that is taken to respond to a terminal inquiry may vary from a second or two (conversational responses) to several minutes, and on most systems some form of response in 2 seconds or so is psychologically desirable [3]. (Fig. 3.4)

An on-demand use of data may or may not be real-time. The on-demand user may be content with a reply in an hour or a reply tomorrow morning. A manager wanting information, on some systems, fills in a form specifying the information he needs. The form goes to the computer center, and a printed response is returned as soon as possible. The response may be returned on the following day. There is then no need for fast access to the files. A group of requests can be processed together if desired, and there is time to load specially formatted files. The physical organization of the data may be very different from that in an interactive system.

SHOULD DATA BE UPDATED IN REAL TIME?   An important question about data which are read interactively is whether they should also be updated interactively. Some data are updated "in real-time" and some are not. If they are not, the interactive inquiry may receive answers which are 24 hours or more out of date. For a few applications the information given must be up-to-the-minute, for example, in a stockbroker system or a police-car-dispatching system. With most systems giving information to management, the data do not need to be up-to-the-minute. It is good enough if the data were updated last night, or possibly last week.

When elaborate searches of the data are necessary in order to respond to spontaneous queries, the data must be structured to facilitate searching. With such structures it can be complex and expensive to update the data in real time and insert new records. It is sometimes better to avoid the complexity of real-time updating and carry out the updating in a later off-line operation.

PRIMARY AND
SECONDARY KEYS

As we shall see, there can be a world of difference between a simple inquiry which relates to the contents of a specified record and a complex inquiry which requires many records of a data base to be searched.

The data item (or items) which a computer uses to identify a record is referred to as a *key*. The *primary key* is defined as that key used to *uniquely* identify a record. The primary keys for the files in Fig. 3.3 would be likely to be ORDER NUMBER, PRODUCT NUMBER, and CUSTOMER NUMBER. These data

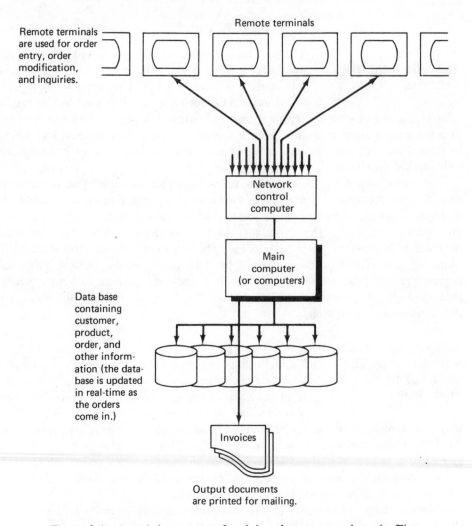

Figure 3.4   A real-time system for doing the same work as in Figs. 3.2 and 3.3. All data-base uses in this diagram are on-demand and not prescheduled.

(handwritten margin note: Primary entity identifier / Key = entity)

items uniquely identify the records in question. Sometimes more than one data item is needed in conjunction to identify a record; for example, both FLIGHT NUMBER and DATE are needed to identify a flight record in an airline reservation system. Neither FLIGHT NUMBER nor DATE alone is enough. The combined data items are referred to as a *concatenated key*.

The primary key is sometimes called an *entity identifier*. In Fig. 2.5, EMPLOYEE NUMBER is the entity identifier.

The computer may also use a key which does not identify a unique record but which identifies all those records which have a certain property. This is referred to as a *secondary key*. A value of the attribute COLOR may be used as a secondary key, for example, BLUE. This key could be used to identify those entities for which the value of the data-item type COLOR is BLUE. Sometimes a file has many secondary keys, which are used to search for records with given properties. Figure 2.5 showed one primary key and two secondary keys.

INVERTED FILES

There are two basic ways in which data can be stored. The first was shown in Fig. 2.5 in which each record contains the attribute values of a given entity. The second way is called an *inverted file* and stores together the entity identifiers which have a given attribute value. The first way of storing data is useful for answering the question: "What are the properties of a given entity?" The second is useful for answering: "What entities have a given property or properties?", for example "What hotels in Maryland have more than 130 rooms?"

A completely inverted file is one which stores the entity identifiers associated with every value of every attribute. In Fig. 3.5, for example, the attributes are GRADE and SKILL-CODE; the employees having each attribute value are listed. A *partially inverted file* is more common than a fully inverted file, and it stores the entity identifiers associated with values of certain attributes, but not all attributes. Some files store the entity identifiers associated with the values of *one* attribute, and this is referred to as an *inverted list*. A partially inverted file may contain several inverted lists.

Figure 3.5 shows a partially inverted file derived from the file in Fig. 2.5. It

Grade	Employee #
03	51883
	53730
	72921
05	28719
07	41618
	53550
08	36453
11	61903
	79632
13	15971

Skill code	Employee #
02	36453
	53550
07	41618
11	79632
21	61903
43	15971
	28719
73	51883
	53730
93	72921

(handwritten note: entity identifiers stored with one value of attribute.)

Figure 3.5 Two inverted lists derived from the secondary key fields in Fig. 2.5.

contains two inverted lists, one for each secondary key shown in Fig. 2.5. The lists in Fig. 3.5 do not contain the other attributes shown in Fig. 2.5. They would have to be used in conjunction with the file in Fig. 2.5 to provide information involving the other attributes.

Many commercial data bases use noninverted files with a small number of inverted lists. Their purpose is to speed up the answering of queries which would take a long time to answer with noninverted files alone.

FORMS OF QUERY

Figure 3.6 shows six forms of simple query relating to entities, E, attributes, A, and their attribute values, V. The examples in this figure concern a file of details about salesmen in which 12 of the attributes are the monthly earnings for each salesman over the last 12 months.

Type 1: $A(E) = ?$ asks; "What is the value of attribute A of entity E?" This is the most common form of inquiry: simply requesting the value of an attribute.

Type 2: $A(?) = V$ is an inverted file inquiry: "What entity, or entities, has a value of attribute A equal to V?"

Type 3: $?(E) = V$ is less common. It asks "Which attribute, or attributes, of entity E has value V?"

Query types 2 and 3 sometimes need a long listing as their answer.

The types with two question marks also require a listing as their answers:

Type 4: $?(E) = ?$ requests the values of all attributes of entity E.

Type 5: $A(?) = ?$ requests the value of attribute A for all entities.

Type 6: $?(?) = V$ is also less common. It requests all attributes of all entities having a value V.

MULTIPLE-KEY RETRIEVAL

The first three query types can have complex forms. Complex forms are most commonly found with type 2, the inverted file query. The query may specify a group of relationships of the form $A(?) \gtreqless V$ and ask what entities satisfy all of them, or what entities satisfy one or more of them. For example, "Which salesmen earned more than $2000 last month AND opened three new accounts?" or "Which salesmen earned more than $2000 in May OR July?"

Where there are type 2 queries relating to multiple attributes, multiple secondary keys may be defined. A variety of *physical* storage organizations of the data is possible to facilitate retrieval or searches based on multiple keys.

Entity = Salesman; Attribute = Aspects about The salesman (handwritten annotation)

	Form	Type of Query	Example
Type 1.	$A(E) = ?$	Common attribute inquiry	How much did Salesman No. 271 earn last month?
Type 2.	$A(?) \begin{matrix} = \\ \neq \\ < \\ > \end{matrix} V$	Which entities have the given value?	Which salesman earned more than $2000 last month?
Type 3.	$?(E) \begin{matrix} = \\ \neq \\ < \\ > \end{matrix} V$	List all attributes having a given set of values for a given entity	Which month's earnings for Salesman No. 271 have exceeded $2000?
Type 4.	$?(E) = ?$	Request for all information about a given entity	List all the information stored about Salesman No. 271
Type 5.	$A(?) = ?$	List the value of a given attribute for every entity	List last month's earnings for every salesman
Type 6.	$?(?) \begin{matrix} = \\ \neq \\ < \\ > \end{matrix} V$	List all entity attributes having a given set of values	For every salesman, list every month when his earnings exceeded $2000

(handwritten "E" with "Salesman" circled in the Type 1 example)

Figure 3.6 Six types of simple query.

$E \equiv$ entity

$A \equiv$ attribute, and,

$V \equiv$ attribute value

Complex queries consist of combinations of these, for example, "Find those values of E_n for which $A_1(E_n) < V_1$ and $A_2(E_n) = V_2$."

BOX 3.1 A Terminal Dialogue for Data-Base Operations that Are Completely Preplanned and Preprogrammed

The display terminal user is attempting to change the delivery date on an order for engineering components:

SCREEN: ENTER CUSTOMER NUMBER IF KNOWN. IF NOT TYPE "N"
USER: N
SCREEN: TYPE FIRST TWO LETTERS OF CUSTOMER'S NAME
USER: GO
SCREEN: WHICH CUSTOMER? ENTER LINE NUMBER
1. GOLDBERG SIDNEY & CO.
2. GOLDEN KAUFMAN SALES CO.
3. GOLDSMITH WALTER & CO.
4. GOODMAN ABE
5. NONE OF THE ABOVE
USER: 3
SCREEN: CUSTOMER NUMBER: 17–8341
GOLDSMITH WALTER & CO.
745, OLD STONE HIGHWAY, SPRINGS,
EAST HAMPTON, N.Y., 11937
REPRESENTATIVE E. S. ROPLEY #543271
PRESS ENTER IF CORRECT
PRESS 1 IF INCORRECT
USER: Presses ENTER key.
SCREEN: WHICH INFORMATION IS TO BE CHANGED?
ENTER LINE NUMBER

1. NEW ORDER	9. INVOICE TO ADDRESS
2. CANCEL ORDER	10. SHIP TO ADDRESS
3. ORDER QUANTITY	11. CUSTOMER ADDRESS
4. DELIVERY DATE	12. CUSTOMER NAME
5. PRIORITY CODE	13. MISC. INSTRUCTIONS
6. ORDER DETAILS	14. REPRESENTATIVE DETAILS
7. DISCOUNT	15. BRANCH OFFICE
8. TAX DETAILS	16. OTHER

USER: 4
SCREEN: WHICH ORDER IS TO BE CHANGED?
ENTER LINE NUMBER

	ORDER #	ITEMS			ORDER DATE	DEL. DATE
1	573824	87289	00241	00029	4/1/79	4/1/81
		00310	77139	04126		
		00900				
2	575931	00391	00700	00421	10/1/79	4/1/80
3	575828	00750	00900		12/1/79	12/1/80
4	579003	02107			6/1/79	8/1/80

Box 3.1—*Cont.*

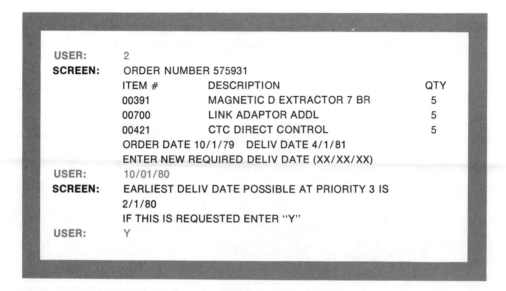

USER: 2
SCREEN: ORDER NUMBER 575931
             ITEM #   DESCRIPTION   QTY
             00391   MAGNETIC D EXTRACTOR 7 BR   5
             00700   LINK ADAPTOR ADDL   5
             00421   CTC DIRECT CONTROL   5
             ORDER DATE 10/1/79   DELIV DATE 4/1/81
             ENTER NEW REQUIRED DELIV DATE (XX/XX/XX)
USER: 10/01/80
SCREEN: EARLIEST DELIV DATE POSSIBLE AT PRIORITY 3 IS
             2/1/80
             IF THIS IS REQUESTED ENTER "Y"
USER: Y

**DOES THE DESIGNER
KNOW HOW THE
DATA BASE WILL
BE USED?**
The bottom subdivision of data usage in Fig. 3.1 relates to whether a demand for data was completely predefined and planned for. On some systems the inquiries are of a simple predictable nature, for example, "How many items of PART 7523 are in stock?" The programmer has anticipated this inquiry and has written a program to answer it.

Often a lengthy dialogue ensues between a terminal user and a data-base system, but the type of data-base operations that occur were entirely preplanned and preprogrammed. Such is the case with the dialogue in Box 3.1.

Sometimes the data-base system designer does not and cannot anticipate all the ways in which the data base will be used. The user may wish to explore the available data in any way that enters his head. In this case a data-base interrogation language is needed. Using the language he can enter spontaneous queries relating to defined data, such as

QUERY THE SALES RECORD FILE;

COUNT THE SALESMEN WITH YEAR-TO-DATE SALES GREATER THAN
    $200000;

(This query could be processed using IBM's IQF query language discussed in
    Chapter 17.)

Languages which permit spontaneous queries to be entered, or allow a non-programmer user to explore the data base and produce reports embodying its data, will become a very important part of data-base technology because they bypass the burdensome process of programming and permit executive questions concerning the data to be answered in minutes rather than weeks.

4 FLEXIBILITY AND INDEPENDENCE

Richard Nolan tells a story in the Harvard Business Review [4] of a marketing vice-president confronted with sales forecasts for a new line of industrial products, similar to the company's existing line. The new line was intended to complement the existing line where competition had been making serious inroads. The forecasts for the new line were more promising than the marketing vice-president had dared to hope, and the forecasting team had shown good reason to take them seriously.

To gain the much-needed profits from the increased sales it was necessary to ensure that the higher sales volume could be manufactured and distributed. Data were needed about plant capacity, personnel, and warehouses. A preliminary examination indicated that the regional warehousing facilities might impose a severe constraint on sales, both in physical space and manpower. The forecasts, however, did not show regional variations in sales in such a way as to make it clear which warehouses would be worst hit and which ones nearby might have excess capacity.

The marketing vice-president had planned an aggressive promotion campaign, and he suspected that if it were successful some regions would need four times their normal warehousing capacity for at least three months. The chief executive officer concluded that it was essential to compute in more detail the impact of the projected marketing campaign on inventory turnover and warehouse crowding. He assumed that this could be computed because the computer already had

1. Inventory simulation programs and several years' data on inventory turnover.

2. Forecasting programs designed to produce forecast sales reports by region and product.

3. A model for market penetration of the new line based on the sales of the old line which it would supplement.

The chief executive officer presented his requirement to the data-processing manager. The results, he said, were needed quickly because the new product line was only a few months from announcement. The DP manager pointed out that, unfortunately, while the data needed did exist, they were not in a form which could be used for the required simulation. The programs for forecasting sales did provide regional projections, but the resulting records did not contain the data necessary for regional inventory simulations. Further, the data about past years' sales were specially coded for the programs with which they had been used in the past and could not be used by the regional inventory simulations without a massive reorganization.

"The Chief Executive Officer looked glum: "How long will it take you to clean up the data and write a simulation program that will give us some answers?"

"Nine months, maybe a year," said the DP manager.

"Because all our data are frozen into these other programs?" the CEO asked.

"That's the main reason," the DP manager replied.

"That's a hell of a reason," the CEO said and stalked toward the door.

"Of course, we could have done it the other way," the DP man called after him. "But now what we'd have to do is. . . ."

But the two men were gone."†

"The other way" would have used data-base techniques instead of letting each department use files designed solely for its own purposes—but it was too late.

MULTIPLE USAGE OF DATA   Figure 4.1 illustrates the way data are organized for computers which do not use data-base techniques. There are many files of records, some on tape and some on direct-access media such as disk. The records contain data items, shown as circles in Fig. 4.1. When a program is written for a new application or a variation of an old application, there may be a file which contains the required set of data items. Often, however, there is not, and a new file has to be created. Suppose that a new user request needs a file with data items A, F, and H. These data items do not appear together in the existing files in Fig. 4.1. Other files must be sorted and merged to obtain the new file, but this will not be straightforward if, as with the above marketing problem, the existing files do not have the required sets of keys. There may not be an H data item for every pair of A and F data items.

†Nolan, *ibid.*

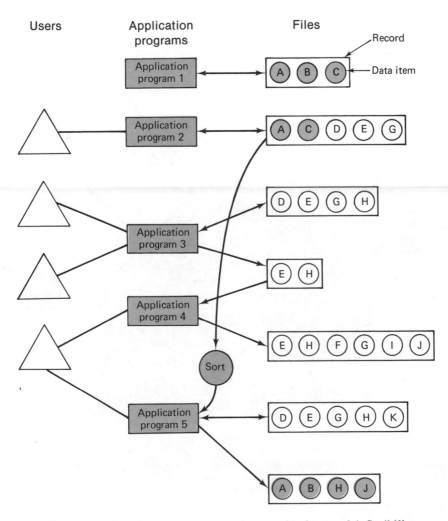

Figure 4.1 A system without a data base: redundacy and inflexibility. Imagine 1000 such files.

AD HOC REQUESTS   Ad hoc requests from management for data, or processing, such as that above, are increasing. As management realizes the potential value of the data that are stored, their requests will be an increasing plague to the data-processing manager. Nonetheless, they must, and should, be readily answered, with minimum disruption.

The concept of data storage shown in Fig. 4.2, if it works as intended, will enable the DP department to be more responsive to such requests.

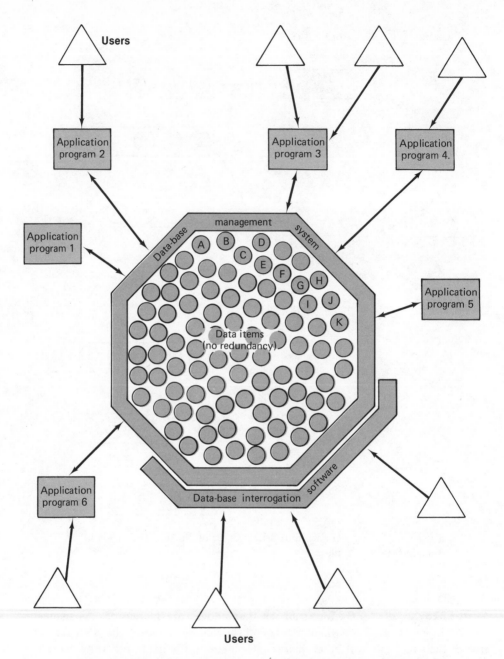

Figure 4.2 The system of Fig. 4.1 with a data base: more responsive and lower development costs. The idea for the form of this figure came from Nolan's article. (*Caution*: This diagram presents a dangerously naive view.)

In the organization of Fig. 4.2, the data items are pooled to form a data base with software that can extract any combinations of data items that a programmer wishes. In reality the data items are usually not stored entirely in isolation, as suggested by the drawing of Fig. 4.2, but in groups of related data items, sometimes called *records*, sometimes *segments*. The software may be able to extract segments and combine them to form the records that an application program uses.

Another important feature shown in Fig. 4.2, at the bottom right, is the data-base interrogation software. This enables some users of the data to interact directly with the data base without application programs having to be written. Instead the user fills in a form expressing a data request, or employs a language, which is part of the interrogation software.

Figure 4.2 suggests that a corporation's data are stored in a large reservoir in which the users can be fishing. Although this figure forms a useful way to explain data-base concepts to management, it is nevertheless a naive view of a data base—in some cases dangerously naive, as we shall see. The data items inside the octagon of Fig. 4.2 have to be organized in such a way that they can be found and accessed with sufficient speed. The organizing introduces many complexities into data-base design and is the subject of Part II of this book. The structuring problems can be sufficiently great that a designer may sometimes elect to employ separate data-base systems, even though they contain much of the same information.

The "reservoir" concept of management information systems, or other information systems, is much easier to conceive than to implement. It is proving a very complex and lengthy operation to build up such data bases, and with current hardware it is expensive to search them sufficiently quickly to give real-time answers to unanticipated queries.

The striving for flexibility, however, is vital. In many corporations, systems (of accounts, organization, methods, responsibilities, and procedures) have been more of a hindrance to change than physical plant and unamortized capital investments. For some, retraining the whole labor force would be easier than changing the system. Quite frequently the computer has contributed to the inflexibility by dressing hallowed procedures in a rigid electronic framework. The computer has been hailed as one of the most versatile and flexible machines ever built, but in many corporations, because of the difficulty and cost of changing their programs and data bases, it becomes a straitjacket which precludes change and even constrains corporate policy. The comment is often heard, "We cannot do that because change is too difficult with our computer system."

One of the most difficult tricks that we have to learn is how to introduce automation without introducing rigidity. The computer industry is only now beginning to glimpse how that can be done. Data-base techniques are an important part of the answer.

REDUNDANCY   Many of the data items in Fig. 4.1 exist multiple times.
                          In most tape or disk libraries a massive amount of
duplication exists in the data that are stored. Many data items are stored redun-
dantly in files for different purposes and in different update versions of the same
data. A large installation often has more than 1000 tapes or disks containing files,
as in Fig. 4.1, and the quantity is constantly increasing.

A data base should remove much of this redundancy, as illustrated in Fig.
4.2. A data base has sometimes been defined as a "nonredundant" collection of
data items, but in reality some measure of redundancy often exists in order to give
improved access times or simpler addressing methods and to provide the capability
to recover from accidental loss of data. There is a trade-off between nonredundancy and other desirable criteria, and so it would be better to use the phrase
"controlled redundancy" or say that a well-designed data base removes "harmful"
redundancy.

Uncontrolled redundancy, as in Fig. 4.1, has several disadvantages. First
there is the extra cost of storing multiple copies. Second, and much more serious,
multiple updating operations are necessary to update at least some of the redundant copies. Redundancy is therefore expensive on files with a large volume of
updating or, worse, in which new items are frequently being inserted or deleted.
Third, because different copies of the data may be in different stages of updating,
the system may give inconsistent information.

In a large data-processing operation without a data base there are so many
redundant data that it is virtually impossible to keep them all at the same level
of update. Too often the users or general management notice the apparent inconsistencies that this causes and distrust the computerized information. Inability to
keep redundant data in the same state of update is a common cause of the anti-
computer stories that managers too often tell.

Redundancy can be reduced in today's data processing systems at three
levels. First, the same data items occur in many records and documents, as shown
in Fig. 4.3. Using appropriate software, different records can be assembled from
a non-redundant data base. Second, the same records and data groupings can be
used for multiple applications as shown in Fig. 4.4. A data-base system enables
the same data groupings to be shared by many applications or users. Third, entire
data bases contain data which can serve the needs of many operations and organizations. Figure 4.5 illustrates how this is so in local government data processing.
The access to and design of data bases, then, should transcend the existing organization boundaries in corporations or government.

Data resources can therefore be designed in a fashion which permits the
data to serve many purposes or users. In this way the data resources are made more
valuable. If the techniques are well designed the data can also be made easier to
use.

RECORDS AND DOCUMENTS

DATA ITEMS	ORDER FROM CUSTOMER	CUSTOMER FILE	WAREHOUSE ORDER	WAREHOUSE TICKET	INVOICE	WEEKLY TOTAL SHIPMENT REPORT	WEEKLY ITEM SHIPMENT REPORT	YEAR-TO-DATE SHIPMENT REPORT	YEAR-TO-DATE ITEM REPORT	ITEM FILE	WEEKLY ITEM INVENTORY REPORT	INVENTORY FILE	BRANCH FILE	MONTHLY BRANCH SUMMARY	YEAR-TO-DATE SALES REPORT	ITEM ON-ORDER REPORT	TOTAL ON-ORDER REPORT	MONTHLY CUSTOMER REPORT	CUSTOMER PAYMENT	ACCOUNTS RECEIVABLE	OVERDUE ACCOUNTS	OVERDUE NOTICES
CUSTOMER NUMBER	•	•	•		•													•	•	•	•	
CUSTOMER ORDER NUMBER	•		•		•														•	•	•	•
ITEM NUMBER	•		•	•	•		•		•	•	•	•				•		•				•
ITEM TYPE AND SIZE	•		•	•	•		•		•	•	•	•				•		•				•
CORPORATE ORDER NUMBER			•	•	•		•											•		•	•	
INVOICE NUMBER					•														•	•	•	•
BRANCH OFFICE NUMBER	•				•								•	•	•		•	•	•	•	•	•
CUSTOMER NAME	•	•			•									•				•	•	•	•	•
ITEM NAME	•		•	•	•		•		•	•	•	•			•	•	•	•				•
DATE OF INVOICE					•															•	•	•
QUANTITY ORDERED	•		•	•	•				•		•	•				•		•				
QUANTITY SHIPPED			•	•	•	•	•	•										•		•	•	•
QUANTITY OUT OF STOCK			•	•	•	•	•	•	•			•					•					
SHIPPING INSTRUCTIONS			•	•	•																	
CODE FOR SHIPPING			•	•	•																	
CUSTOMER ADDRESS		•			•																	
BRANCH OFFICE NAME	•	•			•								•	•	•		•	•	•			•
BRANCH OFFICE ADDRESS	•				•									•								•
PRICE			•	•	•	•	•	•	•										•	•	•	•
INVOICE LINE VALUE					•															•	•	•
DISCOUNT RATE AND QUALIFN					•				•											•	•	•
INVOICE LINE DISCOUNT					•																	•
C.O.D. OR CREDIT CODE	•	•			•														•			•
WEEKLY TOTAL OF ITEM SHIPPED						•	•	•	•		•											
WEEKLY VALUE OF ITEM SHIPPED						•	•	•	•													

Figure 4.3 The same data items are used in multiple records and documents.

APPLICATIONS

RECORDS OR DATA GROUPINGS	ACCOUNT ORIGINATION	ACCOUNT UPDATING	TRANSACTION PROCESSING	CREDIT APPLICATION	CREDIT EVALUATION	LOAN TRANSACTION PROCESSING	STATEMENTS	CASH POSITION MANAGEMENT	PROFIT PLANNING	RESOURCE/LIABILITY FORECASTING	CUSTOMER PROFITABILITY REPORTING	MANAGEMENT FINANCIAL REPORTING
CUSTOMER INFORMATION	•	•	•	•	•	•	•				•	
CHECKING ACCOUNTS		•	•	•	•		•					
SPECIAL ACCOUNTS		•	•	•	•		•					
SAVINGS		•	•	•			•					
DEMAND DEPOSITS		•	•	•			•					
REAL ESTATE LOANS				•		•						
COLLATERAL LOANS						•						
MISCELLANEOUS LOANS						•						
TIDEOVER						•	•					
AUTHORIZATION I.D.	•	•	•									
CREDIT SUPPORT	•			•	•							
ACCOUNT HISTORY						•					•	
⁞												
ACCOUNTS RECEIVABLE								•	•	•		•
GENERAL ACCOUNTING								•	•	•		•
GENERAL LEDGER												
READY RESERVE								•	•	•		•
CENSUS												
CASH INVENTORY								•	•	•		•

Figure 4.4 (Above) The same files or data groupings are used in multiple applications.

Figure 4.5 (Right) An efficiently planned set of data bases may be shared by multiple processes and multiple organizational groups. It should therefore cut across political boundaries. This example is taken from a local government study [5].

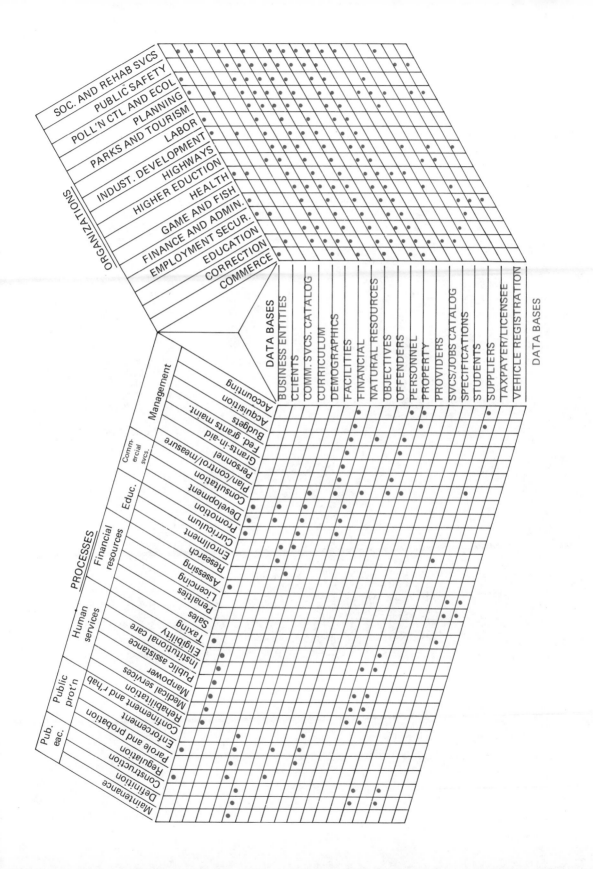

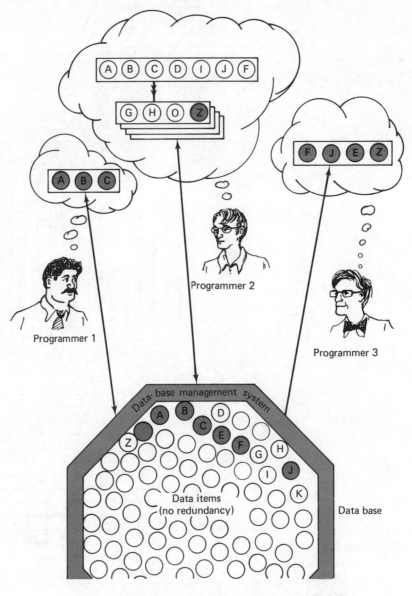

Figure 4.6 The programmers can live in blissful ignorance of how the data are really stored.

ARE YOUR DATA   A data base is intended to make data independent of
INDEPENDENT?   the programs that use them. Either data or programs
                      can be changed without causing the other to have to
be changed. The data can be easily reorganized or their content added to. Old
application programs do not have to be rewritten when changes are made to data
structures, data layout, or the physical devices on which data are stored.

This independence of data is essential if data are to become a general-purpose corporate resource. There are many aspects to data independence, as we will see later in the book. In the past data structures have been devised by a programmer for his own use. He writes a program to create a file of data. Usually when another programmer needs the data for another purpose it is not structured in the way he wants, so he creates another file. Hence the duplication in Fig. 4.1.

Data independence is one of the most important differences between the way data are organized in data bases and the way they are organized in the file systems of computers that do not use data-base management software. The programmers can each have their own logical data structure, as shown in Fig. 4.6, and can program in blissful ignorance of how the data are really organized. When the data organization is changed, *the old programs still work*.

CHANGE AND   A data base in an organization is no more a *static* entity
DECAY   than are contents of the organization's filing cabinets.
                      The details of data stored, and the way they are used,
change continuously. If a computer system attempts to impose an unchangeable file structure on an organization, it is doomed to the types of pressure that will result in most of the programming efforts being spent on modifying existing programs rather than developing new applications.

Figure 4.7 shows how programming costs have tended to change in organizations. The total programming costs in a typical organization have grown, becoming a higher proportion of the total data-processing budget. However, the programming man-hours spent on new applications have fallen steadily. The reason is that the effort to maintain or modify the existing programs becomes greater and greater. It is often thought by systems analysts and data-processing managers that existing programs which work well can be left alone. In reality, however, the data which they create or use are needed for other applications and almost always needed in a slightly different form. New data-item types are added. New record types are needed with data-item types from several previous records. The data must be indexed in a different way. The physical layout of data is improved. Data bases for different applications are merged, and so forth.

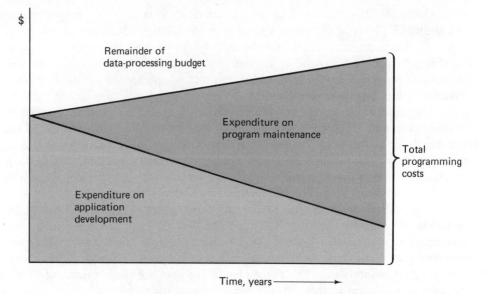

Figure 4.7 New application progress is often deferred by the rising cost of modifying existing programs and files [43]. Some corporations now spend more than 80% of their programming budget just keeping current and only 20% forging ahead.

One of the main objectives of a data-base system is that new programs using the data in a modified form should be able to do so without having any effect on programs which use that same data in their old form. Furthermore, a program may be modified, changing in some way the data it uses, without disturbing any other programs which use that same data. In other words, *each program should be insulated* from the effects of changes to other programs, and all programs should be insulated from the effects of reorganizing the data. If the data are reorganized into pages, moved from a sequential-access to a direct-access device, addressed differently, or stored on new hardware with different track lengths, the program should *not* have to be modified.

This facility makes the data-base software complex. However, without it, new application development can be immensely time-consuming and prohibitively expensive because it makes it necessary to rewrite existing programs or convert existing data. The total number of man-years that a corporation has invested in application programs grows steadily. The programmers are long since gone, and it is too late to complain that their documentation is inadequate. The greater the number of programs, the more horrifying the thought of having to convert them or their data.

In summary, one of the most important characteristics of data bases is that they will constantly need to change and grow. Dynamic restructuring of the data base must be possible as new types of data and new applications are added. The restructuring should be possible without having to rewrite the application programs, and in general should cause as little upheaval as possible. The ease with which a data base can be changed will have a major effect on the rate at which data-processing applications can be developed in a corporation.

It is often easy for a systems analyst to imagine that the data structure he has designed for an application represents its ultimate content and usage. He leaves some spare characters in the records and thinks that these will accommodate any change that will occur. Consequently he ties his data to a physical organization which is efficient for that particular structure. *Time and time again he is proven wrong.* The requirements change in unforeseen ways. The data structures have to be modified, and consequently many application programs have to be rewritten and debugged. The larger an installation's base of application programs, the more expensive is this process.

In some installations at the time of writing 80% of the programming budget is being spent on maintaining or modifying past programs and data; only 20% is being used for new application programming. This ratio is extremely inhibiting to the development of data processing in the organization. It is desirable to write today's programs in such a way that the same ratio will not apply five years hence. If we continue to write programs without data independence, the maintenance difficulties will grow worse as the numbers of programs grow, until the impact cripples the capability to take advantage of the new hardware and techniques that are now under development.

The decade ahead is likely to be an era of great invention in the techniques for storing and organizing data, and many of the new techniques will be highly complex. The greater the rate of introduction of new techniques or modified data organizations, the greater is the need to protect the application programs and programmers from them. This is one of the main reasons why we need *data base* systems rather than merely *file* systems without the data independence.

5 THE CHANGING VIEW OF DATA

We will now summarize the characteristics and advantages that a data-base system should have.

The question is often asked, "Why data base? Why should not my computer system have separate data files as it has always had? Why the added expense and difficulty of replacing files which are easily understood with a data base needing such complex software?" The reader should have clearly in his mind the possible answers to these questions before reading subsequent sections of this book.

EVOLUTION OF DATA-BASE CONCEPTS   Data storage techniques have evolved through several stages, and all the stages are still to be found today, the primitive ones mainly on small systems or mini-computers.

The term *data base* came into popularity about 1970. Prior to that, the data-processing world had talked about files of data and data sets. As often happens when a new term becomes fashionable many users promoted their files by changing their title to "data base" without changing their nature to include some of the most important data-base characteristics:

Data independence

Speedy handling of spontaneous information requests

Nonredundancy

Versatility in representing relationships between data items

Security protection

or, in many cases,

Real-time accessibility

As the employment of better data management software spreads, these characteristics spread with it. For reasons that will emerge later in the book, no single software package yet gives all the characteristics that an ideal data base should have,
and the systems analyst, as often when he designs systems, has to select a compromise between different qualities.

Box 5.1 shows the various ways in which data usage is evolving. The statements at the right-hand side of the box represent the objectives of data-base
management in general and to a lesser extent its accomplishments so far. No
data-base system yet achieves all the desirable features listed at the right-hand side
of the box.

Managers outside the data-processing department perceive only the external
effect of the changes. Where data-base implementation is successful and the systems
are put to good use, these effects can be impressive:

Trend

1.	2.	3.	4.
Managers are provided with long listings, often of little use.	Managers are provided with exception reports highlighting actions required.	Staff are able to make real-time inquiries to certain files.	General requests for information are answered encouraging a manager to use the data creatively.
Managers requesting new types of reports from the computer are told that they cannot have them.	Managers requesting new types of reports are told that programs can be written to provide them in several months	Managers requesting new reports using existing data are given them in several days.	New requests for information relating to existing data are answered by staff with terminals in a few minutes.

BOX 5.1 Trends in The Usage of Computer Data

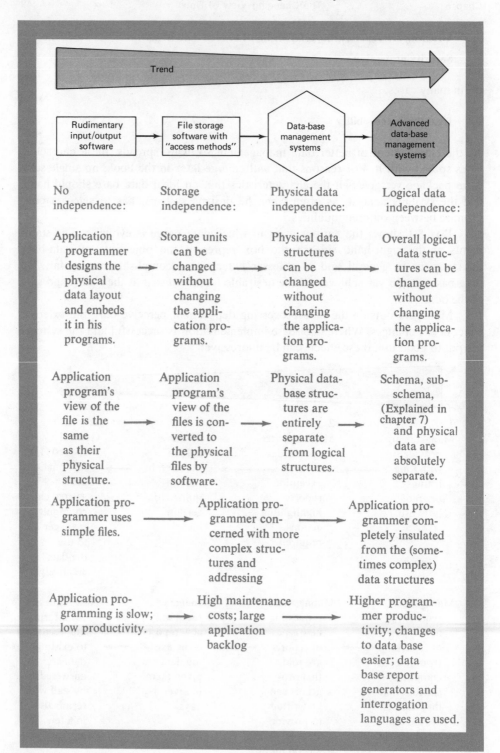

Trend

| Rudimentary input/output software | File storage software with "access methods" | Data-base management systems | Advanced data-base management systems |

No independence:

Application programmer designs the physical data layout and embeds it in his programs.

Application program's view of the file is the same as their physical structure.

Application programmer uses simple files.

Application programming is slow; low productivity.

Storage independence:

Storage units can be changed without changing the application programs.

Application program's view of the files is converted to the physical files by software.

Application programmer concerned with more complex structures and addressing

High maintenance costs; large application backlog

Physical data independence:

Physical data structures can be changed without changing the application programs.

Physical database structures are entirely separate from logical structures.

Logical data independence:

Overall logical data structures can be changed without changing the application programs.

Schema, subschema, (Explained in chapter 7) and physical data are absolutely separate.

Application programmer completely insulated from the (sometimes complex) data structures

Higher programmer productivity; changes to data base easier; data base report generators and interrogation languages are used.

Box 5.1—*Cont.*

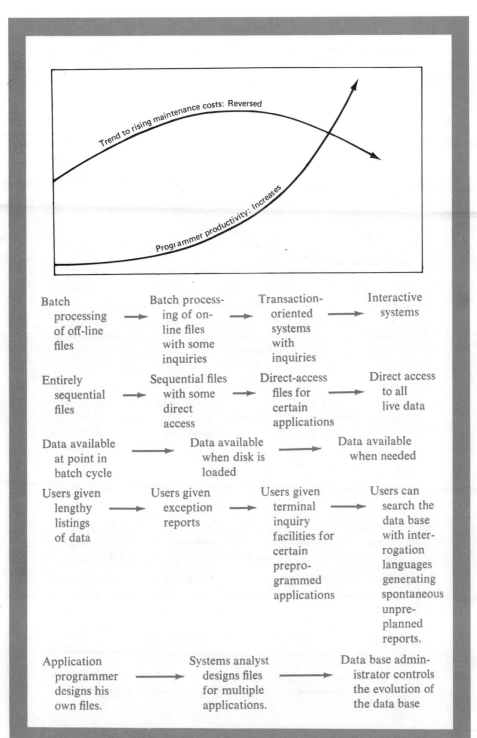

Box 5.1—*Cont.*

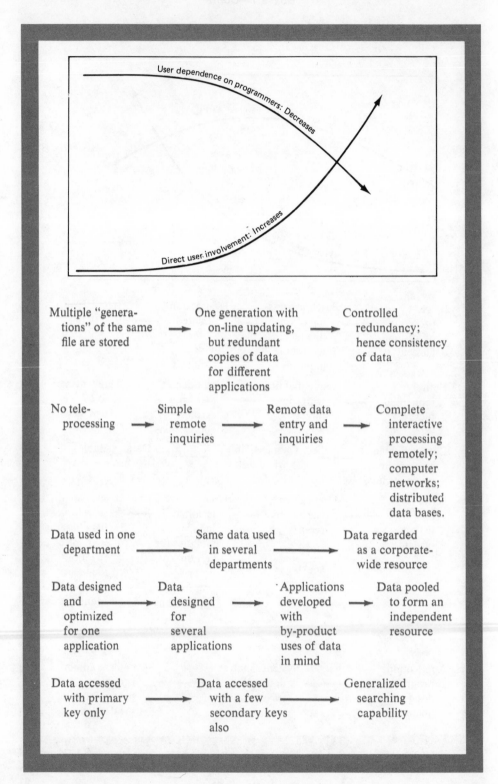

Multiple "genera-tions" of the same file are stored → One generation with on-line updating, but redundant copies of data for different applications → Controlled redundancy; hence consistency of data

No tele-processing → Simple remote inquiries → Remote data entry and inquiries → Complete interactive processing remotely; computer networks; distributed data bases.

Data used in one department → Same data used in several departments → Data regarded as a corporate-wide resource

Data designed and optimized for one application → Data designed for several applications → Applications developed with by-product uses of data in mind → Data pooled to form an independent resource

Data accessed with primary key only → Data accessed with a few secondary keys also → Generalized searching capability

Box 5.1—*Cont.*

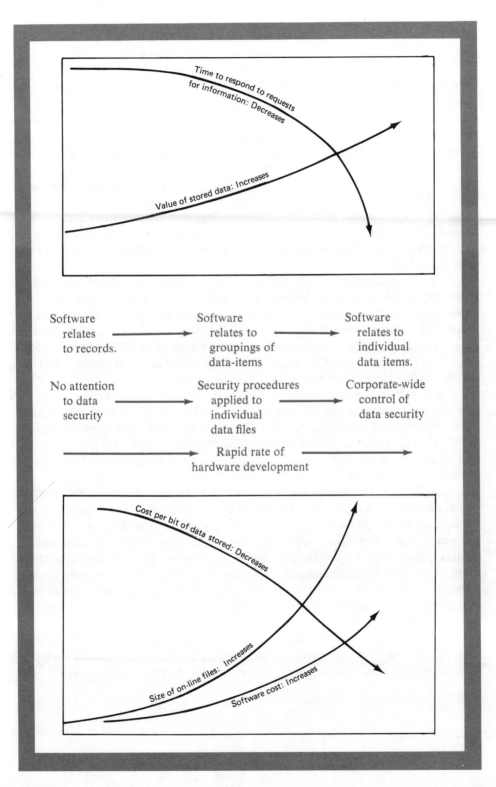

FILE
SOFTWARE

Prior to the use of data-base techniques, computers operated with isolated files each designed for its own application. The software executed the input/output operations of the storage devices and little else. The coding written into the application programs took care of the data organization, and this was done in an elementary manner, usually with simple sequential files on tape. There was no *data independence*. If a change was made to the data organization or to storage units, the application programmer had to modify his programs accordingly and then test the modifications. To update a file, a new file was written. The old one was retained and referred to as the *father*. The previous generation—*grandfather*—was also kept, and often earlier ancestors. Most files were used for one application only. Often other applications used the same data, but they usually needed them in a different form, often with different data items, so different files were created. There was therefore a high level of redundancy with many different files containing the same data items.

Some direct-access storage devices were used which permitted the user to access any record at random instead of scanning the entire file sequentially. The means of addressing them had to be built by the application programmer into his code. If the storage devices were changed, a major upheaval in the application program coding was necessary. In fact, the storage devices did change. New technology brought substantial reductions in the cost per bit of storage, and the sizes of the files often outgrew their earlier storage devices.

New software was introduced which recognized the changing nature of files and their storage devices. It attempted to insulate the application programmer from the effects of hardware changes. The software made it possible to change the physical data layout without changing the "logical" view of the data, provided that there was no change in record contents or in the fundamental structuring of the files.

The files used in this second era were, like the first, generally designed for one application or closely related applications. A set of files, for example, would be designed for the purchasing function in a corporation. A small group of systems analysts and programmers would design these files and include in them the set of data elements needed for the purchasing application. The files would be structured to serve that application as efficiently as possible. The accounts payable application needs much of the same information. A separate small group may design the files for accounts payable. It might be suggested to them that they use the purchasing file. However, they need a number of data items that are not in these files, and they want to permit inquiries to the files that would be difficult with files structured in the manner of the purchasing files. Consequently they produce their own files with separate computer runs. If the accounts payable and purchasing applications could have used the same files, both the total processing time and the total storage requirement would have been less.

WHEN DATA STRUCTURE CHANGES

As commercial data processing evolved, it became clear that it was desirable to isolate the application programs not only from changes in file hardware and the effect of increasing file size but also from additions to the data that are stored, such as new fields and new relationships. If ideal data management software had been used, it would have been possible to develop the purchasing application and the accounts payable application separately and then, later, merge their files without having to rewrite the application programs. Data-base software attempts to accomplish this. It recognizes that a data base is something that is continually evolving and will be used for new applications. New types of records will be added and new data items will be included in existing records. The structure of the data base will be changed to improve its efficiency or to permit new types of inquiries. The users will change their needs and modify the types of inquiries they make of the data.

If it is to be possible to add new data items to records without rewriting the application programs, then the software must relate to the data at the level of data items rather than at the level of records. One programmer's logical description of a record may contain items different from another programmer's description of the same record. The physical record must include both sets of items.

As many different logical files can be derived from the same stored data, the same data may be *accessed* in different ways by applications with different requirements. This often leads to complex data structures. Good data-base software, however, *protects the application programmer from the complexities* of the data structure. Regardless of how the data are organized the application programmer should see the file as a relatively simple structure planned as he needs it for his application. Simplification of the programmer's task is one of the purposes of *data independence*.

LOGICAL AND PHYSICAL DATA INDEPENDENCE

When the early data-base systems had been in use for some time it became apparent that a further level of data independence was needed. The overall logical structure of the data became complex in many cases, and as the data base evolved the overall logical structure inevitably changed. It became important that it should be able to change without forcing a change in the many application programs which used it. On many systems, change in the overall logical structure of the data has become a way of life; it is constantly evolving. Because of this, two levels of data independence are needed. We call these *logical* and *physical* data independence.

Logical data independence means that the overall logical structure of the data may be changed without changing the application programs. (The changes must not, of course, remove any of the data the application programs use.) Consequently one application program's data can be changed without disrupting other application programs.

Physical data independence means that the physical layout and organization of the data may be changed without changing either the overall logical structure of the data or the application programs.

Figure 5.1 illustrates the concept of logical and physical independence, and, glancing ahead to Chapter 7, Fig. 7.2 shows a more detailed illustration. At the center of Fig. 5.1 is the overall logical structure of the data—sometimes referred to as the *global* logical view of the data. It is the data base administration's view. This view is often entirely different from the *physical* structure of the data, shown at the bottom of the figure. The application programmer's views—the application program files—are shown at the top of the figure. These three views of the data are separate. The application programmer may, for example, view the files as a set of master records with subordinate detail records. The data administrator views the data base as a whole, but still in a logical form. The physical organization is concerned with the indices, pointers, chains, and other means of physically locating records (which we discuss in Part II of this book); with the overflow areas and techniques used for inserting new records and deleting records; and with physical layout and compaction techniques.

The data-base software will convert the application programmer's view of the data into the overall logical view and will then map the overall logical view into the physical representation.

The purpose of the separation of views shown in Fig. 5.1 is to permit the maximum freedom to change the data structures without having to rehash much of the earlier work on the data base. Figure 5.2 lists a number of changes that are common on a data-base system and indicates whether they can be accomplished without restructuring the physical storage organization, the global logical view of the data, or the application programs other than the one which initiated the change. The crosses in the columns of Fig. 5.2 represent an objective of contemporary data-base software design.

Figure 5.3 illustrates physical data independence, and Figure 5.4 illustrates logical data independence.

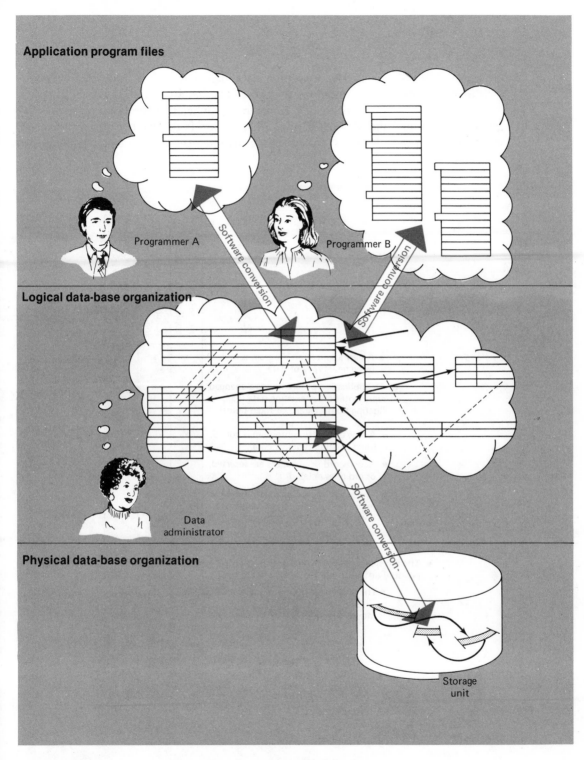

Application program files

Programmer A

Programmer B

Logical data-base organization

Data administrator

Physical data-base organization

Storage unit

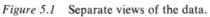

Figure 5.1   Separate views of the data.

CAN YOU FIND IT QUICKLY ENOUGH? The user of a data base may ask a wide variety of questions about the data that are stored. In the majority of today's commercial applications the types of queries are anticipated, and the physical storage organization is designed to handle them with suitable speed. There is an increasing requirement for systems to handle

	No change in (other) application programs	No change in the global logical data description	No change in the physical storage organization
A new application program is added, using new types of data	x	x	x
An application program uses a changed representation of existing data (e.g., floating-point instead of fixed-point)	x	x	x
A new application program is added, using existing types of data	x		
New record occurrences are inserted, or old ones deleted	x	x	x
The global logical data description is improved, or new relationships between data types are created	x		
Two data bases are merged	x		
The physical organization of data is improved; possibly different representations are used	x	x	
The addressing methods are changed	x	x	
The data is moved to a different type of volume	x	x	
The software is changed	x	x	
The hardware is changed	x	x	

Figure 5.2   The data independence capabilities required in advanced data-base systems.

Figure 5.3   Physical data independence.

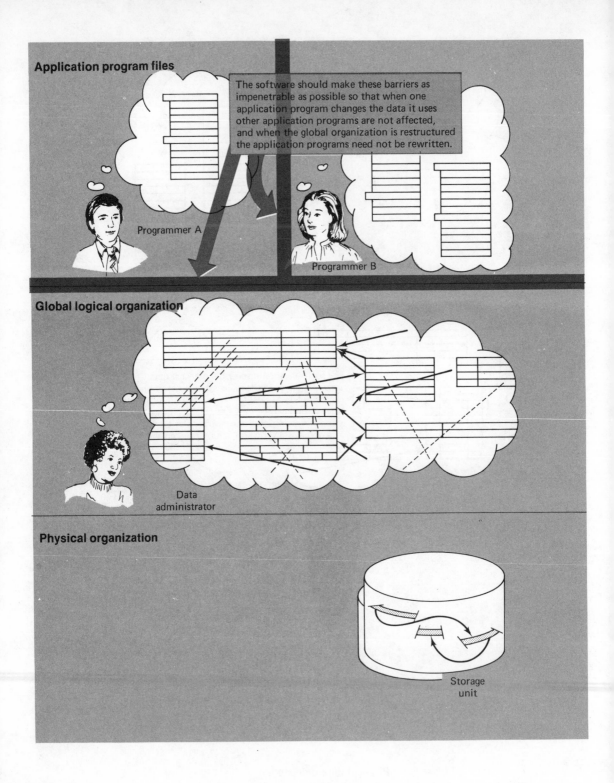

Figure 5.4   Logical data independence.

queries or produce reports that were *not* anticipated in detail. The user may enter spontaneous requests for information at a terminal. Unanticipated queries (and some anticipated queries) make it necessary to search parts of the data base. If a quick answer is needed at a terminal, the search will have to be fast. The capability to search a data base quickly and with different search criteria is highly dependent on the physical storage organization. With many storage organizations the search times are far too long for real-time responses at terminals. An objective of the data-base organization, then, may be to achieve fast and flexible search capability.

As we commented earlier, the ability to search a data base rapidly with multiple search criteria may be time-consuming with today's hardware. It has been too expensive for many systems that would otherwise have used it. As technology improves, the capability to make fast and flexible searches will become a more tenable objective.

TUNING When real-time access is needed to the data, users of the system are very much concerned with the time it takes the system to respond. With batch-processing systems there is concern with how large a throughput the system can handle, or how long it takes to accomplish the work load. These factors are dependent on the time it takes to access the required data, and are dependent on the organization of the data and their positioning in file units. The difference between appropriate and inappropriate organizations can make a very large difference in response times and throughputs.

If the data storage is planned for a specific and well understood set of operations, such as airline reservations, the organization can be selected and data positioned in an optimal manner for those operations. The designer knows precisely what he is designing for. Often a designer is not so fortunate. In some cases he does not know exactly how the files will be used or how the data base will be interrogated, or how often. It is therefore necessary to adjust, or even to fundamentally change, the organization of the storage *after* the system has come into use and the usage pattern has become clear. With many data bases the usage continually changes as different persons become familiar with how the system can be used, or as the application programs evolve. The adjustment of the storage organization to improve its performance is a continuing process.

Adjusting a data base to improve its performance is sometimes referred to as *tuning* the data base. The savings that have resulted from tuning have often, in practice, been great. Sometimes they have been so great as to make the difference between workable and unworkable applications. The data base administrator or his group is responsible for the tuning and operations of the data base, and it is important that he should be free to make what changes he feels necessary without playing havoc with the application programs. Without appropriate software, tuning requires changes to application programs and this can incur unacceptably high costs in program maintenance and testing.

DATA MIGRATION Some data are referenced very frequently and others only occasionally. It is desirable to store the frequently referenced data in such a manner that they can be accessed quickly and conveniently. The rarely accessed data can be stored in a cheaper fashion. In an office the information which is used every day is in the secretaries' filing cabinets; information which is rarely if ever looked at may be in the basement, out of the way and inexpensively stored. The computer equivalent of the basement storage may be magnetic tape, and frequently accessed data may be on disk or drum, always readable in a fraction of a second. A complex data base may have multiple levels of ease of accessibility.

Some stored data, like pop music, rapidly change their popularity rating. In a stockbroker system, for example, there may be a high level of activity on certain stocks which last month had little attention paid to them. On an airline there is a high activity on the records of those flights and passengers which take off in a few days. Ten months before a flight takes off there is little activity, although some bookings will be made. Two days after it takes off there is no activity, although the records must still be kept.

As the popularity of data changes they may be moved to forms of storage, or to positions in the data base, suited to their activity. Two days after an airline flight takes off the records of the flight and its passengers are moved from the real-time disks to *archival* storage on tape. In some cases the data themselves are not moved, but references to them in the indices which are used for addressing them are changed so that they can be found more quickly. The process of adjusting the storage of data to suit their popularity rating is called *data migration*. In some systems it is done automatically. In others it is done by the systems programmers or data-base administrator. In some it is regarded as part of the process of tuning the data base.

PRIVACY It is vitally important to protect certain data from being read by persons who have no right to read them. The privacy of individuals must be preserved, and trade secrets must be securely locked up.

Even more important, data must be protected from being modified by individuals who have no right to modify them. The updating process must be very carefully controlled.

It is more difficult to keep data secure and private in a shared data base than in separate unshared files. Security controls and locks on the data become an essential part of the software. The reason for the difficulty is, first, that the data are more fragmented. Data items, rather than data *records*, are stored and may be individually addressable. Second, the data items can be referenced for any application rather than a single application. As we will discuss later in Chapter 22, a technology of security exists, and the data-base environment makes it essential that it be used. Data can be locked up in a well-designed data base, although in many of today's data-base systems the precautions are poor.

DATA PROTECTION

When machine failures or software failures occur it is essential that they should not cause the loss of an update or the accidental double updating of a record or data item. Ensuring that the updates are correct even during failure periods is referred to as preserving *data integrity*. The stored data must also be protected from accidental damage or loss.

While most causes of damage or loss can be avoided, accidents occasionally happen. The worst type of accident may be fire destroying the data library. When stored data are harmed, it is essential that it should be possible to reconstruct them. In a simple batch-processing environment data could be reconstructed from the tape preserved from previous batch runs—the so-called father and grandfather tapes. When data are updated in place on direct-access files more elaborate precautions are needed in case of damage to the master copy. These precautions usually include journals (logs) with procedures for restarting the process after a failure and reconstructing data from the journals. We shall discuss data protection in Chapter 22.

THE INTERFACE WITH THE PAST

Organizations which have been using data processing for some time have a major investment in their existing programs, procedures, and data. When an organization installs new data-base software it is important that it can work with the existing programs and procedures and that the existing data can be converted. This need for *compatibility* can be a major constraint in switching to a new data-base system. It is essential, however, that the growth of data-base technology not be held back by too much attention to compatibility with the past.

THE INTERFACE   Most important is the interface with the future. In the
WITH THE FUTURE   future the data and their storage media will change
                           in many ways. No commercial organization is static;
change is a way of life. Change has been extremely costly to data-processing
users. *The enormous cost of seemingly trivial changes has held back application development seriously.* This cost has resulted from the need to rewrite application programs, to convert data, and to deal with the many bugs that are
introduced by the changes. Over the years the numbers of application programs
grow in an organization until eventually the prospect of having to rewrite all of
them is unthinkable. One of the most important objectives of data-base design
is to plan the data base in such a way that changes can be made to it without
having to modify the application programs.

Thus, the data independence we have discussed is the key to future development. A data base should be regarded as something which is constantly changing
and improving, the physical data must be severed as completely as possible from
the logical data (Fig. 5.3), and the application programs must be isolated from
the changes in the overall logical structure (Fig. 5.4).

The setting up of data-base techniques is a fundamental step in the evolution
of an organization's data processing. Only with good data-base techniques can an
organization be free to allow its computer data to change and evolve as the users'
needs inevitably require.

6 OPERATIONS SYSTEMS VERSUS INFORMATION SYSTEMS

For practical reasons, given today's hardware, it is not always possible for a single data base to satisfy the needs of all users of the data, as suggested in Fig. 2.2. In particular it is sometimes necessary to distinguish between what are referred to as *operations systems* and *information systems*.

We will use the term information system to refer to a system in which the information needs of the user are not defined precisely at the time the system is designed. The need becomes clear only when the request for information is made and the data base may have to be searched to answer the request. The term operations system refers to one in which the types of information are fully anticipated and programs are written to handle them in an efficient manner.

The Internal Revenue Service, for example, has systems for handling queries and operations relating to individual tax accounts. Such operations are relatively straightforward and entirely preplanned. The IRS also needs an *information system* which will answer ad hoc questions for senators and social planners, such as "What percentage of taxpayers with more than three dependents are in a net income bracket less than $6000?" or "What percentage of short-term capital gains taxes from individuals arose from the sale of land?" or "For persons in a gross income bracket between $5000 and $6000 and paying less than 10% of the income in taxes, what are the three largest categories of deductions; repeat this for larger income brackets going up in steps of $1000 to $100,000." Such questions cannot be anticipated in detail, but it may be necessary to answer them fairly quickly.

In an information system, because the types of queries are not anticipated, lengthy searches through the files may be necessary when the query is made. In an operations system lengthy searches can generally be avoided because the information is stored in the form in which it is needed.

65

EXECUTIVE AND SUPERVISORY SYSTEMS

The terms *supervisory* and *executive* systems are sometimes used with meanings similar to operations and information systems. The former refers to systems—usually *operations systems*—with anticipated processing requirements programmed in conventional computer languages. Executive systems, on the other hand, are those which can respond to ad hoc requests for information (often for executives) which require answering quickly.

If the details of the type of information sought are not known prior to its being requested, then a special capability is required in the system—the capability to process ad hoc requests, possibly by generating quickly a program that will

BOX 6.1 Differences Between Supervisory Systems and Executive Systems

	Supervisory Systems (Operations Systems)	Executive Systems (Information Systems)
Request for data	Anticipated Preprogrammed	Spontaneous Not preprogrammed
Typical examples	Airline reservation Bank teller system system	Sales analysis system Personnel information system
Typical users	Bank tellers Shop foreman First-line management	Information staff Middle management Top management aides
Basic objectives	Support routine operations	Support planning and urgent information needs
Response time	Seconds	Minutes, hours
Application implementor	Programmer	Information specialist
Time to respond to a new request for information by management	Months, weeks	Hours, minutes
Typical languages used	COBOL, PL/I	IQF, GIS, special data-base language faculty

respond to the request. A file may contain details, for example, of all branch office expenditure, and an executive may ask the question "Which branch offices have had the largest expenditures for entertaining customers?" A program may be generated quickly which can search the files to produce a precise answer to this question. The executive might go on to ask "How does this expenditure correlate with their sales performance?" This question could be answered precisely using correlation analysis, or it could be answered in a simpler way, which would probably suffice, by listing performance figures alongside branch office entertainment expenses. In either case *the data exist but the question is new*, so a new program is generated rapidly to answer the question. The program might be generated quickly by means of a data-base interrogation language discussed in Chapter 17.

Box 6.1 summaries the differences between supervisory and executive systems.

FOUR TYPES
OF SYSTEMS
A useful way to categorize systems is by asking two questions from Chapter 3. First: *Is the information produced on a scheduled basis*, for example, once a day, once a week, or once a month? If it is, then the operation will be entirely planned in advance and will fit into the daily timetable of jobs to be run on the computer. If not, then the information will normally be requested *on-line* at a terminal. Second: *Does the program for providing the information exist prior to the time the request is made, or is it a new type of request*? In other words, is the request predefined?

Figure 6.1 categorizes systems according to these two questions. There are four possibilities:

1. *Scheduled production of predefined information.* This is classical data processing with no on-line inquiries.
2. *Scheduled production of nonpredefined information.* Nonpredefined information requests might be satisfied by the visual inspection of the vast listings of data that were characteristic of some batch-processing systems. In general, this is a less-than-satisfactory mode of operation. Some batch processing operations have been designed to process ad hoc requests.
3. *On-demand production of predefined information.* This usually requires terminals for answering specific types of inquiries, using prewritten application programs.
4. *On-demand production of information defined when it is needed.* A major complication is introduced into this category of system: The means for searching the data base to find the information must be generated when the information is requested.

It is this last category that is sometimes referred to as an information system. Category 2 could also be an information system, but with a slower reaction time—too slow to be satisfactory for some purposes. The categories in the left-hand squares of Fig. 6.1 will be called operations systems; they are preprogrammed for well-defined operations.

Figure 6.1 Categories of systems needing different data-base structures.

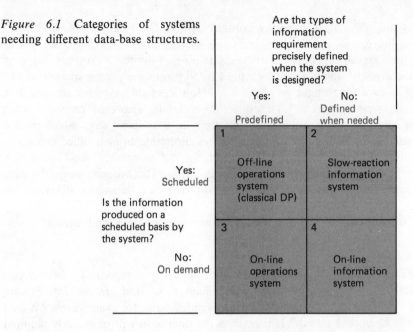

The data base for an *operations system* can be optimized for a precisely predefined set of operations. The data base for an *information system* cannot be tailored to the nature and volume of its use because the use is not predefined in detail.

EXAMPLES   The two types of systems use data bases which are entirely differently structured, as we shall see.

Examples of operations systems are

- A banking system with terminals for tellers
- A factory shop floor system
- An airline reservation system
- A sales order entry and inquiry system
- A credit-checking system
- An air traffic control system
- A police emergency system

Examples of information systems are

- A library information-retrieval system
- A marketing management information system
- A system for searching a litigation data base
- A personnel search data base
- A police detective information system

There are far more operations systems than information systems installed. The cost justification for an operations system is more likely to be tangible than that for an information system.

SEPARATE
DATA BASE
An information system data base may contain the same data as an operations system data base. A firm's marketing management information system, for example, may contain the same data-item types as its sales order entry and inquiry system. However, because one is designed for random searching and the other for precisely defined and relatively simple operations, the data structures needed for the two are very different. They are so different that in practice separate data-base systems are sometimes used, as shown in Fig. 6.2.

The system on the left in Fig. 6.2 might, for example, be a sales order entry system with terminals in branch sales offices. Its files are updated in real time, and many modifications to the data have to be made in real time. The files are

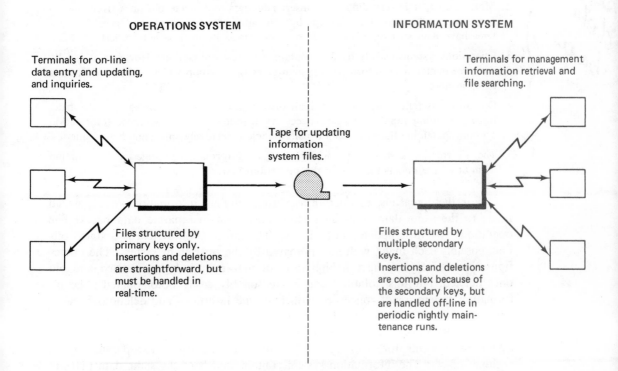

OPERATIONS SYSTEM   INFORMATION SYSTEM

Terminals for on-line data entry and updating, and inquiries.

Terminals for management information retrieval and file searching.

Tape for updating information system files.

Files structured by primary keys only. Insertions and deletions are straightforward, but must be handled in real-time.

Files structured by multiple secondary keys. Insertions and deletions are complex because of the secondary keys, but are handled off-line in periodic nightly maintenance runs.

Figure 6.2   The files of an information system and an operation system relate to the same data. However, they are separated to facilitate maintenance and provide good response time. The same computer may or may not control both sets of files.

all structured and manipulated on the basis of primary keys such as PART-NUMBER and CUSTOMER-NUMBER. New items must be inserted into the files as they arise. There might be a high volume of insertions and deletions, but a fairly straightforward technique can be devised for handling them.

The system on the right in Fig. 6.2 is designed to provide information to management and their staff. It might, for example, answer questions such as "How have the sales of the model 38 in the eastern region to public utilities been affected by the introduction of the new compensation plan?" To answer a diverse set of such questions spontaneously the system uses multiple secondary keys and elaborate file-searching techniques. Why, then, should the systems have separate data bases? The reasons are as follows:

1. The physical data structures used for information systems are such that it is difficult or excessively time-consuming to keep the data up-to-date because multiple lengthy indices or chains are used. Operations systems, on the other hand, have simpler data structures which can be designed for fast updating.

2. More serious, it is very difficult to insert new data and delete old ones from the information system data base, except by a lengthy off-line operation. Operations systems have data structures such that records can easily be inserted or deleted [6].

3. Operations systems usually have to contain the latest transactions. However, it usually does not matter if an information system gives information which is 24 hours out of date, or more.

4. Operations systems may handle a high throughput of transactions so that file structures permitting rapid access are necessary to cope with the volume. Information systems containing the same data usually handle a relatively small number of queries.

5. The information system may contain summary information or digested information without all the details that are in the operations system.

For these reasons an operations system and an information system which relate to the same data sometimes store their data in separate data bases. The operations system is updated in real time. The information system is updated off-line, possibly each night, with files prepared by the operations system. The operations system files may have a high ratio of new records being inserted and old ones deleted, but this volatility can be reasonably easily accomodated. The information system is not concerned with real-time insertions and deletions because new records are inserted off-line.

The IRS information system mentioned earlier is in Maryland, and the IRS operations systems for working on individual tax returns are separate, in ten regional offices. The information system contains much of the same data that are stored in the operations systems; however the data base is structured entirely differently because it is used for entirely different purposes.

SYSTEM EVOLUTION

Operations systems are normally installed before information systems. However, it is worth stressing that in some organizations there has been an evolution from general-purpose information systems to ones which deal with well-specified information requests (i.e., a trend from information systems to operations systems). This is a natural progression and reflects the fact that the information needs of management steadily become better understood. It is a progression that might well be planned for as part of the expected evolution of such systems.

Perhaps the greatest difficulty in building information systems for management lies in finding out what information the management really needs—especially top management—and translating this into the language of the programmer. The systems analyst often does not communicate with the executive in question but with his aide, who is unfamiliar with computer procedures. The systems analyst forms his view of what is needed and passes it on to a program analyst, who writes specifications for the programmers, who then interpret everything according to their own ideas. As if this is not bad enough, the same system when programmed is often used for other executives with different personalities and different styles of operating. It is not surprising that the result sometimes does not fit management's needs.

One of the arguments much used in favor of general-purpose management information systems is that if the system can meet *unspecified* information requirements, then the problems with distortion in the chain of specifications do not arise. The designer does not need to know the precise questions that the user will ask of the system. The user will formulate his needs. There are several flaws in this argument, however. First, information systems which are truly general-purpose and which give an adequate response time tend to be expensive (less expensive however than a non-general system which does not fit management's needs). Second, the user must have an effective means of carrying on a dialogue with the system, and this has often not worked satisfactorily with high-level users, although high-level staff can be trained to use the system to answer management questions. Third, the systems designer must still know the general nature of the user's information needs so that appropriate data bases and mechanisms for manipulating them can be set up.

Faced with these and other problems, general-purpose information systems have sometimes given disappointing results. However, in attempting to solve the problems, more specific needs of management are identified. It slowly becomes clear that the data will be employed for certain specific decisions, and hence an evolution occurs into systems which answer more completely defined information needs. In some cases the capability to generate spontaneously unpreplanned reports from the data has been invaluable to management, and this capability sometimes becomes the most important reason for using data base techniques.

BY-PRODUCT   It is often the case that information of general useful-
INFORMATION   ness can be derived as a by-product of existing data-
                                  processing operations. For example, a local government
data-processing system may carry out a number of operations relating to property,
such as:

> Tax accounts
> Rents accounts
> File of government-owned property records
> File of housing property records
> Records and details of management of government property
> Property demolition records
> File of planning permissions
> Public health inspection records

From these data, secondary information of potential value can be derived.
The data items might therefore be stored in such a manner that they can be
searched to answer unanticipated queries. It may be discovered if this is done
that most of the by-product uses of the data fall into specific categories such as
[7]:

> Land charges search
> Site suitability search
> Trend analysis for overall condition of area
> Centralized inquiry service for public
> Analysis aid for planning decisions (or zoning)
> Analysis aid for tax assessment

In other words, as the value of the data becomes better understood there is
a movement away from *unanticipated* uses toward *anticipated* uses. The data may
therefore be restructured to respond to the anticipated uses more efficiently. In
other words, the information system may evolve into an operations system. There
is often only a vague distinction between the two as data usage clarifies.

If the data base relates to other local government functions also, such as
health, education, parks, and social services, then a much larger and more interesting collection of parasite subsystems could result, giving a highly versatile information system for local government.

It is this type of idea that lies behind much of the enthusiasm for management information systems. Data relating to all aspects of running a corporation
are likely to exist already in some computer storage or other, mostly in systems
designed for routine operations. If only these data could be correlated and analyzed
when needed, then much information could be made available to management
to enable them to make better decisions. We will discuss management information
systems further in Chapter 24.

PART II

DATA ORGANIZATION

Who sees the variety and not the unity, wanders on
from death to death.

Katha Upanishad

7 SCHEMAS AND SUBSCHEMAS

[handwritten: data base must show relationships stored among items.]

*[handwritten: * logical view — for physical without concern — view.]*

If the function of a data base were merely to store data, its organization would be simple. Most of the complexities arise from the fact that it must also show the *relationships* among the various items of data that are stored.

There is a variety of ways in which users represent their views of data relationships. Some of these are very good ways. Others are confusing and liable to mislead. Others are limited in that they cannot represent some of the relationships that exist in reality. Some are inflexible in that they do not easily permit the view of the data to expand and change in the ways a data base ought to develop.

Given the ability of data management software to separate the physical organization of data from the users' view or "logical" organization, the users' view ought, in theory at least, to be formulated *without concern for physical representation*. The users' view of data should be in whatever form is most convenient for them, and the data management software should do the translation between this logical organization and whatever physical organization gives efficient performance.

In practice the computer industry has not yet achieved perfect data management software, and so compromises are sought in the separation of logical and physical data descriptions, as we shall see.

THE SCHEMA

[handwritten: schema — The logical data-base description]

It is necessary to describe the organization of the data in a formal manner. The logical and physical data-base descriptions are used by the data-base management software in extracting from the data base those data items which users require.

The logical data-base description is referred to as a *schema*. A schema is a chart of the types of data that are used. It gives the names of the entities and attributes and specifies the relations among them. It is a framework into which the *values* of the data items can be fitted. Like the display at an airport giving arrival

[handwritten: gives names entities attributes or specifies relations among them]

74

and departure information, the schema will remain the same, while the values fitted into it change from instant to instant. Figure 2.5 could be regarded as a schema if the attribute values inside the box were removed. When the schema framework is filled in with data item values, as in Fig. 2.5, it is referred to as *an instance of the schema.*

We must distinguish between a *record type* and an *instance of the record.* When we talk about a "personnel record," this is really a record type. There are no data values associated with it. Like a schema, it is a framework into which specific data values can be fitted. The data values may change from time to time. At one moment in time the personnel record for Bill Jones may have the data values shown in the top line in the box in Fig. 2.5. We will refer to this as *an instance* of the *personnel record.*

A similar distinction applies to data items, data aggregates, and all other categories of data. In the interest of brevity, this book, like other literature, sometimes uses terms such as "SALARY data item" when it really means "SALARY data-item type," "SUPPLIER record" when it means "SUPPLIER record type," and so forth.

RELATIONSHIPS AND CROSS-REFERENCES   Schemas† are often drawn in the form of a diagram using blocks. Figure 7.1 shows a typical schema. (Like many of the drawings in this book it has been simplified in that the schema for a purchasing system in real life contains many more items than that in Fig. 7.1.)

The solid lines connecting blocks show relationships. The PURCHASE-ORDER record is connected to the PURCHASE-ITEM records of which that

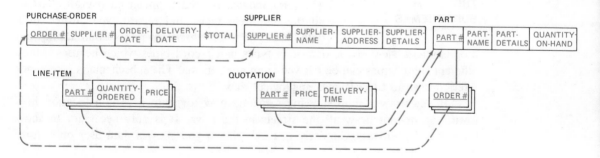

Figure 7.1 A schema. The solid lines between blocks represent relationships. The dashed lines represent cross-references and could be omitted.

---

†The classical plural of *schema* is *schemata.* The plural *schemas* is used in this book in the belief that most readers are happier with it and that a language should evolve toward more logical forms. After all, we no longer say *dogmata* for the plural of *dogma.*

purchase order is composed. The SUPPLIER record is connected to the QUOTA-TION records, showing the parts that a supplier can provide and the price quotations he has given.

The dotted lines show *cross-references*. The PART-NAME or PART-DE-TAILS are not in the PURCHASE-ITEM record but in a separate PART record. Similarly the SUPPLIER-NAME and SUPPLIER-ADDRESS are not in the PURCHASE-ORDER record but in separate SUPPLIER records. In this way it is possible to avoid duplicating SUPPLIER and PART-DETAILS in every PURCHASE-ITEM. Note that the diagram would still represent the information completely if the dotted lines were omitted.

The relationships (solid lines) in the schema *convey information* which is not inherent in the data items shown in the schema by themselves. There is nothing in the PURCHASE-ORDER record of Fig. 7.1, for example, to say what part or quantities of parts the order is for. The information is complete only when the PURCHASE-ITEM records are linked to the appropriate PURCHASE-ORDER records. In some data bases the same two record types can be linked with multiple different relationships.

The cross-references on the other hand do not convey additional information. The PURCHASE-ORDER record does not contain the supplier's name and address. However, it does contain the supplier number. Using this, the name and address can be found from the SUPPLIER file. If the dotted line from SUPPLIER # to SUPPLIER record were removed, no information would be lost. The cross-reference lines indicate pointers in the file which will enable the data pointed to to be located more quickly.

THE SUBSCHEMAS

The term *schema* is used to mean an overall chart of all the data-item types and record types stored in a data base. The term *subschema* refers to an application programmer's view of the data-item types and record types which he uses. Many different subschemas can be derived from one schema. The subschema is sometimes referred to as an *LVIEW* meaning logical view.

If you draw a map showing someone how to go to a certain location in a town, you do not draw all the streets in the town. It is only necessary to show the streets he will use. Similarly in a subschema you show a data user only those data types that he will use.

Figure 7.2 might be a representation of a data base—a schema. It is complex and confusing; you cannot find what you want to find. To show someone how to go to your house you draw a simpler diagram which shows the route, as in Fig. 7.3 —a subschema. The subschema is easy to follow. The user does not mind that there are data which are not shown. He sees what he needs and is not overwhelmed by the complexity of the data base. Many different subschemas can be drawn for different journeys from the overall street map of Fig. 7.2.

Figure 7.2 The overall data-base structure as represented by the schema may be complex and confusing. An application program uses a simpler view of the structure designed for a specific purpose, as in Fig. 7.3. This simpler application-oriented view is called a subschema. Many different subschemas may be derived from one schema.

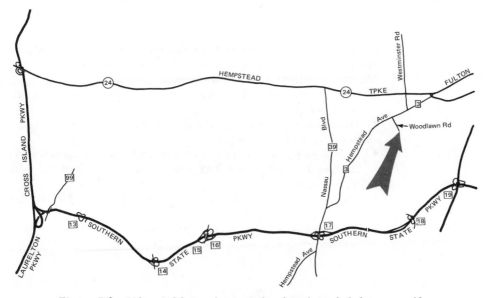

Figure 7.3 (Above) Many views of the data intended for a specific purpose may be derived from the overall data structure (Fig. 7.2).

Figure 7.4 (Right) Different application programs have different views of the data. This figure shows the schema of Fig. 7.1 and two subschemas derived from it by different programmers.

- The schema can evolve without the programmers having to rewrite their programs.
- Programmer A can change the subschema he uses without having any effect on Programmer B.
- A third programmer can add to the data for his own needs without affecting the view of the data seen by the programs of Programmers A or B.
- The programmers neither know nor care how the data are organized physically. The physical organization can be changed without them having to rewrite their programs.

Subschema for programmer B

PARTS-IN-STOCK

PART #	PART-NAME	QUANTITY-ON-HAND

ON-ORDER-DETAIL

ORDER #	SUPPLIER-NAME	QUANTITY-ORDERED	ORDER-DATE	DELIVERY-DATE

Subschema for programmer A

PURCHASE-ORDER-MASTER

ORDER #	SUPPLIER #	SUPPLIER-NAME	SUPPLIER-ADDRESS	DELIVERY-DATE	ORDER-DATE	$TOTAL

PURCHASE-ORDER-DETAIL

PART #	PART-NAME	QUANTITY-ORDERED	PRICE

Software conversion

Software conversion

Programmer A

Programmer B

Schema — The logical data-base description

PART

PART #	PART-NAME	PART-DETAILS	QUANTITY-ON-HAND

PURCHASE-ORDER

ORDER #	SUPPLIER #	ORDER-DATE	DELIVERY-DATE	$TOTAL

SUPPLIER #	SUPPLIER-NAME	SUPPLIER-ADDRESS	SUPPLIER-DETAILS

LINE-ITEM

PART #	QUANTITY-ORDERED	PRICE

QUOTATION

PART #	PRICE	DELIVERY-TIME

ORDER #

Data administrator

Figure 7.4 shows two subschemas for two different application programmers, which are derived from the schema in Fig. 7.1. The programmers have very different views of the data.

The PURCHASE-ORDER-MASTER record of programmer A now contains SUPPLIER-NAME and SUPPLIER-ADDRESS, and the PURCHASE-ORDER-DETAIL record contains PART-NAME and PRICE. The ON-ORDER-DETAIL record of programmer B contains data items from three separate records in the schema.

The application programmers do not necessarily see the schema. The data base administrator, however, must ensure that the subschemas they use are derivable from the schema. The data management software derives the subschema data from the schema data automatically and gives it to the application program.

**THREE DATA
DESCRIPTIONS**
Neither schemas nor subschemas reflect the way the data are stored physically. There are many different forms of physical organization possible for a given logical organization.

There are thus three separate descriptions of the data (illustrated in Fig. 5.1):

1. *The subschema or LVIEW*: A chart of a portion of the data which is oriented to the needs of one or more application programs—a programmer's file organization.

2. *The logical data-base description or schema*: A chart of the entire logical data base. This is the overall view of the data seen by the data base administrator or those systems analysts who see the entire data base.

3. *The physical data-base description*: A chart of the physical layout of the data on the storage devices. The view seen by the systems programmers and the systems designers who are concerned with performance and how data are positioned on the hardware, how it is indexed or located, and what compaction techniques are used.

There is often a fourth view of the data as well—that of the terminal user. Increasingly in the future the terminal user will be a person not trained in the techniques of data processing. The view of the data that he obtains from the system should be as close as possible to the view that is inherent in his job. The way this view is presented to him will depend on the design of the man-computer dialogue that he uses.

Figure 7.5 summarizes these four separate views of the data.

The data-base management system does not employ multiple views of the data just for the sake of multiple views. It permits one view to be changed when necessary while the other views are *preserved*. Only in this way can changes be prevented from dragging the entire set of data views with them. In systems without this facility, the attempt to make seemingly trivial changes in data content or organization has proven appallingly expensive, especially on a complex data base.

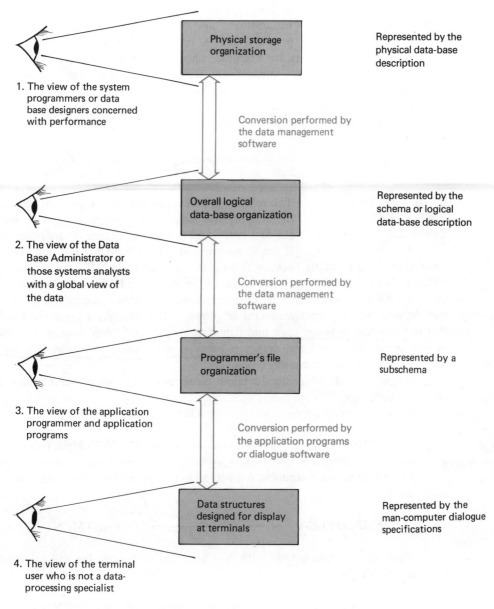

1. The view of the system programmers or data base designers concerned with performance

Physical storage organization

Represented by the physical data-base description

Conversion performed by the data management software

2. The view of the Data Base Administrator or those systems analysts with a global view of the data

Overall logical data-base organization

Represented by the schema or logical data-base description

Conversion performed by the data management software

3. The view of the application programmer and application programs

Programmer's file organization

Represented by a subschema

Conversion performed by the application programs or dialogue software

4. The view of the terminal user who is not a data-processing specialist

Data structures designed for display at terminals

Represented by the man-computer dialogue specifications

Figure 7.5   Four views of the data.

**DATA
LANGUAGES**
A language is needed to represent the schema, the subschemas, and the physical layout of data with pointers, chains, indices, etc. The same language may be used for each of these, as, for example, when IBM's IMS (Information Management System) is employed. Alternatively, different languages may be used, for example, the COBOL Data Division for the subschemas, the CODASYL DBTG Data Description Language for the schema, and the language of some data-base management system for the physical representations. We will discuss such languages in Part III.

Employee # & NAME maps easy

**DATA MAPPING,
SIMPLE AND
COMPLEX**
The relationship between two data types can be simple or complex. By simple we mean that each datum of the first type is related to *one* datum of the other type. If the items are EMPLOYEE-NUMBER and NAME, for example, the mapping between them is simple: Each NAME has an associated EMPLOYEE-NUMBER and vice versa. If the items are EMPLOYEE-NUMBER and DEPARTMENT-NUMBER, the relationship is more complicated because one department can contain several employees. The wording commonly used is that the *mapping* between man and department is *simple* (each man is a member of one department) and the mapping between department and man is *complex* (each department can have many employees).

The schema drawing should make clear which are simple and which are complex mappings.

We will represent a simple mapping by a line with a single arrow on it: *simple*

EMPLOYEE-# ——————⟶—————— DEPARTMENT-#

Simple mapping

We will represent a complex (one-to-many) mapping by a line with a double arrow on it:

Complex mapping

EMPLOYEE-# ——————⟵⟵—————— DEPARTMENT-#

Where the relationships in both directions are of interest we will use arrows pointing in both directions:

EMPLOYEE-# ——————⟵——⟶—————— DEPARTMENT-#

EMPLOYEE-# ——————⟵——⟶—————— EMPLOYEE-NAME

MASTER-RECORD ——————⟶⟶—————— DETAIL-RECORD

STUDENT-# ——————⟵⟵——⟶⟶—————— COURSE-#

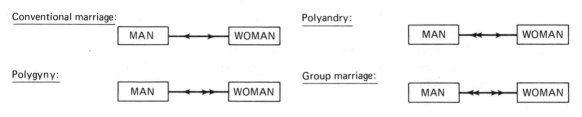

Figure 7.6 Four types of mapping between two entity types—a recommended way to draw simple and complex mappings.

Four types of relations are possible between two sets of items A and B. The mapping of A to B can be simple and the inverse mapping complex. The mapping of A to B can be complex and the inverse mapping simple. Both mappings can be simple, or both mappings can be complex. Figure 7.6 shows four conceivable mappings between MAN and WOMAN using the relationship "marriage."

SCHEMA
DRAWING

A badly drawn schema can confuse rather than clarify, and one often sees badly drawn schemas. When the relationships among records or groups of data items are complex, clarity in schema drawing is very important. Figure 7.7 shows a schema for a purchasing data base with more complex interrelations than those in Fig. 7.1. There is a complex mapping shown from the PART records to the QUOTATION records so that a purchasing officer making an inquiry about a part can see the quotations for that part. There are two complex mappings between the SUPPLIER records and the PURCHASE-ITEM records (which show one item on a purchase order) so that a query may be made about which items are *outstanding* from a supplier and which are *late*. There are two complex mappings between SUPPLIER and QUOTATION to show which suppliers are *candidates* to supply which parts, and which are *actual* suppliers. There is a complex mapping between PART records and ORDER records for those parts.

The cross-reference lines from the PURCHASE-ORDER and PURCHASE-ITEM records to the SUPPLIER and PART records show how supplier name and address and part names are obtained when a purchase order is printed.

Seven relationships are shown in Fig. 7.7, and they are given names. In some cases there are two different relationships between the same records. For example, the suppliers for a given part can be *actual* suppliers or merely *candidate* suppliers for whom a quotation is on file. The relationships between SUPPLIER and QUOTATION records are therefore of two types, one for the actual suppliers and one for the candidate suppliers. The two relationships are given the names ACTUAL-SQ and CANDIDATE-SQ. Similarly, two relations connect the SUPPLIER and PURCHASE-ITEM records, one for orders which are outstanding from a supplier and one for orders which are late. As we will see later, data description languages which are part of data-base management software give (or should give) the capability to specify such relationships.

In a typical commercial data base it can be expected that many more relations than these will develop, needing much more complicated diagrams, so clarity of representation is essential.

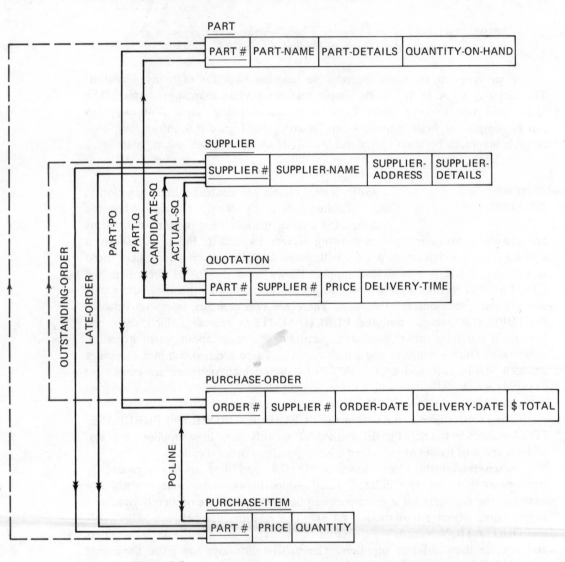

Figure 7.7 A schema for a purchasing data base, with more complex interrelations than those in Fig. 7.1. As before, the solid lines show relationships; the dashed lines show cross-references. The dashed lines could be omitted.

8 TREE AND PLEX STRUCTURES

In the early days of data processing, all files were *flat* files. In a flat file each record contains the same types of data items. One (or possibly more than one) data item is designated the *key* and is used for sequencing the file and for locating records.

In the data-base world many file structures are used which are not *flat*. They are described with words such as *hierarchical files*, CODASYL, *sets, tree structures*, and *networks*. All these types of structures can be classed as either *trees* or *plex structures*.

It may be noted before we begin discussing tree and plex structures that all these more complicated file structures can be broken down into groups of flat files with redundant data items.

TREES

Figure 8.1 shows a tree. A tree is composed of a hierarchy of elements, called *nodes*. The uppermost level of the hierarchy has only one node, called the *root*. With the exception of the root, every node has one node related to it at a higher level, and this is called its *parent* or *father*. No element can have more than one parent. Each element can have one or more elements related to it at a lower level. These are called *children* or sons. Two elements with the same parent are called *twins* or brothers. (Male words are generally avoided since Women's Lib.) Elements at the end of the branches, i.e., with no children, are called *leaves*. The computer industry likes to mix its metaphors.

In Fig. 8.1, element 1 is the *root*. Elements 5, 6, 8–12, and 14–22 are *leaves*. Trees are normally drawn upside down with the root at the top and the leaves at the bottom.

A TREE is composed of a hierarchy of elements called nodes

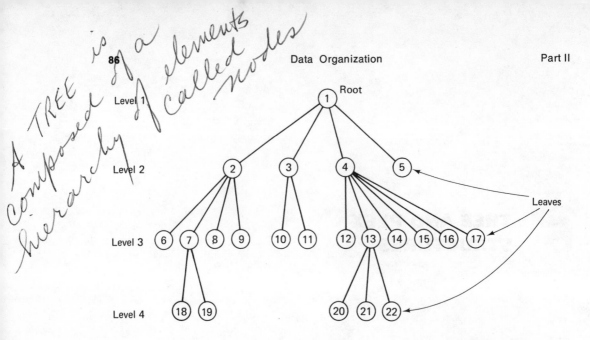

Figure 8.1   A tree. (No element has more than one parent.)

A tree can be defined as a hierarchy of nodes with binodal relationships such that

1. The highest level in the hierarchy has one node called a *root*.

2. All nodes except the root are related to one and only one node on a level higher than themselves.

A tree structure usually implies that there is simple mapping from child to parent (i.e., a child has one parent) and that the inverse mapping is complex (one-to-many), as in Fig. 8.2, which shows a schema and an instance of that schema for a simple two-level tree structure.

MASTER DETAIL file.

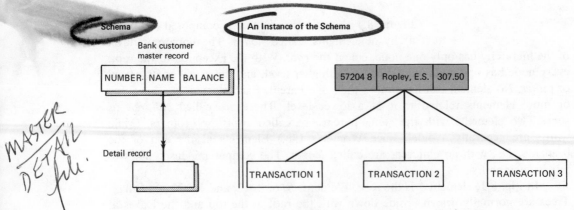

Figure 8.2   A hierarchical file with only two record types.

**HIERARCHICAL
FILES**

The term *hierarchical file* refers to a file with a tree-structure relationship between the records. Figure 8.2 shows a master-detail file—a common type of hierarchical file with two record types. Figure 8.3 shows a four-level hierarchical file. Some data-base software is designed to handle only flat files and hierarchical files. While this is satisfactory for some applications, many important data structures are not of tree form in that one record type can have more than one parent. Hence, software designed solely to handle flat and hierarchical files is limited in its capability.

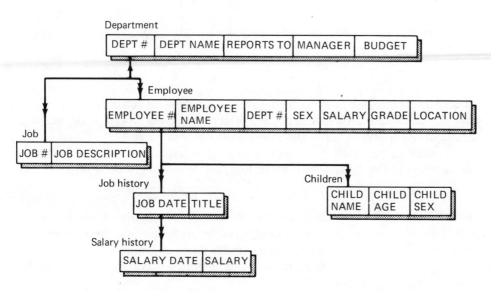

Figure 8.3   A schema for a multilevel hierarchical file.

**PLEX
STRUCTURES**

If a child in a data relationship has *more than one parent*, the relationship cannot be described as a "tree" or "hierarchical structure." Instead it is described as a "network" or "plex structure." The words *network* and *plex structure* are synonymous. We will use *plex structure* because the word network is overworked in teleprocessing.

A family tree is really a plex structure because each individual in the tree has more than one parent. It could be drawn as a tree structure only in the days when women were not included.

Any item in a plex structure can be linked to any other item. Figure 8.4 shows some examples of plex structures.

As with a tree structure, a plex structure can be described in terms of children and parents, and drawn in such a way that the children are lower than the parents, but now a child can have more than one parent. In the first example in Fig.

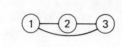

Figure 8.4 Examples of plex structures. One node (or more) has multiple parents.

8.4 each child has two parents. In the second example no indication is given of what the child-parent relationships are. Whichever is the lowest node has two parents. In the fourth example, the lowest node has four parents.

In some plex structures it is natural to refer to levels, as with a tree structure. The examples in Fig. 8.4 have two, three, four, and five levels, respectively.

SIMPLE AND COMPLEX PLEX STRUCTURES

In many plex structures showing the relationships between record types or segment types, the mapping between parents and children is similar to that in a tree: The parent-to-child mapping is complex, and the child-to-parent mapping is simple.

Figure 8.5 shows such a plex structure with five record-types. None of the lines joining the record-types have double arrows *in both directions*. Each relationship can be regarded as a parent-child relationship. The PURCHASE-ORDER record-type is a child of the PART record-type and a parent of the PURCHASE-ITEM record-type.

It is desirable to distinguish between a plex structure in which the child-to-parent mapping is simple or unused and one in which the mapping between any two data-types is complex in both directions. In the latter case one of the lines on the schema will have double arrows going in both directions. We will refer to this type of schema as a *complex plex structure*. A schema in which no line has double arrows in both directions will be called a *simple plex structure*. Figure 8.5 shows a simple plex structure. It becomes a complex plex structure if the mapping from PURCHASE-ORDER to PART is used, because one purchase order can be for many parts. Figure 8.6 shows the schema redrawn as a complex plex structure.

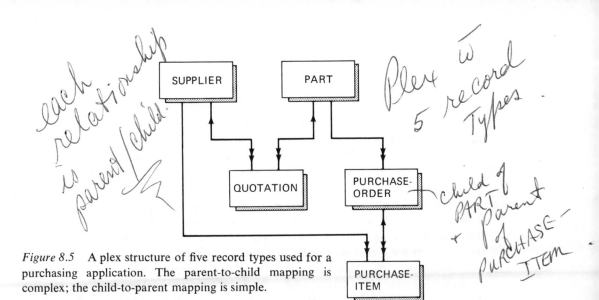

each relationship is parent/child.

Plex w̄ 5 record Types.

child of PART & parent of PURCHASE-ITEM

Figure 8.5 A plex structure of five record types used for a purchasing application. The parent-to-child mapping is complex; the child-to-parent mapping is simple.

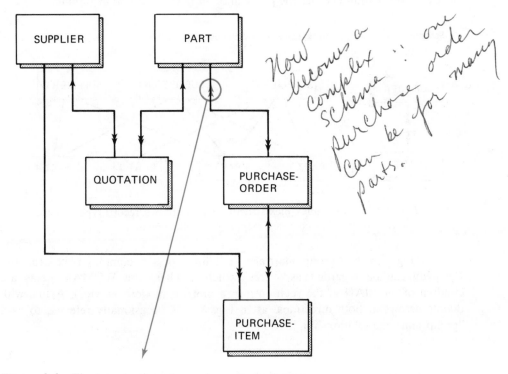

Now becomes a complex scheme ∴ one purchase order can be for many parts.

Figure 8.6 The introduction of complex mapping between the PURCHASE-ORDER record type and the PART record type makes this a complex plex structure. Much data base software cannot handle complex plex structures unless they are restructured.

CODASYL data
description language.
Can describe a simple plex.

The reason for making the distinction between simple and complex plex structures is that the latter need more elaborate methods for representing them *physically* than simple plex structures. Some data-base management software can handle simple plex structures but not complex ones. The data description language proposed by the CODASYL Data Task Group as an industry standard (Chapter 15) can describe simple plex structures but cannot describe complex plex structures without their being modified to a simple form.

The reader might like to think up one or more ways of representing the tree structure of Fig. 8.3 physically, and see if they would work with a simple plex structure; then devise one or more methods which do work with a simple plex structure and see if they work with a complex structure.

A complex plex structure can exist with only two record-types. Figure 8.7 shows an example. The SUPPLIER record can have more than one child because the supplier can supply more than one type of part. The PART record can have more than one parent because the part can be supplied by different suppliers.

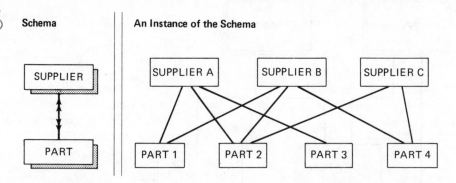

Schema   **An Instance of the Schema**

Figure 8.7   A complex plex structure with only two record types. The one relationship has complex mapping in both directions.

In Fig. 7.6 the "group marriage" relationship is a complex plex structure. *Polygyny* can be regarded as a tree structure where the WOMAN items are children of the MAN in the relationship (a plot for modern movie?). A line with double arrows in both directions, as in Fig. 8.6, is occasionally referred to as a "group marriage relationship."

CYCLES AND LOOPS   Some plex structures contain cycles. A cycle refers to a situation where a node in the structure has as its descendant an ancestor of the node. The parent-child relationships can be followed round in a closed loop. In the schema diagram double-arrow lines form a continuous path as in Fig. 8.8.

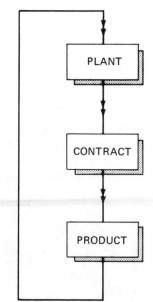

Figure 8.8. A cycle.

Fig. 8.8 shows a cycle. A plant makes many products. Some products may be subcontracted out to other plants. One contract may relate to several products. Representing these relationships gives a cycle. Complicated plex structures occasionally contain multiple cycles. Some data-base software can represent cycles, and some cannot.

A special type of cycle is one which contains only one record-type. The child record-type is the same as the parent. This situation is sometimes called a *loop* (Fig. 8.9).

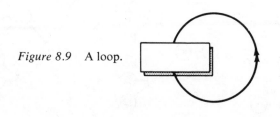

Figure 8.9 A loop.

DECOMPOSITION   A plex structure can be reduced to a simpler form by
INTO SIMPLER FORMS introducing redundancy.

            Figure 8.10 shows how three simple plex structures may be represented as equivalent tree structures. In some cases the redundancy involved in doing so is small and might be tolerated. In other cases it is excessive.

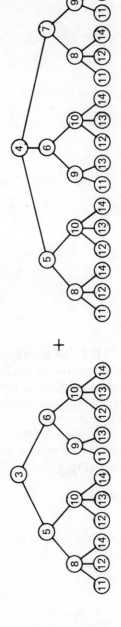

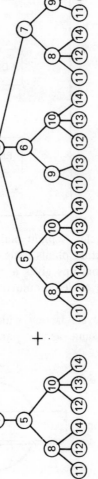

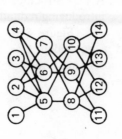

Figure 8.10 Any plex structure can be represented as a tree, or set of trees, with redundant elements. With some structures the amount of redundance can be tolerated; with others it is excessive.

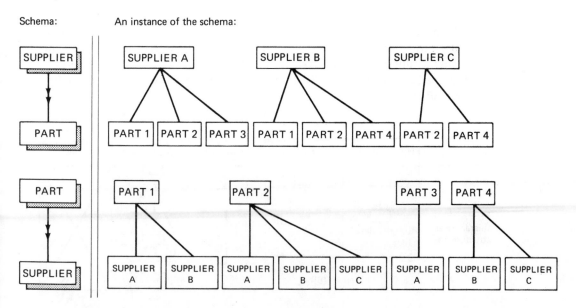

Figure 8.11 The relationship in Fig. 8.7 redrawn as two two-level tree relationships.

A complex plex structure is somewhat more difficult to convert to tree structure. Figure 8.7 requires two trees to represent it, as shown in Fig. 8.11. In general each relationship with complex mapping in both directions needs to be replaced with two tree-structured links.

Note that the duplication of blocks in Fig. 8.11 does not imply redundancy in the manner in which the data are *physically* stored. The diagram, like all schemas, gives a *logical* view of the data and can be mapped into physical storage in a variety of ways, some of which avoid redundancy.

SOFTWARE   The main reason for concern about whether relationships are represented by trees or plex structures is that some data management software can handle plex structures and some cannot. Some can handle trees but not plex structures. The number of levels that can be handled differs from one software package to another. Some software can handle only simple relationships, such as a master-detail file, in which one record-type can be related to only one other record-type. Others can handle compound relationships in which each record-type can be related to multiple other record-types.

Figure 8.12 summarizes the main categories of schema that may be permitted. Different techniques for physical representation have different limitations on which of the types of schema in Fig. 8.12 they can handle. Hence, data-base management systems and data description languages differ in which of the schemas they can handle. Some can handle tree structures but not plex structures. Some can handle simple plex structures but not complex plex structures. The number of levels that can be handled differs from one system to another.

The reader may use Fig. 8.12 to aid in making comparisons of vendors' data-base software.

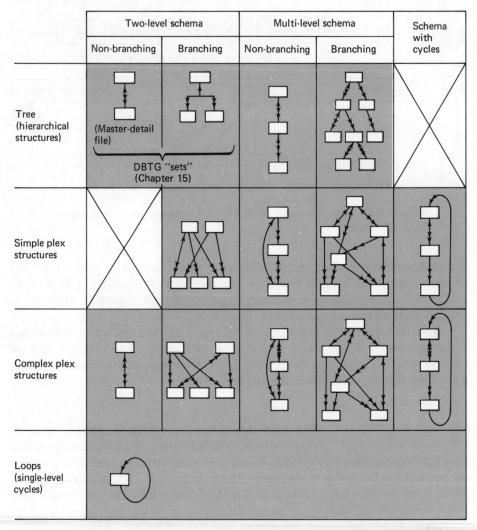

Figure 8.12 Categories of schema. Data-base management systems and languages differ in which of these structures they can handle. Some can handle hierarchical structures but not plex structures. Some can handle simple plex structures but not complex plex structures. The number of levels that can be handled differs from one system to another. Few can handle loops.

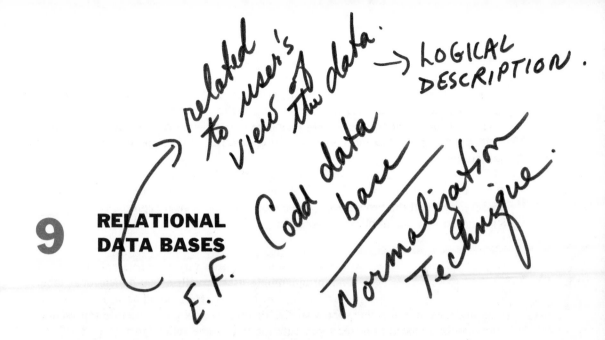

Handwritten annotations: "related to user's views thru data. → LOGICAL DESCRIPTION. Codd data base E.F. Normalization Technique:"

9 RELATIONAL DATA BASES

Most data-base software uses tree or plex structures, so the reader should be fully familiar with them. It is not mandatory, however, to employ tree or plex structures in a data base with complex relationships. There is a simpler and more elegant method—the use of *relational* data bases.

Throughout the history of engineering a principle seems to emerge: *Great engineering is simple engineering.* Ideas which become too cumbersome, inflexible, and problematic tend to be replaced with newer, conceptually cleaner ideas which, compared to the old, are esthetic in their simplicity. When a programmer's block diagram looks like tangled cobweb, the time has come to rethink the entire program.

Data-base systems run the danger of becoming cumbersome, inflexible, and problematic. The logical linkages tend to multiply as new applications are added and as users request that new forms of query be answerable with the data. A high level of complexity will build up in many data-base systems. Unless the designers have conceptual clarity, they will weave a tangled web.

It is possible to avoid the entanglements that build up in tree and plex structures by a technique called *normalization*. Normalization techniques were originally designed and advocated by E. F. Codd [8, 9, 10, 11]. Codd's principles relate to the user's view of the data, or the *logical* description of the data. It is very important to note that they do *not* apply to its physical representation. There are many ways in which a Codd data base could be *physically* structured.

By means of data management software the users' views of data can be kept entirely separate from the physical representation of data, and the physical representation and the hardware can be changed, if necessary, without changing the users' "logical" description of the data. Given this independence, one consideration is of overriding importance in the logical data description: *the convenience of the majority of application programmers and users*. We must search for a way of describing the data that (1) can be understood easily by users with no training in programming, (2) makes it possible to add to the data base without changing the existing *logical* structure and hence changing the application programs, and (3) permits the maximum flexibility in formulating unanticipated or spontaneous inquiries at terminals.

As we will indicate, tree, plex structure, and pointer-linked data representations in general can prohibit many changes to data that may be needed as a data base grows, and the growth can play havoc with the logical representation of data and hence with the application programs.

TABULAR REPRESENTATION

Often the most natural way to represent data to a nonprogramming user is with a two-dimensional table such as that in Fig. 9.1. He is familiar with tables and can understand, remember, and visualize them. Just as a plex structure representation can be reduced to a tree representation with some redundancy (Fig. 8.10), so *any* representation can be reduced to a two-dimensional tabular form with some redundancy. *Normalization* is a step-by-step process for replacing relationships between data such as those in Chapter 8 with relationships in two-dimensional tabular form. The tables must be set up in such a way that no information about the relations between data elements is lost.

The tables in question are rectangular arrays like that in Fig. 9.1, which can be described mathematically. They have the following properties:

1. Each entry in a table represents one data item; there are no repeating groups.

2. They are column-homogeneous; that is, in any column all items are of the same kind.

3. Each column is assigned a distinct name.

4. All rows are distinct; duplicate rows are not allowed.

5. Both the rows and the columns can be viewed in any sequence at any time without affecting either the information content or the semantics of any function using the table.

RELATIONS, TUPLES, AND DOMAINS

The enthusiasts of normalization use a vocabulary different from conventional data-base wording and have a tendency to dress up a basically simple subject in confusing language.

The table, like that in Fig. 9.1, is referred to as a *relation.* A data base constructed using relations is referred to as a *relational data base.* A relational data base is thus one constructed from "flat" arrangements of data items.

The rows of the table are referred to as *tuples.* A tuple is thus a set of data-item values relating to one entity. A tuple of two values is called a *pair.* A tuple containing *N* values is called an *N-tuple.* The tuples shown in Fig. 9.1 are 9-tuples.

This Table is a relation.

A 9-Tuple

Employee-number	Name	Sex	Grade	Date	Department	Skill-code	Title	Salary
53730	JONES BILL W	1	03	100335	044	73	ACCOUNTANT	2000
28719	BLANAGAN JOE E	1	05	101019	172	43	PLUMBER	1800
53550	LAWRENCE MARIGOLD	0	07	090932	044	02	CLERK	1100
79632	ROCKEFELLER FRED	1	11	011132	090	11	CONSULTANT	5000
15971	ROPLEY ED S	1	13	021242	172	43	PLUMBER	1700
51883	SMITH TOM P W	1	03	091130	044	73	ACCOUNTANT	2000
36453	RALNER WILLIAM C	1	08	110941	044	02	CLERK	1200
41618	HORSERADISH FREDA	0	07	071235	172	07	ENGINEER	2500
61903	HALL ALBERT JR	1	11	011030	172	21	ARCHITECT	3700
72921	FAIR CAROLYN	0	03	020442	090	93	PROGRAMMER	2100

Prime key

Tuple

Domain

Relation

Figure 9.1 The wording used in relational data bases. (Note: In a well-designed data base, this relation would be split into more than one relation in *third normal form*; an explanation of third normal form is given in Chapter 14 of *Computer Data-Base Organization* by James Martin.)

A column

9 Tuples

A Tuple is a set of data items.

rows are Tuples

A relation is Two domains is a relation degree 2.

A *flat file* is thus one relation and consists of a set of tuples. Files which involve relationships between data items more complex than *flat* two-dimensional relations can be broken into groups of associated two-dimensional relations, as we will illustrate later.

A column in Fig. 9.1, i.e., the set of values of one data item, is referred to as a *domain*.

A relation consisting of two domains, i.e., two data-item types, is referred to as a relation of degree 2.

If there are *N* domains, it is of degree *N*. Relations of degree 2 are called *binary*, degree 3 are called *ternary*, and degree *N* are called *N-ary*.

Precise mathematical notations exist based on relational algebra or relational calculus for describing such relations and operations among them. Codd has devised a sublanguage for manipulating such a data base [4]. A more conventional man-computer dialogue could be translated into this sublanguage. We will use nonmathematical language to describe the way the tables may be manipulated.

Different users of the same data base will perceive different sets of data items and different relationships between them. It is therefore necessary to extract subsets of the table columns for some users, creating tables of smaller degree, and to join tables together for other users. Codd's sublanguage carries out these operations. As some of the tables may have many columns, the ability to extract subsets is important. These cutting and pasting operations give a degree of flexibility that is not possible with most tree structures and network structures.

The logical view of the data base can thus consist of sets of two-dimensional tables with operations for extracting columns and joining them. In Codd's words, *"Both the application programmer and the interactive user view the data base as a time varying collection of normalized relations of assorted degrees"* [2].

REPEATING GROUPS

It sometimes comes as rather a shock to the conventional data-base specialist steeped in tree and plex structures to hear that [*all files can be represented as flat files.*] It sometimes strains his credulity; we had better consider some examples.

First a file which is flat except for a repeating group can be normalized by removing the repeating group into a separate table or flat file, as shown in Fig. 9.2. The new file or *relation* so formed is given a name. The tuples in it must have keys which uniquely identify them. The data item ORDER-# is repeated in the PURCHASE-ITEM file, and this combined with PART-# forms a unique identifier.

It might be objected that redundancy is increased because the data item ORDER-# appears twice. Normalization does require that some data items appear in more than one record in order to identify the records. This duplication does not necessarily imply an increase in storage requirements because normalization

A group of data items which is repeated a specified number of times.

flat except for a repeating group

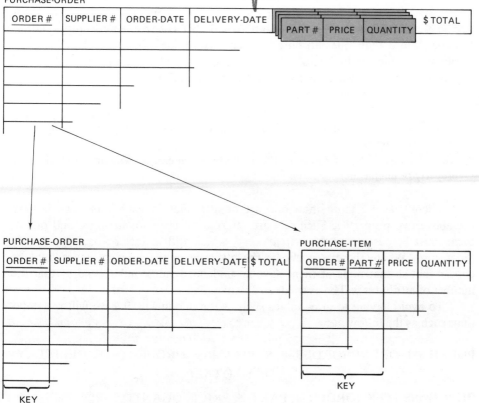

Figure 9.2   A repeating group is removed by
splitting the file into two relations.

is concerned with *logical* structure—the users' views of data—not with the way
they are physically represented in storage.

If repeating groups are not separated out in this way when a data base
is initially designed, there is a danger that subsequent evolution in the way the
data base is used will necessitate their separation. For example, programs may
have to be added in the future in which the individual PURCHASE-ITEM tuples
in Fig. 9.2 are associated with a different record. The PURCHASE-ORDER data
base may evolve as shown in Fig. 7.8 so that an association between SUPPLIER
records and the PURCHASE-ITEM tuples is used. In Fig. 7.8 the PURCHASE-
ITEM tuple must be a separate record rather than a repeating group of the
PURCHASE-ORDER records. If repeating groups have to be separated out at a
time after application programs have been written using them, then these application programs must be substantially modified and retested. Normalization
coupled with data independence in the software will avoid this maintenance cost.

KEYS   Each tuple must have a key with which it can be identi-
                          fied. The tuple may be identifiable by means of one
attribute. ORDER-# in Fig. 9.2 identifies a PURCHASE-ORDER tuple. Often,
however, more than one attribute is necessary to identify the tuple. No single
attribute is sufficient to identify a PURCHASE-ITEM tuple in Fig. 9.2, so the
key would consist of two attributes ORDER-# and PART-#.

The key must have two properties:

1. *Unique identification*: In each tuple of a relation, the value of the key must uniquely
   identify that tuple.
2. *Nonredundancy*: No attribute in the key can be discarded without destroying the
   property of unique identification.

There may be more than one set of attributes in each tuple which have
the above two properties. Such sets are referred to as *candidate keys*, and one of
them must be designated the *primary key*, which will in fact be used to identify
the record. Where there is a choice the attribute in the primary key should be
chosen first so that none of them have an undefined value and second so that the
number of attributes will be as small as possible.

To avoid having to draw tables such as the one in Fig. 9.2 we will use notations such as the following: *names of the domains*

PURCHASE-ORDER (ORDER-#, SUPPLIER-#, ORDER-DATE, DELIVERY-
                          DATE, $-TOTAL)

PURCHASE-ITEM (ORDER-#, PART-#, PRICE, QUANTITY)

The item prior to the parentheses is the *name of the relation*. The items
inside the parentheses are the *names of the domains*. The underlined *items are the
keys* which are necessary to identify the tuples (i.e., the primary keys).

primary key.

TREE   A tree structure can be normalized in a similar fashion.
STRUCTURES   Figure 9.3 illustrates a four-level tree and shows how it
                          is replaced by six relations. The key of a relation may
incorporate the key of the relation immediately above it in the tree. JOB-
HISTORY, for example, has a key (EMPLOYEE-#, JOB-DATE) which incorporated the key of the item above it (EMPLOYEE-#). The EMPLOYEE relation,
however, has a key of its own (EMPLOYEE-#), which uniquely identifies the
EMPLOYEE tuples and so does not need to incorporate the key of the relation
above it.

Normalize Tree (handwritten)

a four-level tree (handwritten)

A schema for a tree structure:

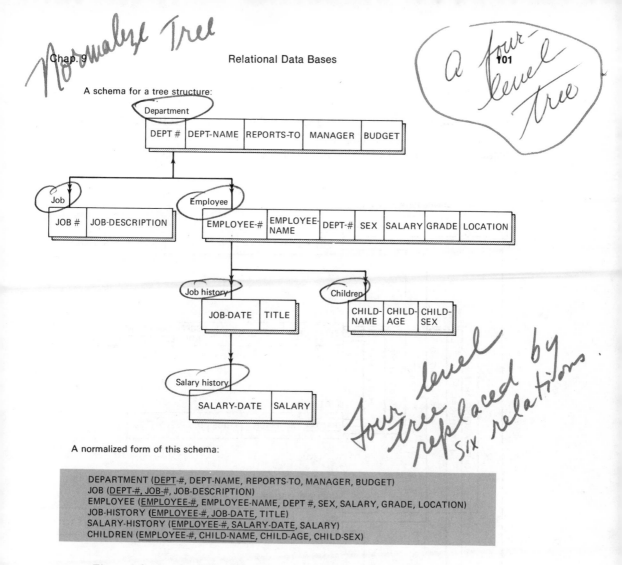

Four level tree replaced by six relations. (handwritten)

A normalized form of this schema:

DEPARTMENT (<u>DEPT-#</u>, DEPT-NAME, REPORTS-TO, MANAGER, BUDGET)
JOB (<u>DEPT-#, JOB-#</u>, JOB-DESCRIPTION)
EMPLOYEE (<u>EMPLOYEE-#</u>, EMPLOYEE-NAME, DEPT #, SEX, SALARY, GRADE, LOCATION)
JOB-HISTORY (<u>EMPLOYEE-#, JOB-DATE</u>, TITLE)
SALARY-HISTORY (<u>EMPLOYEE-#, SALARY-DATE</u>, SALARY)
CHILDREN (<u>EMPLOYEE-#, CHILD-NAME</u>, CHILD-AGE, CHILD-SEX)

Figure 9.3 As the following chapter will indicate, a further normalization step should be applied to these relations.

PLEX STRUCTURES

Figure 9.4 shows the plex schema used earlier and gives one of several possible normalized forms of it.

A variety of directed links is shown in the schema, some of them with one arrow, showing simple mapping, and some of them with two arrows, showing complex mapping. Some of the links show relations among the data. The link from PART to PURCHASE-ORDER shows which purchase orders include an order for that part. The link from PURCHASE-ORDER to PURCHASE-ITEM shows which parts are listed on a given order. To reconstruct the order the supplier name and part names are required, and so there are single-arrow cross-reference (dotted) links from PURCHASE-ITEM to PART and from PURCHASE-ORDER to SUPPLIER. Similarly, each PART record is linked to quotations for that part. The QUOTATION record does not contain the supplier name and hence is linked to the SUPPLIER record.

A schema for a plex structure:

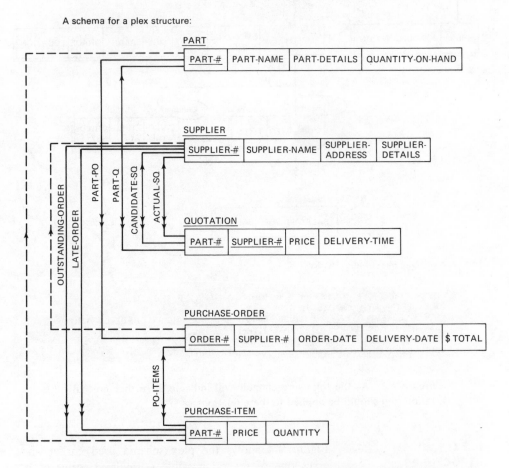

A normalized form of this schema:

PART (<u>PART-#</u>, PART-NAME, PART-DETAILS, QUANTITY-ON-HAND)
SUPPLIER (<u>SUPPLIER-#</u>, SUPPLIER-NAME, SUPPLIER-ADDRESS, SUPPLIER-DETAILS)
ACTUAL-SUPPLIER (<u>PART-#</u>, <u>SUPPLIER-#</u>, PRICE, DELIVERY-TIME)
CANDIDATE-SUPPLIER (<u>PART-#</u>, <u>SUPPLIER-#</u>, PRICE, DELIVERY-TIME)
PURCHASE-ORDER (<u>ORDER-#</u>, SUPPLIER #, ORDER-DATE, DELIVERY-DATE, $ TOTAL)
PURCHASE-ITEM (<u>PART-#</u>, <u>ORDER-#</u>, PRICE, QUANTITY)
ORDERS-OUTSTANDING (<u>PART-#</u>, <u>SUPPLIER-#</u>, <u>ORDER-#</u>, LATE?)

Figure 9.4

Some of the links in Fig. 9.4 are labeled to have special meanings. For example, the links between SUPPLIER and QUOTATION indicate whether the supplier actually supplies the part in the QUOTATION record or is merely a candidate to supply it. The links from SUPPLIER to PURCHASE-ITEM show the outstanding and late orders for each supplier.

PROBLEMS WITH In Codd's view there is no need at all for directed links,
DIRECTED LINKS such as those in Fig. 9.4, in the users' or application
programmers' description of the data. They tend to confuse rather than to clarify.

Some of the links in Fig. 9.4 are *unnecessary*. The link from PURCHASE-ITEM to PART is unnecessary, for example, because the PURCHASE-ITEM record contains the attribute PART-#, which could be used for accessing the PART record. The inclusion of the link from PURCHASE-ITEM to PART results from a confusion of the logical description of data with the physical description in which a physical pointer might be used. The same is true with all the single-arrow pointers in Fig. 9.4.

In most data bases there are many cross-referencing associations that could be shown. To depict them all with lines and arrows would result in an impossibly tangled web of connections.

The links drawn on schemas generally imply a relation of degree 2. For example, the line labeled PO-ITEMS from the PURCHASE-ORDER to the PURCHASE-ITEM tuple could be represented by a relation PO-ITEMS (OR-DER-#, PART-#). Where parallel links with different labels are drawn, as with OUTSTANDING and LATE on the links from SUPPLIER to PURCHASE-ITEM, they imply a relation of degree 3 (SUPPLIER, PURCHASE-ITEM, STATUS). Such links imply a different treatment of relations of degree 2 (or 3) to relations of higher degree, whereas in fact they may be treated identically. If they *are* treated differently by the computer, for example, with different addressing methods, this difference should be the concern of the designer of the *physical* data structure, not the designer of the *logical* structure.

As the data base grows, a relation which is at one time of degree 2 may become a relation of higher degree. If the degree 2 relations are *lines with arrows* in the logical data description, this growth is difficult to represent. It entails replacing a line in a schema by a new relation, thus disrupting some application programs.

Where lines with arrows are drawn from one block to another and then to a succeeding block, the user tends to follow these lines and assume that they represent a ternary relation. Drawing such lines offers the temptation to represent a ternary relation as two binary relations, but to do so may be invalid. Codd refers to this as "the connection trap" [8]. Consider case 1 in Fig. 9.5. Arrows go from PART 4 to SUBASSEMBLY C and from SUBASSEMBLY C to PRODUCT 5. A casual user may draw the implication from the arrows that PRODUCT 5 contains PART

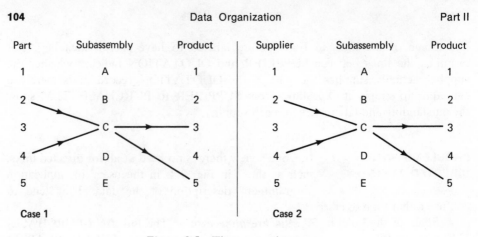

Figure 9.5   The connection trap.

4, and he would be correct. Now, however, consider case 2 in Fig. 9.5. This case is identical to case 1 except that the left-hand column is now headed SUPPLIER instead of PART. Arrows go from SUPPLIER 4 to SUBASSEMBLY C and from SUBASSEMBLY C to PRODUCT 5. The user may draw the implication from the arrows that PRODUCT 5 has SUPPLIER 4 as one of its suppliers. This time he may be wrong. The SUBASSEMBLY C used in PRODUCT 5 may be supplied by SUPPLIER 2, not SUPPLIER 4; that in PRODUCT 3 alone may be supplied by SUPPLIER 4.

Ternary relations are needed to clarify the situation, as follows:

Case 1			*Case 2*		
PART	SUBASSEMBLY	PRODUCT	SUPPLIER	SUBASSEMBLY	PRODUCT
2	C	3	2	C	5
2	C	5	4	C	3
4	C	3			
4	C	5			

In general, lines with arrows offer the designer of the logical data base the temptation to draw structures which are inflexible, misleading, and sometimes invalid. A relational representation can be flexible, easily comprehensible, and mathematically rigorous.

BILL-OF-MATERIALS NORMALIZATION

In many cases the normalized form appears much simpler than a conventional schema. This is the case with the bill-of-materials schema shown in Fig. 9.6.

A schema for a bill-of-materials file:

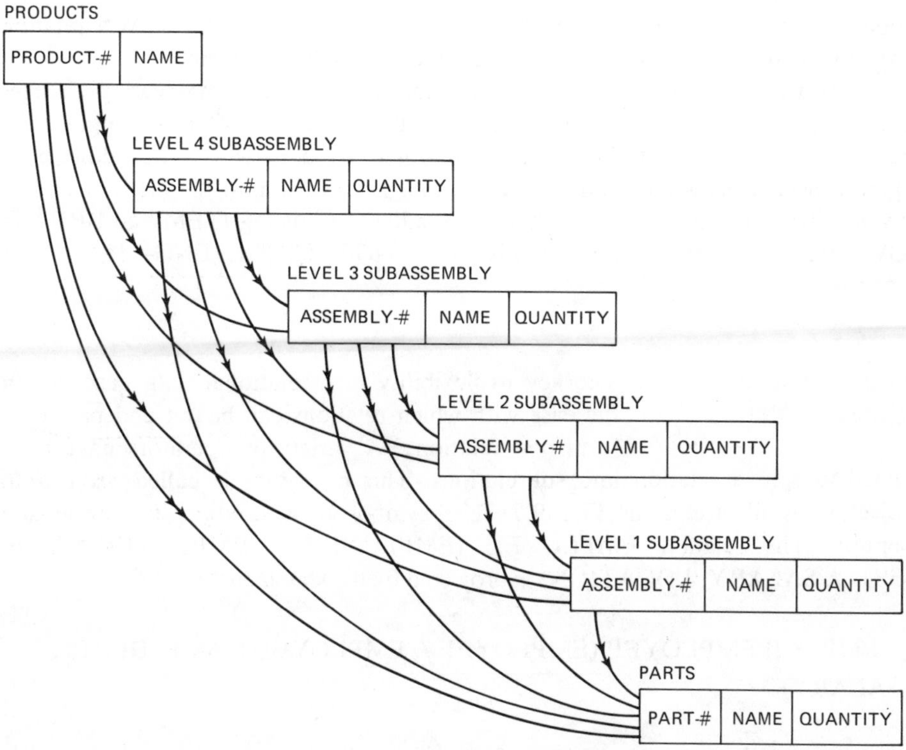

A normalized form of this schema:

ITEM (ITEM-#, CATEGORY, NAME)
BREAKDOWN (ITEM-#, COMPONENT-ITEM-#, QUANTITY)

Figure 9.6 In some cases the normalized form can be much simpler than the unnormalized schemas. The more complex the relationships the more the user needs normalization to keep his head straight.

The products made by a factory consist of parts, such as screws or rods, and subassemblies, such as drive units and door catches. A subassembly may itself be composed of parts and other subassemblies. Level 4 subassemblies may contain level 3 subassemblies, which may contain level 2 subassemblies, and so forth. The bill-of-materials file shows what the products and subassemblies are composed of.

The normalized form of this file contains two relations: an ITEM relation which contains the ITEM-#, NAME, and an attribute saying whether the item is a product, part, or level 1, 2, 3, or 4 subassembly, and a BREAKDOWN relation giving the quantity of each item that is a component of another item.

It is a characteristic of many bill-of-materials files that engineering changes occur frequently. The product breakdown both before and after the engineering change will be stored. If the file is represented by a network, the addition of engineering changes will be complex. In the normalized form of the file it is simple. Any new items introduced by the change are added to existing ITEM and BREAK-DOWN relations, and a third relation is used: ENG-CHANGE (ENG-CHANGE-# ITEM-#).

MANIPULATIONS OF RELATIONS   The key to flexibility in a relational data base lies in the ease with which relations can be cut and pasted to form new relations. A variety of operators have been defined to split a relation into subrelations. This operation is called *projection*. Projection is illustrated in Fig. 9.7. The symbol Π is used as the projection operator. The relation EMPLOYEE (EMPLOYEE-#, EMPLOYEE-NAME, DEPT-#, SALARY, LOCATION) is projected by the statement

EMP = Π EMPLOYEE (EMPLOYEE#, EMPLOYEE-NAME, DEPT#, SALARY)

to form a new relation called EMP, as follows:

EMP (EMPLOYEE-#, EMPLOYEE-NAME, DEPT-#, SALARY)

Similarly, the statement DEPT = Π EMPLOYEE (DEPT-#, LOCATION) forms the relation DEPT (DEPT-#, LOCATION). In this case the result contains fewer tuples than the original because all duplicate tuples are removed.

The converse of splitting relations is connecting different relations together with a NATURAL JOIN operation. * is the symbol used as the JOIN operator. The statement EMPLOYEE = EMP * DEPT does the opposite of the operation shown in Fig. 9.7 and forms the relation EMPLOYEE from the relations EMP and DEPT.

A user may wish to form a relation out of two or more separate relations, which does not use all the attributes of these relations. For example, in joining EMP and DEPT he may wish to create a relation which gives only the employees' names and locations. This can be done with the statement

EMPLOC = Π EMP * DEPT (EMPLOYEE-NAME, LOCATION)

Π is the projection operator. (handwritten)

EMPLOYEE

EMPLOYEE-#	EMPLOYEE-NAME	DEPT-#	SALARY	LOCATION
53702	BLANAGAN J E	721	1200	NEW YORK
53703	ROPLEY E S	721	2300	NEW YORK
53791	MUSSOLINI M	007	5000	DETROIT
53800	FRANKENSTEIN W	402	1100	MIAMI
53805	DUNNE J	721	1900	NEW YORK
53806	JONES P L	402	1000	MIAMI

split relation into sub relations (handwritten)

EMP = Π EMPLOYEE (EMPLOYEE #, EMPLOYEE NAME, DEPT #, SALARY)

DEPT = Π EMPLOYEE (DEPT #, LOCATION)

EMP

EMPLOYEE-#	EMPLOYEE-NAME	DEPT-#	SALARY
53702	BLANAGAN J E	721	1200
53703	ROPLEY E S	721	2300
53791	MUSSOLINI M	007	5000
53800	FRANKENSTEIN W	402	1100
53805	DUNNE J	721	1900
53806	JONES P L	402	1000

DEPT

DEPT-#	LOCATION
721	NEW YORK
007	DETROIT
402	MIAMI

Figure 9.7 An illustration of projection. The relation EMPLOYEE is split into two relations.

Figure 9.8 shows a natural join operation on three relations. The resulting relation may be much smaller than relations which are joined.

Caution is needed when a JOIN operation is used to ensure that the result is indeed valid. It is quite possible to JOIN relations which logically should not be joined.

Many other operations are possible on relations. A calculus [10, 11] exists for the manipulation of relations, which might become the basis of future data-base languages enabling data to be spontaneously searched or manipulated.

P123

IDENTIFIC-ATION#	CONVICTION-DATE	CONVICTION-TYPE	CONVICTION-LENGTH
817.42315	1.12.75	RAPE	12
817.42815	2.2.76	THEFT	24
817.43001	10.12.73	THEFT	36
817.44051	11.1.76	DRUGS	LIFE
817.46172	3.5.75	RAPE	36

A117

IDENTIFIC-ATION#	NAME	ADDRESS	ZIP-CODE
817.53711	JENKINS L	10.E.51	10017
817.42815	SMITH A	24.E.51	10017
817.60712	ROPLEY E S	201.E.51	10017
817.31179	ELIOT K	402.E.51	10017
817.44051	DOE J	497.E.51	10017

A125

IDENTIFIC-ATION#	NAME	PROFESSION	INCOME-RANGE
817.42815	SMITH A	ACCOUNTANT	10 000
817.77112	WILLIAMS S	REALTOR	30 000
817.73119	NELSON H	SAILOR	10 000
817.44051	DOE J	DIPLOMAT	50 000
817.91254	MARTIN P	PROGRAMMER	10 000

k = P123 * A117 * A125 (NAME, ZIP CODE, PROFESSION, CONVICTION TYPE, CONVICTION DATE)

NAME	ZIP-CODE	PROFESSION	CONVICTION-TYPE	CONVICTION-DATE
SMITH A	10017	ACCOUNTANT	THEFT	2.2.76
DOE J	10017	DIPLOMAT	DRUGS	11.1.76

Figure 9.8   A natural join operation.

✳ = ⋈ NATURAL JOIN

PAY AS LITTLE AS

55¢ AN ISSUE

Try Newsweek for as little as 55¢ an issue and save up to 71% off the $1.95 cover price.

☐ 3 YEARS–55¢/ISSUE
(156 Issues)

☐ 2 YEARS–65¢/ISSUE
(104 Issues)

☐ 1 YEAR–75¢/ISSUE
(52 Issues)

☐ 6 MONTHS–75¢/ISSUE
(26 Issues)

Mr./Mrs./Ms. (circle one)

Street

City   State   Zip

☐ Check enclosed   ☐ Bill me   ☐ Renewal (Attach label)

75¢ is Annual Basic Rate   Offer good in US only and subject to change

7143053730

Newsweek

ADVANTAGES　　　　　　Normalized data structures have important advantages over other data structures, especially when third normal form is used. They are:

1. *Ease of use.* The easiest way to represent most data to users not trained or talented in the techniques of data processing is with two-dimensional tables.
2. *Flexibility.* Operations such as PROJECTION and JOIN permit cutting and pasting of relations so that the different logical files wanted by different application programmers can be given to them in the form they want them.
3. *Precision.* The directed links which are common today in logical data representations can sometmes be misleading, as in Fig. 9.5. Relations are precise in meaning and can be manipulated with the precise mathematics of relational algebra or relational calculus.
4. *Security.* Security controls can be more easily implemented. Security authorizations will relate to relations. Sensitive attributes, such as SALARY in an employee file, could, for example, be moved into a separate relation with its own authorization controls. If the authorization requirements are met, SALARY will be JOINed back to the other employee attributes.
5. *Relatability.* The maximum flexibility is possible in relating attributes from different sets of tuples, or different "files."
6. *Ease of implementation.* The physical storage of flat files can be less complex than the physical storage of tree and plex structures. As more elaborate physical techniques come into use, the simplification offered by normalization will probably pay major dividends. Hardware devices to assist in rapid file searching are more feasible with files which avoid complex pointer linkages.
7. *Data independence.* There will be need for most data bases to grow by adding new attributes and new relations. The data will be used in new ways. Tuples will be added and deleted. New data-item types will be added and old ones deleted. If the data base is in a normalized form with data independence in the software, the data can be restructured, and the data base can grow without, in most cases, forcing the rewriting of application programs. This is important because of the excessive and growing costs of maintaining an organization's application programs and its data from the disrupting effects of data-base growth, then as its quantity of application programs increases the cost of maintaining them will rise to prohibitive levels. Good data independence can probably be achieved more easily with normalized logical structures than with tree or plex structures.
8. *Data manipulation language.* A data manipulation sublanguage can be based on relational algebra or relational calculus. If the data were organized so that a variety of non-flat structures were permitted, the data sublanguage would either be unnecessarily complex for the user or else be limited in its capability.
9. *Clarity.* The logical data-base representations using arrows, such as those in Figs. 9.3 and 9.4, may be clear as long as the number of records is low. The ultimate objective of data-base growth, however, is to produce data bases which encompass many of the related activities of an organization. An attempt to represent the details of the interrelations of many files using schemas with arrows becomes exces-

sively complicated. One occasionally finds data base administrators plastering the walls with vast cobweb-like arrow diagrams. As data bases grow to encompass more and more activities it is essential that we break away from logical representations using pointers to pointers to pointers. Relational data bases seem the best alternative.

THIRD NORMAL FORM   Normalization needs to be taken a step further than is described in this chapter. It is necessary to select the attributes in each tuple in such a way that the tuple will be *stable* as the data base grows, changes, and is used for new applications. A relation can have new data-item types (new domains) added to it without affecting existing programs if the right software exists. However, the contents of a relation should be chosen so that they are not likely to split into two or more relations. Codd applies two rigorously defined steps of further normalization which result in a structure called *third normal form*. A reader interested in this should read Reference 9 or J. Martin, *Computer Data-Base Organization*, Prentice-Hall, Inc., Englewood Cliffs, N.J., 1975.

A third normal form structure protects the data base and programs which use it as much as possible from the disrupting effects of future change, and hence from the spector of maintenance costs rising to prohibitive levels.

SOFTWARE   Most of today's data-base management systems are not designed around normalized data structures, or *rational data bases*. Eventually, one hopes, they will be. There are many prototype or custom-built relational data bases. Most of today's software could nevertheless be used to implement normalized structures but lacks the capability to cut and paste the relations so that their usage can be made highly flexible.

10 FILE ADDRESSING

We have seen that our naive picture of a data base in Fig. 4.2 does not reveal the complexity of representing relationships among data. In this chapter we will deal with another cause of data-base complexity: How do you find the data you are looking for in the data base?

As we described earlier, records are *identified* by means of a unique group of characters called a primary *key*. It may be an account number in a bank or a part number in a factory. It may be necessary to join two or more data items together in order to produce a unique key. (This is called a *concatenated key*.) The basic problem of file addressing is this: *Given a primary key, how does the computer locate the record for that key?*

There are several techniques for locating a record. Each has a major effect on the *physical* organization of a data base. This chapter discusses them.

Technique 1: Scanning the File

The simplest and crudest way of locating a record is to scan the file, inspecting the key of each record. This method is far too slow for most purposes and is only likely to be used on a batch-processing operation using a serial file such as tape where each record must be read anyway.

Technique 2: A Block Search

Where the records are sequentially organized by key not every record need be read when scanning the file. The computer might, for example, examine every hundredth record in ascending key sequence (Fig. 10.1). When a record is found with a key higher than the key used for searching, the 99 records that were skipped

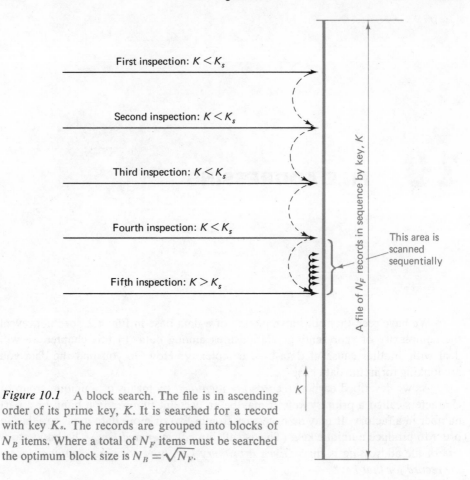

First inspection: $K < K_s$

Second inspection: $K < K_s$

Third inspection: $K < K_s$

Fourth inspection: $K < K_s$

Fifth inspection: $K > K_s$

This area is
scanned
sequentially

A file of N_F records in sequence by key, K

K

Figure 10.1   A block search. The file is in ascending
order of its prime key, K. It is searched for a record
with key K_s. The records are grouped into blocks of
N_B items. Where a total of N_F items must be searched
the optimum block size is $N_B = \sqrt{N_F}$.

are then searched. This is called a *block search*, the records being grouped into
blocks, and each block is inspected once until the correct block is found. It is
also sometimes called a *skip search*.

A block search is unlikely to be used for searching a large file, but it is an
important technique for searching a relatively small portion of a file located by
another technique such as indexing.

Technique 3:   A Binary Search

A binary search can be used when the records are ordered in the sequence of
their keys. A binary search goes to the midpoint of the area to be searched and
compares the key of that record with the search key. It then halves the search
area and repeats the process (Fig. 10.2). It continues halving the area until the
required record is found.

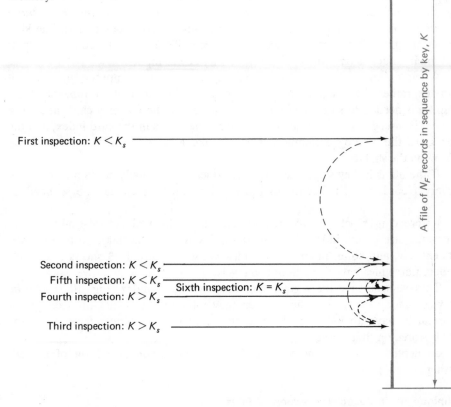

Figure 10.2 A binary search. The file is in ascending order of its prime key, K. It is searched for a record of key K_s. Each inspection of the file halves the area to be searched. A binary search may be unsuitable for searching a file on direct-access storage because of the seeks it incurs. It is commonly used for searching an index which is entirely within main memory.

A binary search is generally inappropriate for searching electromechanical storage devices because it necessitates time-consuming movements of the access mechanism backwards and forwards. It can be useful, however, for searching items in main memory or in a solid-state storage, because no mechanical movement occurs.

As with a block search, binary searching is more likely to be used for searching an index to a file than searching the file itself.

Technique 4: Indexed Sequential Files

If a file is laid out in key sequence, the usual method of addressing it is by means of a table called an *index*. The input to the table is the key of the record sought, and the result of the table look-up operation is the address of the record on the file unit.

An index may be defined as *a table which operates with a procedure that accepts information about certain attribute values as input and gives information as output which assists in quickly locating the record or records that have those attribute values*. A primary index is one which uses a record identifier (prime key) as input and gives information concerning the record's physical location as output. A secondary index is one which uses a secondary key as input.

When an index is used for addressing a file, the computer must search the index rather than search the file. A considerable amount of time is saved, but space is needed to store the index. It is rather like the use of a card index in a library. The user looks up the name of the book he wants in the card index, and the index gives the catalogue number, which is like a relative address of the book position on the shelves.

If the file is in key sequence, the index does not normally contain a reference to every record but a reference to blocks of records which can be scanned or searched.

Referencing blocks of records rather than individual records substantially reduces the size of the index. Even so the index is often too large to be searched in its entirety, and so an index to the index is used. Figure 10.3 shows two levels of index. Large files have more than two levels.

To save seek time the segments of the lower-level index (Fig. 10.3) may be dispersed among the data records which they refer to. On a disk-file example, it is normal to have an index track on each cylinder, containing references to the records stored on that cylinder.

Sequential files with indices constitute the most common form of file addressing.

Technique 5: Indexed Nonsequential Files

A nonsequential file can be indexed, as can a sequential file. A much larger index is needed, however, because it must contain an entry for every record rather than an entry for every block of records. Furthermore, it must contain *complete* addresses (or relative addresses), whereas an index to a sequential file can truncate the address it contains because the high-order characters of succeeding addresses are the same. Figure 10.4 illustrates an indexed nonsequential file.

Compared with an indexed nonsequential file, an indexed sequential file is more economical of both index space and the time needed to search the index. Why then would a nonsequential file be used? The main reason is that the file may have to be addressed by more than one key. If it is in sequence for one key,

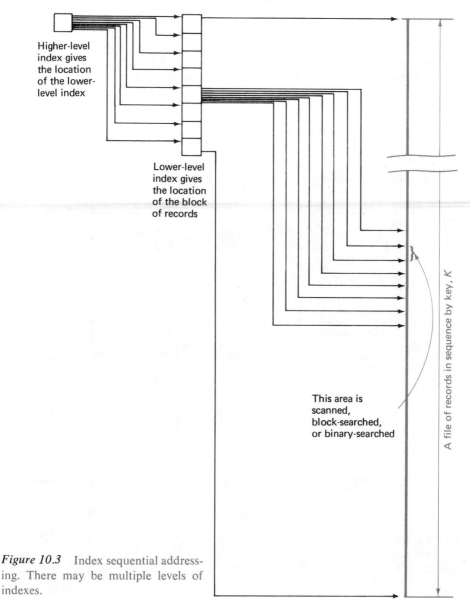

Higher-level index gives the location of the lower-level index

Lower-level index gives the location of the block of records

This area is scanned, block-searched, or binary-searched

A file of records in sequence by key, K

Figure 10.3 Index sequential addressing. There may be multiple levels of indexes.

then it is out of sequence for another. A second reason is to avoid having to sort the file. An index may be used for each key, the index for the sequential key having one entry per block of records and the other being longer with an entry for every record. The key that is used most frequently for addressing the file is usually the one that is used for sequencing it because fast access is possible with the short sequential index.

The analogy of a library card index is better suited to an indexed nonsequential file than to an indexed sequential file. Two keys are used in the card index—book title and author's name—and neither key is used for sequencing the books on the nonfiction shelves. There must therefore be an entry for *every* book in both of these indices.

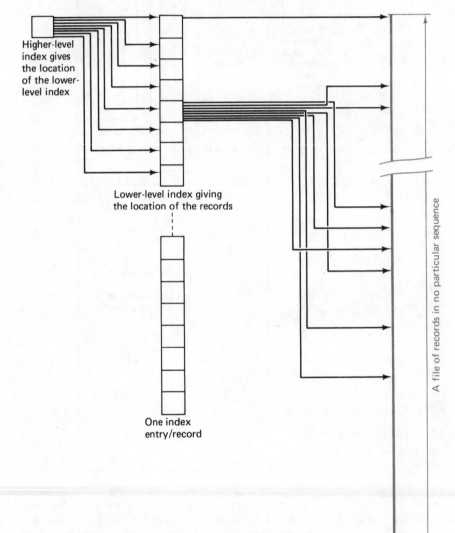

Figure 10.4 Indexed nonsequential addressing. The index is much larger than that in Fig. 10.3. On some systems there are many such indices for *secondary* keys.

The books are in sequence by catalogue number. When the user has found the catalogue number of the book he wants, he searches through the rows of shelves. Each *row* usually contains a sign giving the beginning or ending numbers of the books in that row. The user compares the catalogue number he has obtained from the index with the numbers posted on the rows. Upon locating the correct row, he searches for the *shelf* that contains the book. When he finds it, he looks at the individual book numbers on the shelf. A computer narrows down its search of the files in a similar way, going, for example, from a master index to a cylinder index and thence to a track index.

The library index does not give the *physical* location of the book on the shelves. Instead it gives what might be regarded as a *symbolic address*, the catalogue number. The reason the actual shelf address is not given is that the books change their location, and if a physical address were used, the library index would have to be frequently updated. Indexed nonsequential files also sometimes use a symbolic address rather than an actual address for a similar reason. The records change their location as new records are added and old ones deleted. When more than one key is used in the records a secondary index (i.e., on a nonprime key) may give as its output the *prime key* of the record. The prime key is then used for locating the record using any other addressing technique. This method is slower than if the index gave the physical address of the record, but on files in which the records change their positions frequently this indirect addressing can be worthwhile.

Another reason for using a nonsequential record layout is that the file has a high proportion of new records being inserted and old ones deleted. The continued insertion and deletion of records into a sequentially ordered file would be too difficult or too time-consuming. If books were stored on the library shelves in alphabetical order, maintenance would be too time-consuming because many books would have to be moved on the shelves each time a new book was inserted.

Technique 6: Key-Equals-Address Addressing

There are various methods of converting a key directly into a file address. Where this can be done it provides the fastest means of addressing, and there is no need for file searches or index operations.

The simplest way to solve the addressing problem is to have in the input transaction the relative machine address of the record in question. In some early banking applications the account numbers were changed so that the account number or part of the number *was* the file address of the account record. The address was equal to the key, or derivable from it simply.

In many applications this direct approach is not possible. The item numbers in a factory could not be changed to suit the computer because they have a significance to the firm in question. Furthermore, such an approach is highly inflexible and destroys data independence.

Sometimes a *machine reference number* can be used in an input transaction without any need for it to be a customer number or item number, The file address of the account record may, for example, be printed on the passbook of a savings bank customer and keyed in by the teller who operates the terminal. When an airline reservation computer sends a teletype message to another airline it includes, in some cases, a machine reference number of the passenger record. A teletype message received in reply, for example, confirming a reservation, should include the machine reference number so that the passenger record is speedily found.

Such schemes are referred to as *direct addressing*, although this term has been extended to include any algorithm which converts a key directly into a machine address and so includes technique 7 and, sometimes, technique 8.

Technique 7:   Algorithm for Key Conversion

Almost as fast as the key-equals-address technique is the use of an algorithm for converting the key into the address. The address on some applications may be computed from entity identifiers such as street location and number or airline flight number and date. This is not possible on the majority of applications, but where it can be done it is a simple and fast method. It is most commonly found on interactive systems where file reference time is critical.

It usually has the disadvantage that it does not completely fill the file. Gaps will be left because the keys do not convert to a continuous set of addresses. An airline may, for example, have 150 flight numbers. The algorithm uses them and the date to calculate the file address. However, not every flight flies on every day; hence, some of the addresses generated will not contain a record.

A situation particularly amenable to a calculation of the file address is one in which the records form a matrix. A corporation may have many distributors, for example. Each distributor handles 200 products, and records are kept about the sales of each product for each distributor for each week of the year. If the records are 100 bytes long, the relative byte address of the record for the Ath distributor, the Bth product, and the Cth week may be calculated to be

$$(A - 1) \times 200 \times 52 \times 100 + (B - 1) \times 52 \times 100 + (C - 1) \times 100 + 1$$

A program would convert this relative address into a machine address.

A disadvantage of direct addressing schemes is their inflexibility. The machine addresses of the records may change as files expand, or are moved to a different unit, or merged or modified. To combat the inherent inflexibility, direct addressing is usually carried out in two stages. The first converts the key to an *ordinal number*. The second converts the ordinal number to the machine address (Fig. 10.5). The ordinal numbers used are such that the second stage can be modified easily when the machine addresses of the records are changed.

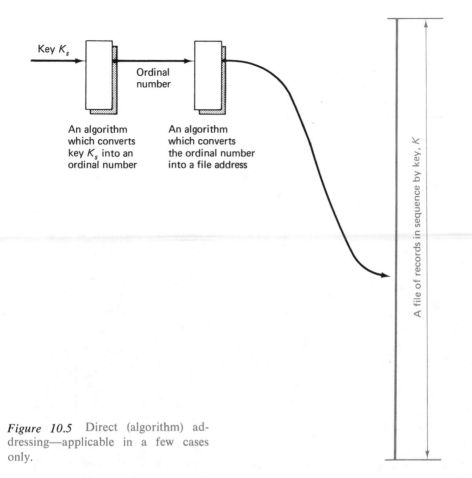

Key K_s

Ordinal
number

An algorithm
which converts
key K_s into an
ordinal number

An algorithm
which converts
the ordinal number
into a file address

A file of records in sequence by key, K

Figure 10.5 Direct (algorithm) addressing—applicable in a few cases
only.

Technique 8: Hashing

An ingenious and useful form of address calculation technique is called
hashing (sometimes *randomizing* or *scrambling*). With this technique the item's
key is converted into a near-random number, and this number is used to determine
where the item is stored. The near-random number could refer to the address
where a record is stored. It is more economical for it to refer to an area where a
group of records is stored, referred to as a *bucket* (sometimes *pocket* or *slot*). See
Fig. 10.6. The number of logical records stored in this area is referred to as the
bucket capacity.

When the file is initially loaded the location in which the records are stored
is determined as follows:

1. The key of the record is converted into a near-random number, n, that lies within
   range 1 to N, where N is the number of buckets usable for storage. Many hashing
   algorithms are possible for this operation, and one must be selected that suits the key
   set of the records in question.

119

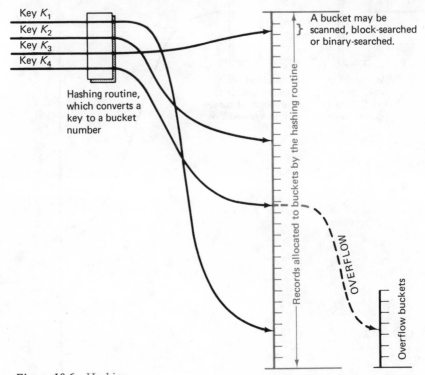

Figure 10.6 Hashing.

2. The near-random number, n, is converted into the address of the nth bucket, and the physical record which constitutes that bucket is read.

3. If there is space remaining in the bucket, the logical record is stored in the bucket.

4. If the bucket is already full, the record must be stored in an *overflow bucket*. This could be the next sequential bucket, or it could be a bucket in a separate area with a pointer to it.

   When records are read from the file, the method of finding them is similar, i.e.,

1. The key of the record to be found is converted into a near-random number, n, using the same algorithm.

2. The near-random number, n, is converted into the address of the nth bucket, and its contents are read.

3. The bucket is searched to find the required logical record.

4. If the required record is not in the bucket, then the overflow bucket is read and searched. It will occasionally be necessary to read more than one overflow bucket to find the record.

Because of the random nature of the algorithm, this technique will not usually achieve 100% packing density; 80% or 90% packing, however, can be achieved with most files, and no space is needed for indices. Most records will be found with one seek, but some need a second (overflow) seek. A very small proportion need a third or fourth seek.

**INSERTIONS
AND DELETIONS**

A major concern in the design of file-addressing schemes and their associated record layouts is how new records will be inserted into the file and old ones deleted. This presents little problem when *hash* addressing is used, but is more difficult to handle with those organization methods which operate with files which are sequential.

To insert new records into a sequential file, variations on two techniques are employed: *overflows* and *distributed free space*. With overflow methods the new items are stored in a separate area, and an indication is left of which area should be searched. With distributed free space, unused areas are scattered throughout the file, waiting for the possible arrival of new records.

**COMBINATIONS OF
TECHNIQUES**

With some files, combinations of the above techniques are used to address the records. An index, for example, may locate an area of the file and that area is then scanned or binary-searched. A direct-addressing algorithm may locate a section of an index so that it is not necessary to search the entire index.

**ASSOCIATIVE
MEMORY**

There is a type of storage device with which no addressing of the types discussed is necessary. It is called *associative* storage. Associative memories are not accessed by an address but by *content*. Associative storage is not widely used yet because complex and expensive logic is needed for construction. As the cost of mass-producing such logic drops associative storage modules may become an important part of data-base systems.

11 SEARCHING

Often it is necessary to search a data base in order to find a piece of information, just as you might have to search a large mail-order catalogue to find something you wanted to buy. How long it takes you to find what you want in such a catalogue depends on whether it has an index and how effectively the index relates to your needs. In a data base there may be many indices tailored to many different information needs.

In the computer industry the term *search engine* is sometimes used to refer to a mechanism for searching a data base rapidly for widely differing information requirements. It is known theoretically how to build data-base hardware which would facilitate fast searching [12] but the cost would be high. We will have to wait some time before effective hardware search engines are available. Meanwhile data-searching facilities are built for conventional storage devices with software [13].

When a file is to be searched in multiple ways, multiple *keys* will be used. The file organizations discussed in Chapter 10 relate to a single key, and that key uniquely determines the location of records in the storage. It is referred to as a *unique identifier* or *primary key*. When multiple keys are used, only one key can be used to uniquely identify records. The other keys which are used for searching the file are referred to as *secondary keys*. Unlike the primary key, there will often be many records with the same secondary-key value. A prime key might be *PART-NUMBER*. It identifies a part record uniquely because no two parts have the same part number. A secondary key might be PART-TYPE. There are many parts of the same type; nevertheless, PART-TYPE may be an important key with many inquiries based on it.

One way of finding a record by a secondary key is to use an index for that key. An index based on an attribute other than the prime key is referred to as a *secondary index*. In some information systems it is desirable to index many different attributes, and so many secondary indices are used.

EXAMPLE OF A MULTIPLE-KEY DATA BASE

A typical example of an information system with secondary indices is one for providing information about sales in a corporation. The users ask questions of the system such as the following:

"Give me the top 10 customers in the southern region on net sales."

"Give me this year's sales and on-order figures for customers in Branch Office 74."

"List the on-order items for transportation industry customers in District 5."

"Which customers in the Detroit area have ordered more than 500 of Item No. 721?"

"What have been the net sales to the cosmetics industry in July?"

"Which branch offices have net sales in excess of $100,000 for last month?"

Customer name and location together form a prime key for addressing the customer records. Item number forms a prime key for addressing the item records. Secondary indices are needed for linking these two files and for indexing items such as *region, net sales, number of items sold, number of items on order, industry category*, and so forth.

When a batch-processing system is used there is often not necessarily any need for secondary indices. The records can be scanned periodically and a variety of listings produced. When the information system becomes on-line large quantities of queries cannot be gathered together and sorted, as they would be in a batch system. A means must be provided for going directly from the query to those records which permit it to be answered.

The designer of an information system needs to decide which data items will be made into secondary keys and what secondary indices will be used. He could make most of the data items into secondary keys and have many secondary indices. In this case more of the storage space might be taken up with indices than with data. Furthermore, some of the indices might refer a user to too many records to be useful.

FOOD FOR THOUGHT

To illustrate the trade-offs in the design of searching techniques we will consider a very simple information system.

Suppose that you are driving through France in an Aston Martin. It is your opinion that computers should be used to improve the enjoyment of life and you would like to use a data base to help you partake of some of the world's finest food and wine.

You have a small radio terminal by the dashboard and want to use it for locating those restaurants, dishes, and wines that provide a second religion to Frenchmen who can afford them.

To construct the data base we use several documents. First, there is the red *Michelin Guide* [14]. Figure 11.1 shows a typical page from the guide, and Fig. 11.2 explains some of the printed symbols used. Second, we need a menu for each of the restaurants in the guide. Third, we need a French-English dictionary. Fourth, we need some detailed information about wines; the *Schoonmaker Encyclopedia of Wines* will suffice. Fifth, we need an explanation of the nature of some of the French dishes.

Figure 11.3 shows a possible logical file structure for the data base. It is drawn in a normalized form (Chapter 9). The reader might like to draw it with tree or plex structures if he prefers. Many variations of the structure are possible.

The question must now be answered: What secondary indices should be set up to facilitate searching the data base? To answer this it is necessary to ask what queries will be answered using the data.

Some of the queries will relate to the locations of the places, for example, "What is the nearest town with a one-star restaurant?" or "How far is Talloires?" To answer such questions the location indications of the guide have been changed. For each town and establishment the latitude and longitude are recorded. In the query dialogue, the user would be asked his present location, and he could enter either the name of a town or his present latitude and longitude. Because many of the queries would be of the form "What is the nearest . . .?" or "Is there . . . within 10 miles?," a file is used relating to grid squares one-tenth of a degree square. One-tenth of a degree is about 6 miles. The file lists each place of interest within each square and gives the exact position of it so that distances can be calculated. To find the nearest establishment to a given location the grid square containing that location will be inspected, and then, if necessary, the adjacent grid squares, and then squares successively farther from the location, until an establishment of the required type is found.

There are many data items for which a secondary index could be useful because the user might make queries relating to them. If he asks, for example, "List the three-star restaurants south of Lyon," it would be much quicker to inspect the 12 three-star restaurants to see whether they are south of Lyon than to inspect the towns or grid squares south of Lyon to see whether they have a restaurant with three stars. A secondary index for three-star restaurants would be quite small—only 12 entries. A secondary index for one-star restaurants would be much larger; it would have over 500 entries and so would take much longer to search. A secondary index for restaurants which allow dogs would be too long for

Tain-Tournon *(fin).*

  Tournon ◉ **07** Ardèche. ⑦-① - 8 127 h. Alt. 123 - ⌷⊡⌷.
  ▭ Promenade Farconnet (été) ⳾ 3.35.

🏨 **Paris** (fermé vend. hors saison), pl. Lycée ⳾ 4.32, Rep 12,50/35 **stc** ♦ 4,50 - 21 ch 25/
    75 **stc** - P 37/55 **stc** - ▥ 🍽 ⊖wc 🛁 wc ⳾. Change. . . . . **z z**

🍴 **Gare** (fermé 1ᵉʳ quinz. de sept.), av. Gare ⳾ 0.93, Rep 3. 8,50/12 ♦ 1,50 - 10 ch 12,50/
    25 - P 22 - ▥ 🍽 ⊖. 🅿. Radió. ⌂ (ch). **z x**

✕✕ **Chaumière** (5 mars-15 oct.) (fermé lundi sauf en été) (avec ch.), quai Farconnet
    ⳾ 1.53, (Cadre rustique), Rep 3,50. 9,50/18 ♦ 4 - 9 ch 12/30 - ⊖ 🍽 ▥. Radió. . . **Y v**

▭ Achette, av. Lyon ⳾ 1.24 . . . . PEUGEOT. | Fournier, r. Valentine ⳾ 2.61. . . . . .
Cotte, av. Beaucaire ⳾ 1.67 . . . . RENAULT. | . . . . HOTCHKISS, SIMCA.
Gélibert, quai Farconnet ⳾ 0.75. CITROËN-PANHARD. |

  TALAIS **33** Gironde. ⑦-⑥ - 541 h. Alt. 7.
Paris (par Bordeaux) 649 (par Royan) 519 - Bordeaux 86 - Lesparre-Médoc 23 - Royan 17.

🏨 **Château Talys** (Pâques-15 sept.) (fermé lundi et mardi hors saison), ⳾ 6, ⌂,
    Rep 3,50. 10,50/12 ♦ 1,50 - 10 ch 10/18 - P 30/32 **stc** - ▥ 🍽 ⊖. 🅿. Radió.

  TALENCE **33** Gironde. ⑦⑧-① - ✕✕✕ voir à Bordeaux p. 3.

  TALLOIRES **74** H.-Savoie. ⑦-⑥. G. Alpes - 659 h. Alt. 447 - Site ★★★. **Env. :** E : Chap.
St-Germain ★ (site ★★) 4 puis 15 mn. **Exc. :** Tour du lac d'Annecy ★★★ 39 - NO : ▥ du lac
d'Annecy (⳾ 45.82.89). - Paris 560 - Albertville 33 - Annecy 13 - Chamonix 83 - Megève 48.

🏨◉ **Abbaye** (Tiffenat) (mai-sept.), ⳾ 45.87.84 « Terrasse ombragée avec belle vue
    sur le lac » ⌂, plage aménagée, Rep 25 bc/45 bc. **Spéc. :** Omble grillé beurre blanc. Gratin
    de queues d'écrevisses, Côte de bœuf savoyarde. **Vins :** Crépy, Seyssel - **60 ch** 40/100 **stc** - P 80/
    100 **stc** - 🅿. Change. Radió. ⌂ (rest).

🏨◉ **Le Cottage** (Georges Bise) (avril-sept.), bord du lac ⳾ 45.88.10 « De la terrasse,
    belle vue sur le lac » ⌂, Rep 5. 25/42 ♦ 4. **Spéc. :** Mousse de foies de volailles truffée,
    Mousseline de brocheton aux queues d'écrevisses, Chateaubriand poêlé. **Vins :** Apremont, Seyssel -
    40 ch 25/70 - P 50/80 - 🅿. Change. Radió. ⌂ (rest).

🏨 **Manoir-Bellevue** Ⓜ, ⳾ 45.88.05, ⌂, Rep 14/18 **stc** ♦ 4 - **22 ch** 25/40 **stc** - P 40/60
    stc - ▥ 🍽 ⊖wc 🛁 wc ⳾. ⊖ 🅿. Change. Radió.

🏨 **Lac** (juin-fin sept.), ⳾ 45.88.08, ⌂, Rep 4. 15/18 ♦ 3,50 - **50 ch** 15/40 (22 %) - P 40/
    64 **stc** - Asc ⊖wc 🍽 wc ⳾. ⊖ 🅿. Change. Radió. ⌂ (rest).

🏨 **Beau Site** (25 mai-sept.), ⳾ 45.88.04, ⌂, ⌂, plage aménagée, Rep 4,50. 14/20 **stc**
    ♦ 3,50 - 37 ch 15/40 **stc** - P 43/57 **stc** - ▥ 🍽 ⊖wc 🛁 wc ⳾. ⊖ 🅿. Change. Radió. ⌂ (rest).

🏨 **Aub. Chamois** (mars-oct.), ⳾ 45.88.17, Rep 11/22 **stc** ♦ 2,60 - **17 ch** 16/28 **stc** - P 34/
    40 **stc** - ⊖ 🍽 ⳾. 🅿. Change. Radió. ⌂ (rest).

✕✕✕✕◉◉ **Auberge du Père Bise** (Marius Bise) (avril-2 oct.) (avec ch.), bord
    du lac ⳾ 45.88.01 « Repas sous l'ombrage, face au lac » ⌂, Rep 5. 55 et carte.
    Spéc. : Gratin de queues d'écrevisses, Omble chevalier, Poularde braisée à la crème d'estragon.
    Vins : Crépy, Roussette de Seyssel - **11 ch** 30/65 (25 %) - P 95/110 (25 %) - ▥ 🍽 ⊖wc ⳾.
    ⊖ 🅿. Change. Radió.

✕✕◉ **Garcin** (15 mars-15 nov.)(Rest. de plein air) (avec ch.), ⳾ 45.88.24, ⌂, Rep 4. 13,50/
    22 **stc** ♦ 3,50. **Spéc. :** Pâté de foies de volailles pistaché, Quenelle « New-Burg », Poularde à la crème
    Rosemonde. **Vins :** Apremont, Gamay - 5 ch 18/35 **stc** - P 35/45 **stc** - ▥ 🍽 ⊖ ⳾.
    Change. Radió.

  À Echarvines (NO : 1,5 km par N 509) - Alt. 500 - ▢ Talloires :

🏨 **Dents de Lanfon** (fermé nov.), ⳾ 45.82.56, ⌂, Rep 3,50. 10/18 **stc** ♦ 2 - 16 ch 13/24 **stc**
    - P 30/34 **stc** - ▥ 🍽 ⊖. 🅿.

  Au Sud : 4 km - ▢ Doussard :

🏨 **Relais du Lac** (avril-sept.), à Glières-Doussard ⳾ 38 Doussard, ⌂, Rep 4,50. 13/
    20 **stc** ♦ 2 - **16 ch** 16/33 **stc** - P 38/42 **stc** - ▥ 🍽 ⊖wc 🛁 ⳾. Radió.

  TALMONT **17** Ch.-Mar. ⑦-⑥. G. **Côte de l'Atlantique** - 128 h. Alt. 23 - ▢ Cozes -
Église Ste-Radegonde ★.
Paris 500 - Pons 33 - Rochefort-s-Mer 54 - La Rochelle 84 - Royan 16 - Saintes 35.

🏨 **L'Estuaire** (fermé du 1ᵉʳ oct. au 15 nov. et lundi du 15 nov. à Pâques), au Caillaud
    ⳾ 4 Talmont, ⌂, Rep 3,50. 13/20 **stc** ♦ 1,50 - 10 ch 15/22 **stc** - P 35 **stc** - ▥ 🍽 ⊖. 🅿. ⌂.

🍴 **Promontoire**, ⳾ 1, Rep 2. 8/25 ♦ 1 - 12 ch 10/15 **stc** - P 30 **stc** - ▥. 🅿. ⌂.

  TALMONT Ⓒ **85** Vendée. ⑥⑦-⑪. G. **Côte de l'Atlantique** - 1 046 h. Alt. 22. - ⌷⊡⌷
(saison). - Paris 457 - Fontenay-le-Comte 64 - La Roche-sur-Yon 29 - Les Sables-d'Olonne 13.

🍴 **Boule d'Or** (fermé du 26 déc. au 25 janv.), r. Château ⳾ 23, Rep 2,50. 8/14 **stc** ♦ 1,70
    - 13 ch 9/11,70 **stc** - P 24/28 **stc** - ▥ 🍽 ⊖. 🅿. Radió. ⌂ (ch).

▭ Herbert, rte des Sables ▥ ⳾ 21. . . . . CITROËN-PANHARD.

  TALUYERS **69** Rhône. ⑦⑧-⑪ - 695 h. - Paris 488 - Givors 8 - Lyon 18 - St-Étienne 40.

✕✕ **Les Acacias** (fermé du 1ᵉʳ au 15 août et lundi), ⳾ 6, Rep (dim dîner à la carte)
    12/35 **stc** ♦ 2,50 - ▥. 🅿. Radió. ⌂.

Figure 11.1

TOWNS

F	"Flower town" (1965 Concours).
P	Prefecture.
SP	Sub-prefecture.
C	Local administrative town.
63	Postal number.
⑩-⑤	Number of the appropriate sheet and section of the Michelin Road map.
G. Jura	See the Michelin Green Guide: **Jura**.
1 050 h.	Population.
Alt. 175	Altitude (in metres).
Stat. therm.	Health resort.
— baln.	Bathing resort.
— hiv.	Winter resort.
⊠ Ars	Local post-office.
BX **A**	Letters giving the location of a place on the town plan.
☀ ⟨	Panoramic view. Viewpoint.
⛳	Golf links and number of holes.
⚓	Shipping.
🛈	Local information office.
T. C. F.	Touring Club de France.
A C.	Automobile Club.

Comfort

	Luxury **hotel**.
	Top class hotel.
	Very comfortable hotel.
	Good average hotel.
	Plain but fairly comfortable hotel.
	Very plain but adequate hotel.
M	**Modern hotels** (see p. 18).
XXXXX	Luxury **restaurant**.
XXXX	Top class restaurant.
XXX	Very comfortable restaurant.
XX	Fairly comfortable restaurant.
X	Plain but good restaurant.

We have classified the hotels and restaurants with the travelling motorist in mind. In each category they have been listed in order of preference.

Cuisine

✿✿✿	One of the best tables in France, well worth the journey.
✿✿	Excellent cuisine, worth a detour.
✿	A good restaurant in its class.

"Spécialités"

A maximum of three are indicated for any hotel or restaurant recommended for its cuisine. They are not all served in the same menu and often only "à la carte", or in the most expensive set meal.

Local wines

A maximum of two are shown. They should be of good quality and reasonably priced. They are usually of a recent vintage and are often served "en carafe".

Amenity

Red print is used to indicate:

Pleasant hotels.
Pleasant restaurants.
Exceptionally attractive view.
Exceptionally extensive view.
Very pleasant surroundings.
Quiet and secluded situation.

Dinner at the hotel

30 ch	Hotels prepared to provide rooms for over-night guests not taking dinner have the number of rooms shown in heavy type.

Figure 11.2

The most important sights

★★★	Worth a special journey.
★★	Worth a detour.
★	Interesting.
Voir :	To be seen in the town.
Principales curiosités :	If time is short, at least see these.
Autres curio.:	If you have more time, see these also.
Env. :	In the neighbourhood of the town.
Exc. :	Excursions in the area.
N, S, E, O	The sight is situated to the North (N), South (S), East (E), West (O) of the town.
①, ②	Sign on town plan and on the Michelin Road Map indicating the road leading to a place of interest.
2	Distance in kilometres.
h, mn	Time to go there and back on foot (h: hours, mn: minutes).

Dates open and situation

(mai-octobre) (été) (été-hiver)	Period during which seasonal hotels are open. Where no date nor season is shown, the hotel is open all the year round.
(sais.)	Probably open for the season.
⟨ ⟨	Beautiful or extensive view.
⟨ ⟨	Exceptional view.
⧈	Quiet situation.
⧈	Quiet and secluded situation. (If particularly attractive, a brief description is added.)
BV g	Reference letters giving the location of the hotel on the town plan.

Hotel facilities

For hotels in categories 🏨🏨, 🏨, 🏨, no details are given. They usually have every modern comfort.

M (sans rest.)	Modern hotels (see p. 18). The hotel has no restaurant or serves meals to residents only.
(avec ch.)	The restaurant has bedrooms.
☏ 43	Telephone number.
30 ch ou **30 ch**	Number of rooms (See page 18 : Dinner at the hotel).
Asc	Lift (elevator).
🔲	Central heating.
	Air-conditioning.
⛲wc	Bidet with running water. Bedroom with private bathroom and lavatory.
⛲	Bedroom with private bathroom but no lavatory.
🛁	Bathroom for general use.
🚿wc	Room with private shower and lavatory.
🚿	Room with private shower but no lavatory.
🚿	Shower for general use.
☏	External phone in room.
🚗	Free garage (one night only) for those having the 1966 Guide.
	Charge made for garage.
P	Free parking: customers only.

⌣ ⌣	Outdoor or indoor swimming-pool.

For the few hotels without hot or cold running water we specify:

⚱	Cold running water only.
⚱	No running water.

Dogs

Dogs are not allowed :

🐕	in any part of the hotel.
🐕 (rest)	in the restaurant.
🐕 (ch)	in the bedrooms.

Wireless

Radio.	No TV or radio played during meals.

Town — TOWN-ID | TOWN-NAME | POPULATION | GRID-REF | DESCRIPTION (FRENCH) | DESCRIPTION (ENGLISH)

Hotel — HOTEL-ID | HOTEL-NAME | TOWN-ID | GRID-REF | ADDRESS | RATING | DESCRIPTION-CODES | FACILITIES-CODES

Restaurant — REST-ID | REST-NAME | TOWN-ID | GRID-REF | ADDRESS | FOOD-RATING | LUXURY-RATING | AVERAGE-PRICE | DESCRIPTION-CODES

Environs — ENVIR-ID | ENVIR-NAME | TOWN-ID | GRID-REF | ADDRESS | DESCRIPTION (ENGLISH) | DESCRIPTION (FRENCH)

Garage — GARAGE-ID | GARAGE-NAME | TOWN-ID | GRID-REF | ADDRESS

Menu — REST-ID | DISH-CODE | PRICE | CONDITION CODE

Wine-list — REST-ID | WINE-CODE | YEAR | HALF-BOTTLE-PRICE | FULL-BOTTLE-PRICE | CARAFE-PRICE

Dish — DISH-CODE | DISH-NAME (ENGLISH) | DISH-NAME (FRENCH) | DISH-DESCRIPTION (ENGLISH) | DISH-DESCRIPTION (FRENCH)

Wine-descr — WINE-CODE | WINE-NAME | WINE-DESCRIPTION (ENGLISH) | WINE-DESCRIPTION (FRENCH)

Wine-vintage — WINE-CODE | YEAR | VINTAGE-REPORT (ENGLISH) | VINTAGE-REPORT (FRENCH)

Town-hotel — TOWN-ID | HOTEL-ID

Town-rest — TOWN-ID | REST-ID

Town-envir — TOWN-ID | ENVIR-ID

Town-garage — TOWN-ID | GARAGE-ID

Grid-square — GRID-SQ | TOWN-ID

Figure 11.3 A possible normalized data-base structure (keys are underlined).

127

reasonable purposes. The designer must decide where he draws the line in setting up secondary indices. Some possible candidates are as follows:

> Restaurant: food rating (number of stars)
>
> Restaurant: luxury rating
>
> Hotel rating
>
> Quiet and secluded location
>
> Average meal price
>
> Exceptional view
>
> Swimming pool
>
> Bathroom and toilet facilities
>
> Modern hotel
>
> Golf course
>
> Automobile club
>
> Number of bedrooms
>
> Parking facilities
>
> Menu items

If the user asks "Where is the nearest restaurant which serves *truite au bleu*?", the computer might have a secondary index for restaurants serving *truite au bleu* or it might search the menus of the nearby restaurants looking for *truite au bleu*. If very few restaurants serve *truite au bleu*, the index will be small and quickly searchable. On the other hand, few persons may make queries about *truite au bleu*. If *truite au bleu* is a greatly sought after but rare delicacy, then the index will be useful as well as small and efficient.

A long secondary index which takes too long to search can be shortened by lessening the degree of resolution of its responses. For example, the *truite au bleu* index may not list every restaurant serving *truite au bleu* but every grid square containing such a restaurant. This index could be searched more quickly, but then restaurant menus in one or more grid squares would also have to be searched.

The worth of a possible index, then, relates to its frequency of use, its degree of resolution, and the time required to search it.

CHAINS   A secondary index is usually much larger than a primary index relating to the same number of keys. The records in an indexed sequential file are sequenced by the primary key and consequently not all primary key values need be included in the index (Fig. 10.3). The records cannot be sequenced by secondary key, and so the same method cannot be used for reducing the size and search time of secondary indices.

An alternative to large indices is the use of chains of pointers embedded in the data records. Figure 11.4 illustrates a chained file. The example relates to a manufacturer of plastic toys. The prime key in this example is PART NUMBER. The secondary key is PRODUCT TYPE, and items of the same type are chained together. Such an organization would work efficiently for responding to certain categories of information requests. It would be good for the request "List the part numbers of all toy cars." For the request "What cars have part numbers between 1500 and 2000?" it would be less efficient. The computer would start at the record for part number 1500, or the first one after that number, and would then scan forward until the CAR chain is found. If only a small proportion of the part numbers are for cars, then many records which are not for cars might have to be examined before the CAR chain is found. The question would be answered more efficiently with a secondary index for cars. On the other hand, if a high proportion of the part numbers are for cars, say one-third, then the chain organization would be reasonably efficient, whereas a secondary index for cars would be very lengthy.

If the file is volatile, new links have to be added to the chain and old links removed. When a new CAR product is added to the file, the computer will scan backward from the location where the record is added until it reaches the closest link of the CAR chain. It will then change the pointer in this record to point to the new record, and the previous pointer will be written in the new record so that the chain is relinked. Similarly, when records are deleted the chain must be relinked, or else the deleted record marked and the relinking left for a periodic file reorganization. In Figure 11.4, relinking the chain appears easy because the computer does not have to scan far to find the chain. In practice on some systems the chain links may be very far from one another, and a lengthy scan is needed.

The chain in Fig. 11.4 is shown as being a one-way chain. Often two-way chains are used instead, each item having a pointer to the previous link as well as to the next link. Two-way chains give protection against the accidental destruction of pointers and also facilitate the removal of records from the chain. With the one-way chain of Fig. 11.4, if a pointer is lost, it can be recovered only by a lengthy operation of scanning the secondary keys of the file.

MORE THAN ONE SECONDARY KEY   A chain such as that in Fig. 11.4 is satisfactory for certain systems which employ a *single* secondary key. Where the requests relate to more than one secondary key, lengthy chains may be very inefficient.

Figure 11.5 shows the same file, using the same technique, but with two secondary keys. Key 3 is the *color* of the plastic toys. The organization in Fig. 11.5 may be satisfactory for requests concerning key 1 and either of the other keys but is less attractive for requests concerning key 2 and key 3.

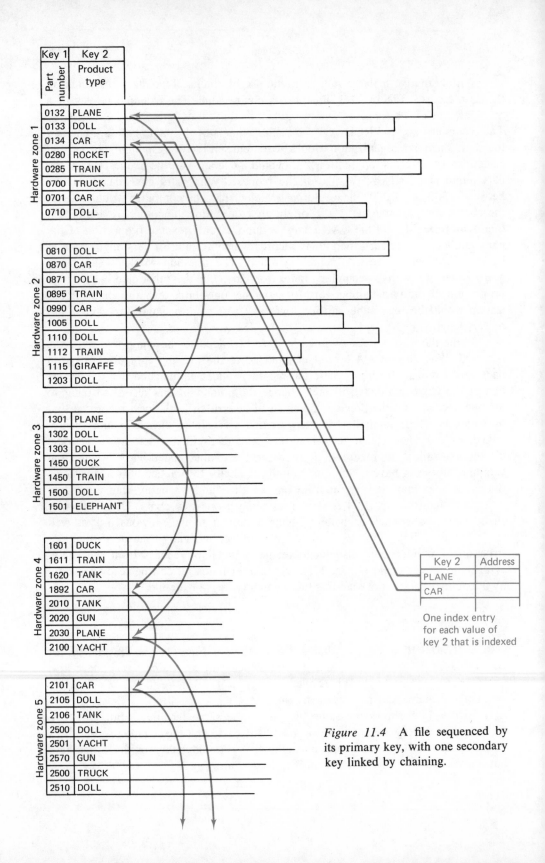

Key 1	Key 2
Part number	Product type

Hardware zone 1

0132	PLANE
0133	DOLL
0134	CAR
0280	ROCKET
0285	TRAIN
0700	TRUCK
0701	CAR
0710	DOLL

Hardware zone 2

0810	DOLL
0870	CAR
0871	DOLL
0895	TRAIN
0990	CAR
1005	DOLL
1110	DOLL
1112	TRAIN
1115	GIRAFFE
1203	DOLL

Hardware zone 3

1301	PLANE
1302	DOLL
1303	DOLL
1450	DUCK
1450	TRAIN
1500	DOLL
1501	ELEPHANT

Hardware zone 4

1601	DUCK
1611	TRAIN
1620	TANK
1892	CAR
2010	TANK
2020	GUN
2030	PLANE
2100	YACHT

Hardware zone 5

2101	CAR
2105	DOLL
2106	TANK
2500	DOLL
2501	YACHT
2570	GUN
2500	TRUCK
2510	DOLL

Key 2	Address
PLANE	
CAR	

One index entry
for each value of
key 2 that is indexed

Figure 11.4 A file sequenced by
its primary key, with one secondary
key linked by chaining.

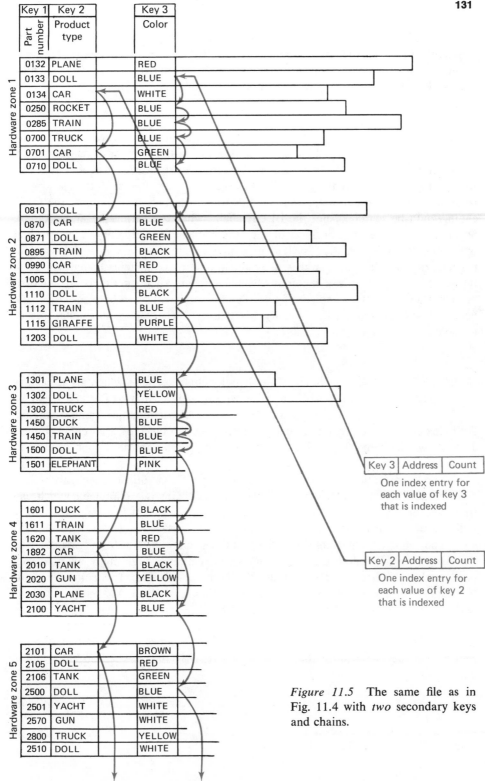

Figure 11.5 The same file as in Fig. 11.4 with *two* secondary keys and chains.

Consider the request "List details of blue cars." Records concerning blue cars may be found either by searching the BLUE chain or by searching the CAR chain. In either case the entire chain has to be searched, and so the machine must seek and read many records which are not for blue cars.

COUNT

It will help if the machine can always follow the shortest chain. A *count* of the number of records in the chains should therefore be included in the index entries, as shown in Fig. 11.5. In practice the count of the chain links serves two purposes in data-base organization. First, it permits the shortest chains to be selected. In Fig. 11.5, the CAR chain would be searched, not the BLUE chain, when answering the above query. Second, it can give an indication of the reasonableness of a query. The terminal operators of an information system may unwittingly enter queries which could trigger extremely lengthy searches or result in an excess of items being printed in reply. The system may use the count field to prevent such queries being handled on-line; they are better handled off-line. The operator will often be pleased to have been warned so that *he can modify his query* to encompass a smaller set of all items.

MULTILIST ORGANIZATION

Some of the lengthy chain searches which are necessary with an organization such as that in Fig. 11.5 can be shortened if the chains are divided into smaller lengths. An index entry is then required giving the start of each piece of each chain. Figure 11.6 shows the same file as Fig. 11.4 with the lengths of the chains limited to three items.

The organization is sometimes referred to as a multilist organization (*list* referring to the *chain* of items). The length of the chains is a parameter which can be varied in a multilist file to give the best compromise between large secondary indices and lengthy chain searches.

The inquiry "What cars have part numbers between 1500 and 2000?" can now be answered without the risk of having to search through many records from part number 1500 onward before the CAR chain is found. The computer finds the address of the record for part number 1500, and the CAR index gives the address of the chain which starts prior to that (the second dashed chain in Fig. 11.6). This chain is followed, and it is quickly found that part number 1892 (only) satisfies the requirements. The number of records read which do not satisfy the request can never be more than $L - 1$, where L is the number of links in the chains.

133

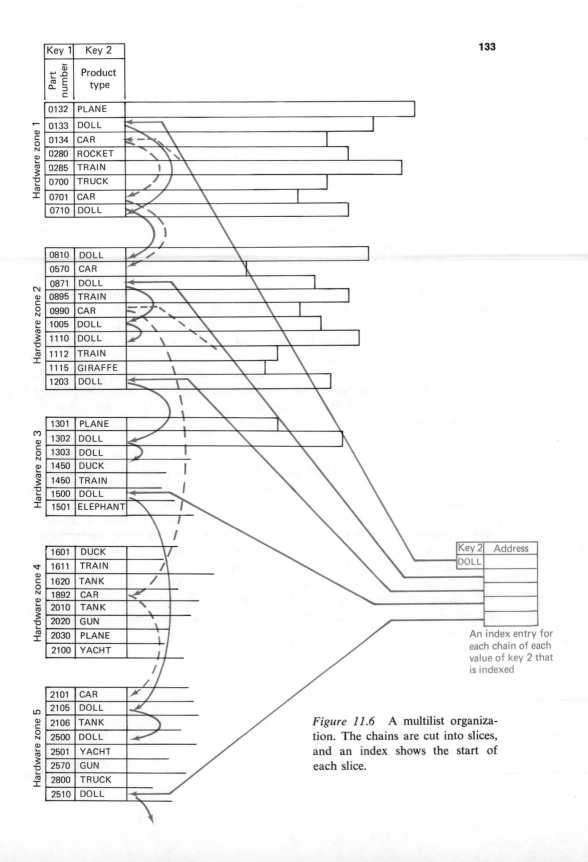

Figure 11.6 A multilist organization. The chains are cut into slices, and an index shows the start of each slice.

HARDWARE-LIMITED
CHAINS

Chains, indices, and searching techniques, in general, can be tailored to the file hardware. It may be decided, for example, that chains should not stretch heedlessly from one cylinder to another of a disk file or from a page to another in an organization in which large pages are read into main memory for searching. The chains are therefore fragmented not by number of items in a chain as in Fig. 11.6 but by the size of hardware zones as in Fig. 11.7. In this way the time-consuming seeks which would occur when chains are followed from one zone to another can be avoided. The zones could be separate cylinders on a disk file, separate cards on a magnetic card file, some other hardware subdivision, or a software division such as large paging blocks.

To answer a request such as "List all black dolls" with the organization in Fig. 11.7, the indices will first be examined to see which hardware zones contain both a BLACK item and a DOLL. Zone 4 does not contain a DOLL; zones 1, 3, and 5 do not contain any BLACK items. Thus, of the five zones shown only zone 2 need be examined. The count fields show that there are five DOLLs in zone 2 but only two BLACK items. The two BLACK-item records will therefore be inspected to see which are black dolls.

To answer an inquiry such as "Which item numbers between 1500 and 2000 are cars?" the key 1 addressing mechanism will indicate that these item numbers extend over zones 3 and 4. Only zone 4 contains a CAR. The inquiry can therefore be answered without any chain searching.

VARIATIONS

There are many variations on this theme, resulting in many search techniques involving scanning records, searching chains, and using indices [12]. In future hardware, blocks of data to be searched may be brought into special searching hardware, associative memory, which, in effect, addresses a record by its contents [13]. In some systems many search operations can go on in parallel; for example, chains are organized so that many pieces of chain can be searched at the same time.

The options available for the design of a multiple-key file permit the designer major trade-offs among increasing the quantity of secondary storage used, increasing the utilization of main memory, and increasing time needed to locate the required records.

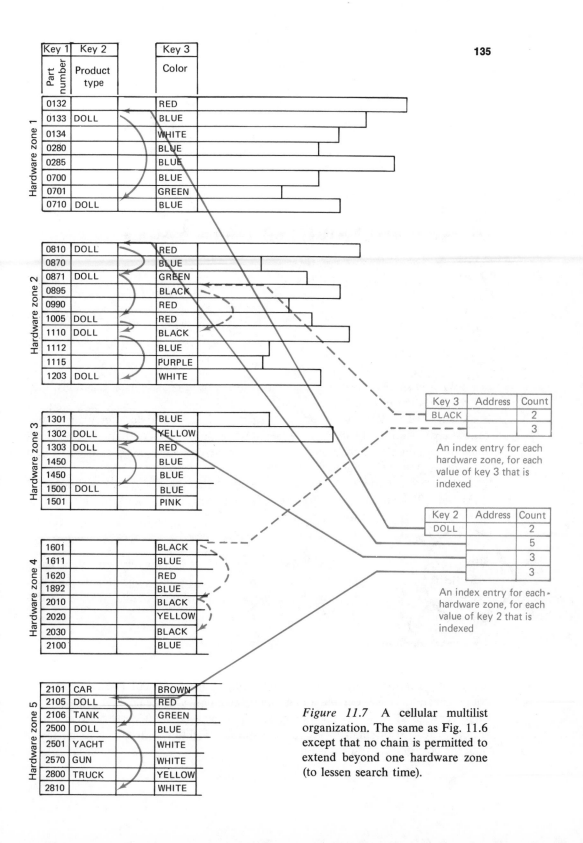

Figure 11.7 A cellular multilist organization. The same as Fig. 11.6 except that no chain is permitted to extend beyond one hardware zone (to lessen search time).

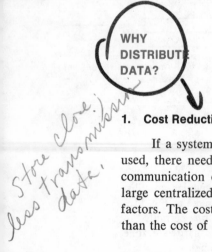

A Single System : data bases in separate locations.

A single system data bases in different locations.

12 DISTRIBUTED DATA BASES

When a single system has data bases in separate geographical locations, they are referred to as *distributed data bases.*

Until the mid-1970s almost all systems with on-line data kept them in one centralized location. If there were separate locations where data were stored, separate and unrelated computers looked after the data. The complexities involved in scattering the data geographically were too great.

There is a variety of types of distributed data-base systems, and some of them are still inadvisable on grounds of complexity. The arguments in favor of distributing data are, however, growing.

WHY DISTRIBUTE DATA?

The pros and cons of geographically split data bases vary greatly from one type of application to another. Possible reasons for distributed data bases are as follows:

1. Cost Reduction

Store close.) less transmission data.

If a system stores its data close to the locations where they originate or are used, there need be less transmission of data, with subsequent reduction in telecommunication costs. On the other hand, economies of scale favor the use of large centralized data storage facilities. There is a cost trade-off between these factors. The cost of small localized data-storage facilities is dropping much faster than the cost of data transmission.

2. Load Considerations

On a few systems the traffic load is greater than the capacity of today's database software. Separate systems may be used, serving different areas, but with identical data structures and capability to pass transactions between systems.

3. Localized Management

A factory or district office may desire to keep its own data in its own computer. The data are nevertheless used in other parts of the organization, possibly by means of telecommunication links. Localized management and control of the data can have substantial advantages. The local organization is fully *responsible* for its accuracy and safekeeping. They cannot blame malfunctions on some far distant group of people. Some of the programs using the data may be best developed locally because only local systems analysts can be *intimate with local problems and requirements*. Separate local data users may, however, be required to conform with centrally agreed data definitions, formats, and schemas.

The problems associated with excessively large system development can be alleviated if local organizations develop local data-base systems and make them work, albeit under central constraints about the nature of the data.

4. Minicomputers

The local development and storage of local files has gained popularity and economic viability with the spread of minicomputers with data transmission capability. In many applications the majority of the data stored on a local minicomputer is employed solely in that location, and a relatively small proportion is transmitted to computers at other locations.

The term "data base" implies *data independence*. On systems with the advantages we described in Part I there must be both logical and physical data independence. This should be contrasted with the term "file system" which implies the straight-forward storage of the programmers' files in a format similar to that used by the programmer. Many minicomputers use *file storage* rather than *data base storage* with data base management software. Networks of such minicomputers should therefore be described as *distributed file systems*, or *fragmented file systems* rather than *distributed data base systems*. The designer must judge whether, taking the long term view, the features of *data base* as opposed to *file* software are desirable.

5. Separate Information Systems

As we commented in Chapter 6, there can be good reasons for keeping *operations system* and *information system* data bases separate. If they are separate, they may or may not be in separate geographical locations. Large organizations may develop the pattern of having local or regional *operations systems* which feed a separate centralized *information system* with differently structured data bases designed for fast spontaneous searching.

A corporation may have head office information system data bases linked to the local data-base systems in factories, storage depots, or regional sales offices. The IRS and other government agencies will have information systems for dealing with the complex queries of policy makers, separate from the operations systems which serve and collect data from the public.

The operations and information system data bases may nevertheless contain some of the same information and be connected by data transmission links. In some cases the information system is a data base system whereas the operations systems are merely file systems.

6. Man-Computer Dialogue

One of the important trends in interactive computer systems is the trend to *distributed intelligence*. Distributed intelligence means that terminals and other devices in a terminal network, instead of being dumb machines like teleprinters or simple multiplexors, may have associated with them a miniature computer programmed to make the far-flung tentacles of the network behave more "intelligently." *Distributed intelligence* has multiple uses, but one of the most important is to provide a dialogue between the terminal and terminal user which is as well adapted to his psychology as possible [15].

The use of distributed intelligence to enhance dialogue is a complex subject. One aspect of it is the use of well-worded English phrases or well-composed tables or graphics to help the terminal user. To transmit these a long distance by telecommunications can be prohibitively expensive. They may therefore be stored at the periphery of the network, possibly at the terminal locations, in a relatively small file attached to peripheral minicomputers.

Similarly, in some systems, data collected from terminal users is stored peripherally in small local storage units and then transmitted in a block to the central computer and central data base. The efficiency and cost of transmitting the data are enhanced. The data may be divided into those which can be stored locally and are of no value centrally and those which are needed centrally because of central control or because other users will employ them.

In this type of system the use of distributed data is related to "distributed intelligence".

In some cases the storage of the local *dialogue* computer is loaded from the central data base at the terminal user's request. For example, in a graphics application the files of manipulatable displays may be transmitted on request from the central data base.

In some cases distributed local files are necessary to provide the fast response time that an effective dialogue needs.

7. Availability

To a much greater extent than with batch-processing systems, systems which serve terminal users need to be free from failures. A terminal user becomes infuriated if his terminal is constantly "going on the blink" or being cut off from the data which he is using. Storage mechanisms do fail, however; and to provide high data *availability* the systems designer may store vital data in duplicate in more than one machine. To circumvent telecommunication failures he may store the duplicate copies in different locations.

Small inexpensive storage units are used close to the terminal locations on some systems to provide a backup when the central data storage is unavailable. Alternatively, there may be two or more main systems.

8. Security

The protection of data has been an argument for splitting a data base on some systems. In certain systems it would be utterly disastrous if the data base were destroyed by fire or sabotage. Vital data may be stored in two widely separate locations. Alternatively, data needed to reconstruct the files may be stored separately.

9. Terminal Versatility

The ability to reach many different data bases can provide a terminal user with a rich array of capabilities. A head office terminal may be connectable to data bases in many parts of a corporation. Often they would be regarded as separate data-base systems rather than one distributed system. If a head office computer is used to manipulate the data from remote data bases, however, these may be designed with common schemas.

10. Computer Networks

Computer networks which interconnect a wide array of heterogeneous computer systems are coming into use. The ARPA network interconnecting university computers [16] was one of the first multicomputer networks. Such networks permit the interlinking of many separately developed data bases.

DIFFERENT TYPES OF SYSTEMS

The above reasons for using distributed data give rise to different categories of systems. Figure 12.1 shows four common types of systems employing geographically scattered data.

In the first the data types and structures may be largely the same, but the physical storage is split geographically. The same schemas may be used for each of the separate data bases.

(1) Split file system

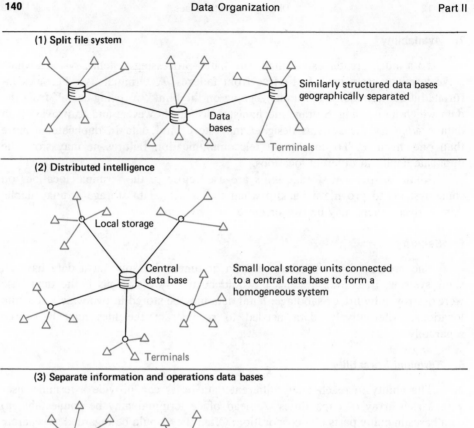

Similarly structured data bases geographically separated

Data bases

Terminals

(2) Distributed intelligence

Local storage

Central data base

Small local storage units connected to a central data base to form a homogeneous system

Terminals

(3) Separate information and operations data bases

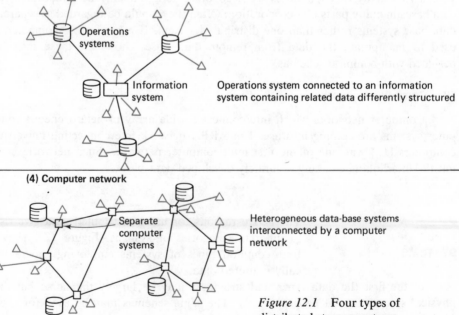

Operations systems

Information system

Operations system connected to an information system containing related data differently structured

(4) Computer network

Separate computer systems

Heterogeneous data-base systems interconnected by a computer network

Figure 12.1   Four types of distributed storage systems.

In the second, small peripheral storage units are employed to enhance the function of a central data base. The subschema used in the peripheral storage units may be derived from the schema used in the central system.

The third diagram of Fig. 12.1 shows separate operations systems feeding part of their data to a central information system. Here the operations systems have schemas in their own right and, unlike the second case, each could be a stand-alone system. The data types and formats used in the systems are, however, closely related and planned in an integrated fashion.

The final diagram shows a computer network in which both the computers and the data bases could be entirely heterogeneous, as they are, for example, on the ARPA network.

HOW SIMILAR ARE THE DATA STRUCTURES?

Distributed data bases differ in their degree of homogeneity. At one extreme they may have identical structures, as could be the case in the top diagram in Fig. 12.1. At the other extreme they could have entirely unrelated structures, as perhaps in the bottom diagram in Fig. 12.1. Between these extremes are systems in which separately structured data bases are combined to serve a common set of functions.

A pattern which is emerging in some corporations is that many localized data bases are constructed, with their own data structures, but the data items used all conform to a centrally agreed definition and format. In some cases the records or segments used are also centrally standardized.

It is desirable to strike an appropriate balance between centralized and decentralized control. Enough decentralized control is needed to permit the local resolution of local problems and to encourage local initiative and innovation. Local problems are often well understood only by the systems analysts who work at the location in question. Enough centralized control is needed to make it possible to pass data and programs from one location to another. As new application programs are developed they should be able to work with existing data from any of the locations.

CENTRALIZED SCHEMAS?

The arguments concerning logical and physical data independence apply to distributed data bases just as to any other types. Without data independence, high costs may be incurred in future development. As sure as life new programs will require the data in new forms. Schemas must be able to evolve without playing havoc with existing programs.

The relations among the subschemas, schemas, and physical data organization may be similar to those in the figures of Chapter 5 except that now the physical organization is geographically split. Figure 12.2 illustrates this concept.

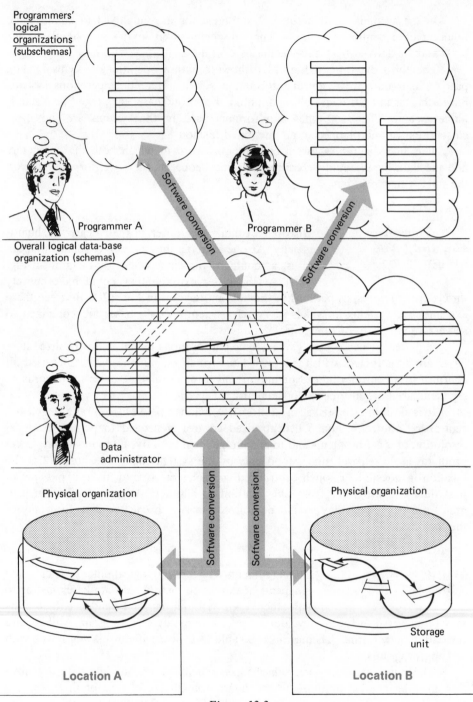

Programmers'
logical
organizations
(subschemas)

Programmer A

Programmer B

Overall logical data-base
organization (schemas)

Data
administrator

Physical organization

Physical organization

Software conversion

Software conversion

Software conversion

Software conversion

Storage
unit

Location A

Location B

Figure 12.2

The overall logical structure (schema) can still evolve without the programs or subschemas having to be changed. The physical structure or geographical location of the data can be modified without the overall logical structure having to be changed.

The software needed to provide the physical data independence with distributed data (the bottom conversion in Fig. 12.2) is complex. Most data-base software does not yet provide true data independence in a distributed system.

The situation becomes still more complicated if subschemas and schemas are held in separate locations. Figure 12.3 shows four possibilities.

The upper diagram of Fig. 12.3 shows a situation that avoids software complexity. The subschemas and schemas are held separately at each data-base location. Terminals have access to different data bases over some form of telecommunication network. Many different network structures are possible.

The second diagram of Fig. 12.3 shows the schemas and subschemas at one location and the data at multiple locations as in Fig. 12.2. Terminals could have access to their local data base only or could be given access to data bases elsewhere.

The third diagram is similar except that the subschemas are prepared at the locations where the data reside. Only the schema is centralized.

The fourth diagram, like the first, shows separate schemas and subschemas at each location but now controlling data at different locations.

Some advocates of distributed data bases (or at least distributed files) have claimed simplicity and ease of implementation as advantages of the distributed approach. The individual data bases are smaller, localized, and hence more comprehensible than a large centralized data base. While this is true, the software is not likely to be simple unless many of the principles we have described in previous chapters are ignored. It is likely that highly complex software for distributed data bases will gradually come into existence, giving logical, physical, and possibly geographical data independence.

HOW ARE THE DATA LOCATED?   A system whose data are scattered geographically must have some means of determining where any required piece of data is stored. As with other aspects of distributed data bases, finding the location of data can range from being a very simple operation to a highly complex one.

A simple method is for the user to specify the location of the data when he makes a request to use them. His transaction may then be transmitted to a computer at the location of the data, or alternatively the data may be transmitted to a location where they can be processed—possibly the location where the transaction originates.

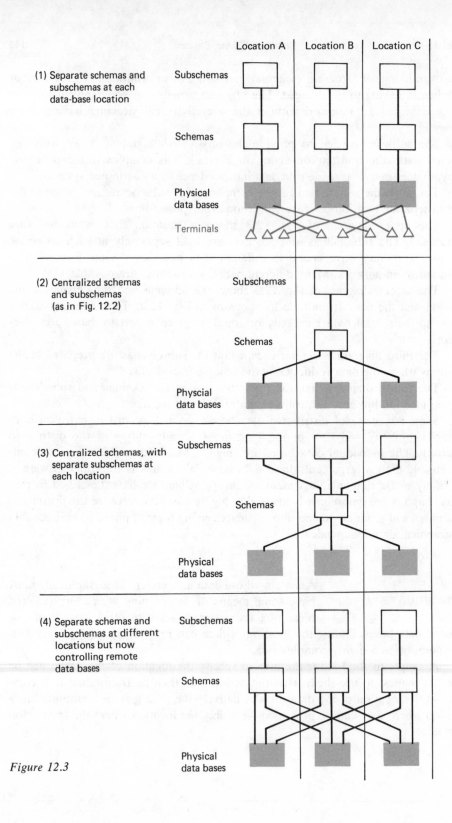

Figure 12.3

Slightly more complicated, the user may specify information about the data from which their location can be simply determined. In a large bank with multiple data centers, for example, a customer may indicate which branch he banks with, and this information determines where his account records are stored.

In some systems of the second configuration in Fig. 12.1, the data which can be given to a terminal are always stored either at the terminal location or at the central location. The program in the computer at the terminal location determines whether it needs to pass the request on to the central computer or not.

Locating the data becomes more complex in the type of system in the bottom diagram of Fig. 12.1 when the user does not know where the data are located. The system must contain some form of catalogue or directory, like a telephone directory, which permits the data to be found. The directory may exist in one particular computer in the network, the request for data being passed to this computer and the location of the data established. Alternatively, every computer in such a network may have a complete directory, listing each file in the network and indicating where it is physically located. Disadvantages of having a directory in every computer are first the storage space required for such directories and second the work of keeping them all up-to-date. In addition the local computers may not be so well equipped for searching the directories rapidly as a specialized or larger computer.

In some systems, most of the transactions received by a local computer relate to the data kept at that location, whereas a few transactions are for data in other locations. In this case the computers may each have a directory of their own data only, and pass the request on to another computer if it relates to data they do not have.

TRANSMISSION OF DATA FILES?   When a transaction reaches a computer which does not possess the data it requires, there are three possibilities:

1. The transaction may be transmitted to the location of the data and processed there.

2. The data may be transmitted to the location of the transaction for use there.

3. Both the transaction and the data may be transmitted to a third location for processing.

The choice of which method is employed will depend partly on the volume of the data and how frequently transmission is required. It would be expensive to move large files of data too often. More important sometimes is the question of keeping control of the data. If the data are to be updated by transactions from different locations, they should remain in one place so that the updating process with its potential conflicts and deadlocks can be controlled. It is undesirable to have more than one copy of data being updated, in different places at the same time. On the other hand, if data are only read, not updated, by the users, the users may have multiple copies, and it may be economical to transmit files to a terminal location for use at that location.

KEEP
IT SIMPLE

In general, data-base software becomes more complex when it permits *logical files* to be split geographically. If every logical file is kept intact in one of the many locations, the severe problems of how to address a geographically dispersed logical file are avoided.

The computer industry does not yet have software which can do everything that might one day be desirable with distributed data bases. The rule with such systems for the time being ought to be "Keep it simple." To do all that may be theoretically advantageous is exceedingly complicated.

PART III

DATA-BASE SOFTWARE

Bloody instructions which, being taught,
return to plague the inventor.

Macbeth

13 TYPES OF DATA-BASE LANGUAGES

To implement and utilize a data base successfully there has to be some complex communication between different categories of people. In the data-processing department the data-base administrator must communicate with the systems analysts and programmers and both must communicate with the data-base management system, sometimes with the help of systems programmers (Fig. 13.1). In the user departments, managers or systems analysts must give statements of their requirements to the data-processing staff, and to the staff who use terminals. The terminal users must have a means of interrogating the data base.

A variety of languages is used to assist in describing data, and constructing and using a data base. The computer industry is expending much money, energy, and argument in developing these languages. Computer users and vendors have formed groups to study the subject—notably the ACM Special Interest Group on File Definition and Translation, the Joint Guide–Share Data Base Requirements Group, and the CODASYL Data Base Task Group. CODASYL is the organization that developed COBOL, the world's most widely used language for commercial programming. Hoping for an encore, the CODASYL Data Base Task Group, known as DBTG, has specified a data description language (described in Chapter 15) and a data manipulation language (Chapter 14) which it believes should form the basis of industry standards [1, 17]. The languages have been criticized as being unsuitable for industry standards because, on the one hand, they are unnecessarily complex and, on the other hand, they do not provide adequate data independence [18].

148

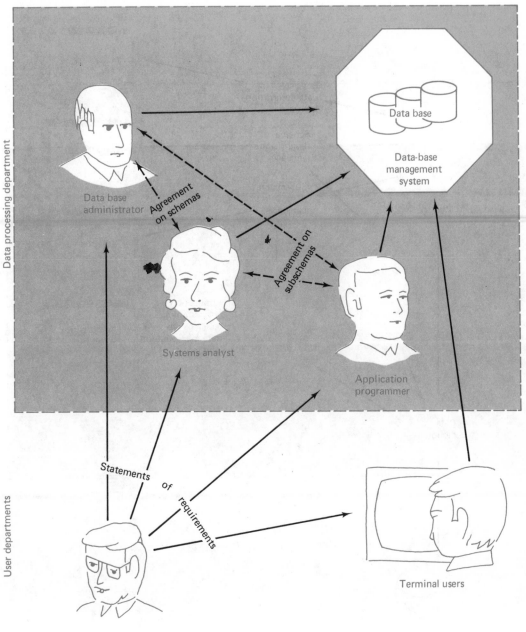

Data processing department

User departments

Data base administrator

Agreement on schemas

Systems analyst

Agreement on subschemas

Application programmer

Data base

Data-base management system

Statements of requirements

Department managers and user analysts

Terminal users

Figure 13.1 Complex communication is necessary between different categories of people.

149

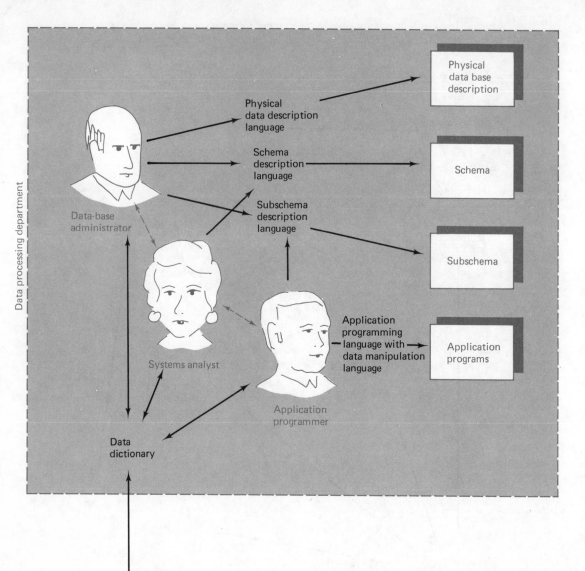

Figure 13.2 Language facilities employed in setting up the data-base system.

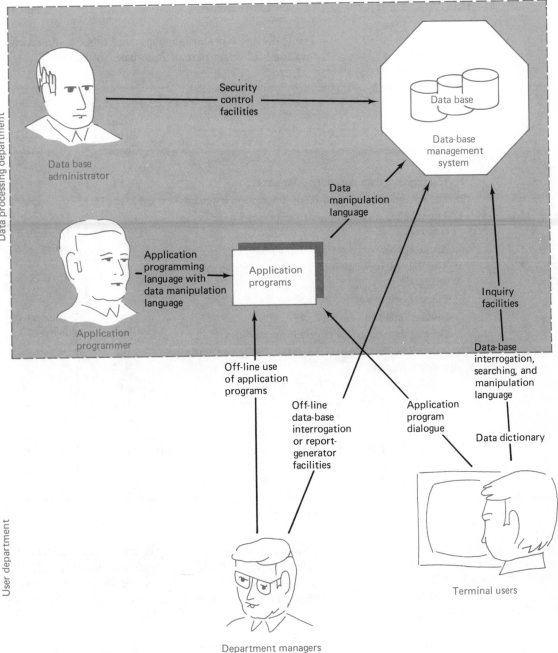

Data processing department

User department

Security
control
facilities

Data base
administrator

Data base

Data-base
management
system

Data
manipulation
language

Application
programmer

Application
programming
language with
data manipulation
language

Application
programs

Inquiry
facilities

Off-line use
of application
programs

Off-line
data-base
interrogation
or report-
generator
facilities

Application
program
dialogue

Data-base
interrogation,
searching, and
manipulation
language

Data dictionary

Department managers
and user analysts

Terminal users

Figure 13.3 Language facilities
employed in *using* the data base.

151

CATEGORIES OF DATA-BASE LANGUAGES

The following types of languages and other communication facilities form part of data-base software:

(handwritten margin note: to set up data base)

	Discussed in Chapter	
1. The physical data description language.	13	
2. The schema (logical data-base) description language.	13, 15, 16	
3. The subchema (programmers' data view) description language.	13, 15, 16	Illustrated in Fig. 13.2
4. Application programming languages.		
5. The data manipulation language used by the application programs.	14	
6. The data dictionary.	18	
7. Inquiry facilities.	17	Illustrated in Fig. 13.3
8. Off-line data-base report-generator facilities.	17	
9. An on-line data-base interrogation, search and manipulation language.	17	
10. Application program dialogue facilities.	17	
11. Security control facilities.	22	

Facilities 1 to 6 in this list are employed in setting up the data base, as illustrated in Fig. 13.2. Facilities 4 to 11 are employed when the data base is in use, as illustrated in Fig. 13.3.

(handwritten note: like skin of onion)

LAYERS OF SOFTWARE

Complex systems have many layers of software, like the skins on an onion. The communication *between* the different layers takes place in a rigorously defined manner which is standardized either within the computer industry or within one manufacturer. This rigorous definition permits any one skin of the onion to be replaced with an alternate layer using different techniques without harming the rest of the onion. The capability to substitute different layers is very important because both the hardware and the software are evolving at a rapid rate.

We will describe the language facilities used in data-base systems starting with the innermost layers of the onion.

(handwritten margin note: Can substitute different layers.)

1. Physical Data Description Language

Some means is needed to specify the physical layout and structure of the data on the storage devices. Some data-base management systems have their own language for specifying this. The CODASYL DBTG refers to a language for this purpose as a *device media control language.* Such a language would specify the assignment of data to devices and media space; would specify how buffering, paging, and overflow is controlled; and would specify addressing and searching techniques such as indexing and chaining. At some future time systems may become clever enough to do the physical layout of data entirely automatically. However, the state of the art is far from that capability at present. Today different data-base management systems use widely differing means of specifying the physical data structure.

Figure 13.4 illustrates this innermost software layer.

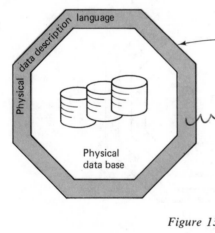

Device Media Control Language
(DMCL) in CODASYL terminology.
Physical Data Base Description
(Physical DBD) is IBM's Data
Language/1.

Figure 13.4

2. Schema Description Language

As we saw in Chapter 7 (Fig. 7.4), the application programmer's view of the data is represented by a subschema and is often different from that represented by the global logical data-base description (schema). Furthermore, the view represented by the schema is different from the physical organization of the data.

The data-base management system uses the data descriptions to derive the global logical records (described in the schema) from the physical records and to derive the records required by the application programs (described in subschemas) from the global logical records. The schema description language, like the subschema language, could be

a. A data declaration facility in the application programming language, possibly an extension of the Data Division of COBOL or the DECLARE statements of PL/I.

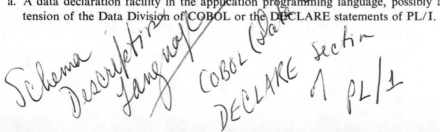

b. A facility provided by the data-base management system, which is independent of which *host* programming language used. IBM's IMS (Information Management System), for example, provides this host-independent subschema description facility in its *program specification block*.

c. An independent data description language which could be employed by any future data-base management system.

In practice different data-base management systems have widely differing facilities for describing schemas. There is a strong case for having an independent language for the schema descriptions because it is desirable that they should not have to be rewritten when the data-base management software, or hardware, is changed. It is also desirable that they should be accessible in various programming languages.

Figure 13.5 illustrates the schema layer of software.

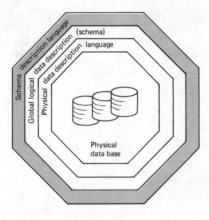

Figure 13.5

3. Subschema Description Language

The application programmer must be able to describe the data that he uses, i.e., declare his subschema. Again one of three types of facility may be employed for this:

a. A programming language (e.g., COBOL) extension.

b. A facility of the data-base management system.

c. An independent language.

Figure 13.6 illustrates the subschema layer in the software.

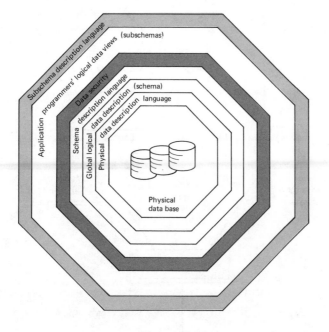

Figure 13.6

Figure 13.7 illustrates the relationships among the three data descriptions. One subschema may be shared by several applications programs. Many subschemas may be derived from one schema, and hence from one physical data base.

4. Programming Languages

The application programmer will write his programs in a conventional programming language such as COBOL, PL/I, or possibly assembler language.

5. Data Manipulation Language

The application program must give instructions to the data-base management system and have a means of interpreting the status messages with which it replies, saying whether the request has been satisfactorily accomplished. For these purposes the data-base management system will provide a set of macroinstruc-

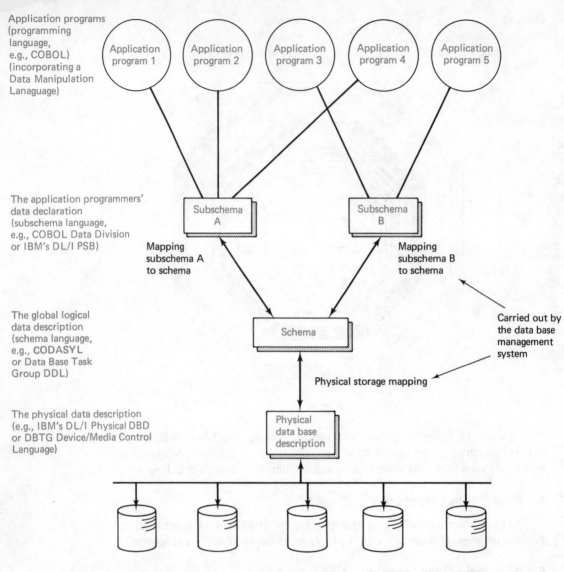

Application programs
(programming
language,
e.g., COBOL)
(incorporating a
Data Manipulation
Lanaguage)

Application
program 1

Application
program 2

Application
program 3

Application
program 4

Application
program 5

The application programmers'
data declaration
(subschema language,
e.g., COBOL Data Division
or IBM's DL/I PSB)

Subschema
A

Subschema
B

Mapping
subschema A
to schema

Mapping
subschema B
to schema

The global logical
data description
(schema language,
e.g., CODASYL
or Data Base Task
Group DDL)

Schema

Carried out by
the data base
management
system

Physical storage mapping

The physical data description
(e.g., IBM's DL/I Physical DBD
or DBTG Device/Media Control
Language)

Physical
data base
description

Figure 13.7

tions or call statements for the application programmer. These may be regarded as an extension of the application programming language, as a separate sublanguage, or merely as a set of call statements provided by a particular data-base management system.

If they are an extension of a programming language, they could be independent of any particular data-base management system. If they are facilities of a data-base management system, they could be basically independent of any programming language. If a separate sublanguage forms the interface between the application programs and the data-base management system, it could, theoretically, be independent of either.

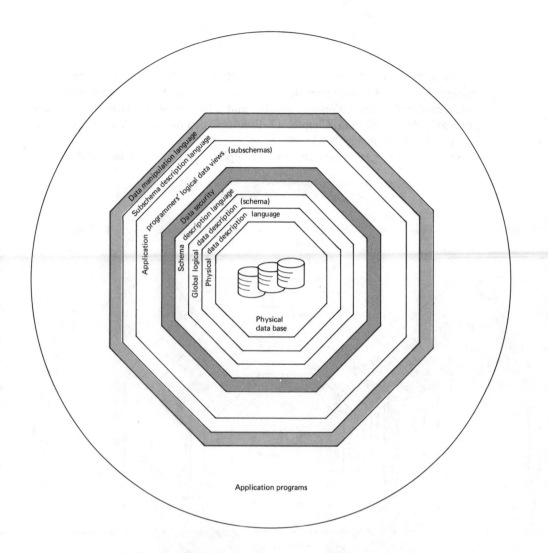

Figure 13.8 The data-base facilities which application programs use.

Some data-base management systems provide an interface which is application-program-independent. The CODASYL Data Base Task Group has proposed an extension of COBOL called a *data manipulation language* (DML) which, it claims, could be implemented for a wide variety of data-base management systems. It is highly desirable that any such sublanguage should permit full data independence, and the CODASYL DML has been criticized on the grounds that it does not do so [18].

Figure 13.8 illustrates the data manipulation layer of software.

6. Data-Base Interrogation Facilities

Figure 13.8 shows the data-base facilities which the application programmers use. A feature of data-base technology which will become increasingly important in the future is the ability to use the data base without involving the application programmers. Figure 13.9 indicates three such means, an off-line report-generator facility, a facility for making on-line queries, and a facility for interrogating, searching, or manipulating the data. Chapter 17 discusses such facilities. A variety of data-base interrogation languages are in use.

Both the interrogation facilities and the application programs use the data-base

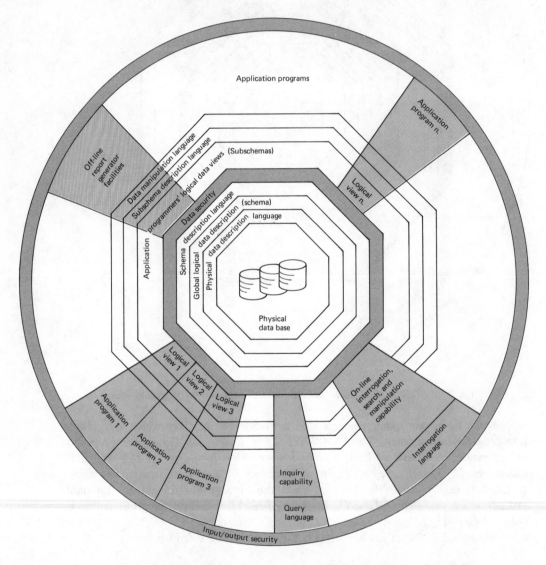

Figure 13.9 Access to the data is provided not only via the application programs, but also—increasingly important—via separate data interrogation facilities.

schema. Figure 13.9 shows them interfacing to the schema software layer but being separated from it by a layer labeled data security. The data base must be protected from all types of users to ensure that unauthorized or incompetent persons do not gain access to the data. A variety of security techniques are in use, some involving access controls built into the schema description language. A further layer of security is drawn in Fig. 13.9 outside the application programs and interrogation facilities. This layer is designed to prevent unauthorized persons gaining access to the programs or interrogation facilities.

7. Security Control Facilities

The data-base administrator controls who has access to what data, and under what conditions. He needs a mechanism to enable him to establish and maintain in the system the tables controlling who has authorization to do what, and to monitor that the system is being used according to the rules. This may be an on-line facility, possibly in the form of a language for security control. It is indicated by the line from the data-base administrator in Fig. 13.3. Data-base security is discussed in Chapter 22.

8. Data Dictionary

A data dictionary is a catalogue of all of the data types in the data base, giving their names, definitions, and characteristics. It may be used by any of the individuals in Fig. 13.1. It may form part of the data-base interrogation facilities. Data dictionaries are discussed in Chapter 18.

9. Teleprocessing Facilities

Much of the use of data bases is via telecommunications links, and more layers of software (and hardware) are used in controlling the teleprocessing. Figure 13.10 indicates first a network management layer. This is designed to set up and control a path through whatever form of network is used. Transmission control, the next layer in Fig. 13.10, is designed to control the transmission of data on each circuit that is set up, to detect any transmission errors that occur, and retransmit the data that was in error. The terminals or their control units today often have microcomputers inside them which permit programs to exist at the terminal location to assist in the application, in the man-computer dialogue, or in the data-base interrogation. The relation between these peripheral programs and the programs in Fig. 13.9 needs to be carefully thought out.

The remote terminals, or their control units, may themselves contain data. We are then concerned with the distributed data issues discussed in the previous chapter. Systems with terminal data today usually have simple *files* rather than *data bases* at the terminal locations.

Another layer of security is drawn in Fig. 13.10 surrounding the terminal facilities.

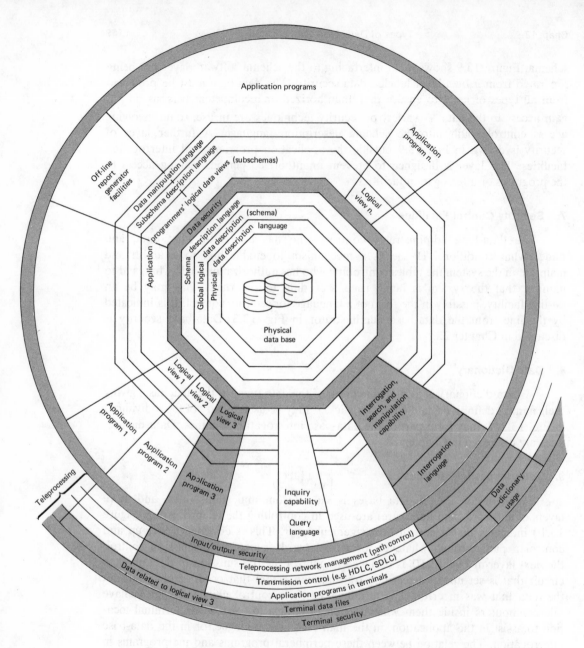

Figure 13.10 The structure of data-base/data-communications software.

RESTART AND RECOVERY

Failures of many different types occur on data-base data-communications systems. The system must be able to restart after such failures and recover in a manner which ensures that no data or transactions are lost, and that no data is accidently updated twice by the same transaction (e.g., the same money paid into a bank account twice). Many systems have the capability to operate in a degraded mode (referred to as *fallback* operation) during a temporary period of failure, and after-

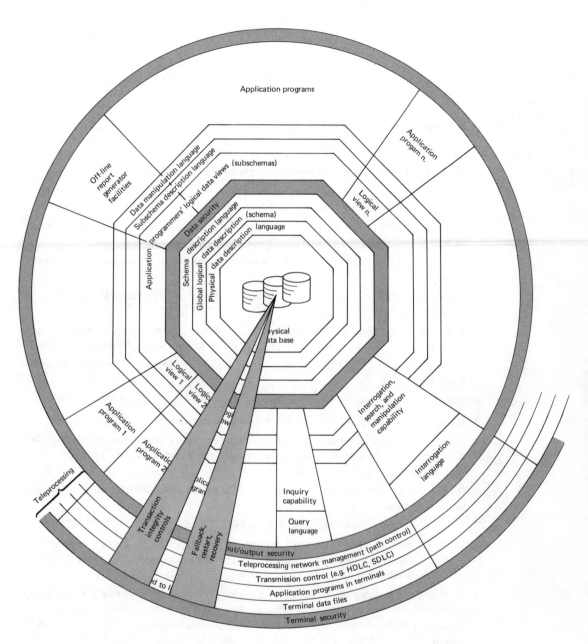

Application programs

Off-line report generator facilities

Data manipulation language

Subschema description language

Application programmers' logical data views (subschemas)

Data security

Schema description language

Global logical data description (schema)

Physical data description language

Physical data base

Logical view 1

Logical view 2

Application program 1

Application program 2

Interrogation, search, and manipulation capability

Interrogation language

Inquiry capability

Query language

Input/output security

Teleprocessing network management (path control)

Transmission control (e.g. HDLC, SDLC)

Application programs in terminals

Terminal data files

Terminal security

Teleprocessing

Transaction integrity controls

Fallback, restart, recovery

Application program n.

Logical view n.

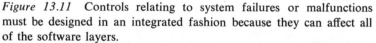

Figure 13.11 Controls relating to system failures or malfunctions must be designed in an integrated fashion because they can affect all of the software layers.

wards recover from this ensuring that no transactions are unprocessed and that all data is updated correctly.

As there are many types of failure possible the fallback, restart, recovery, and integrity control procedures are complex. It is important that they are controlled in an integrated fashion as they relate to *all* of the software layers, as shown in Fig. 13.11.

**WHAT DOES A
DATA DESCRIPTION
LANGUAGE DO?**

A data description language giving a *logical* data description should perform the following functions:

1. It should identify the types of data subdivision such as data item, data aggregate, segment, record, and data-base file. (The types of data subdivision differ from one language to another; "data-aggregate" is a CODASYL group of data items; segment" is a group of data items used in other data description languages.)

2. It should give a unique name to each data-item type, segment type, record type, file type, data base, and other data subdivisions.

3. It should specify which data-item types are in a data-aggregate type, segment type, or record type and should specify their sequence.

4. It should specify which data-item types or combinations of data-item types are used as keys.

5. It should specify how the segment types or record types are related in tree, plex, or other structures.

6. It should give names to the relationships between segment types or record types (i.e., names to the lines connecting blocks on the schema and subschema diagrams).

7. It should define the type of encoding in the data items (binary, character, numeric, floating-point, etc.).

8. It may define the length of the data items.

9. It may define the range of values that a data item can assume.

10. It may specify the number of data items that compose a vector, specify the number of dimensions and size of a matrix, or specify the number of data aggregates in a repeating group.

11. It may specify the sequence of records in a file or the sequence of groups of records in the data base.

12. It may specify means of checking for errors in the data.

13. It should specify privacy locks for preventing unauthorized reading or modification of the data. These locks may operate at the data-item, segment, record, file, or data-base level.

14. A *logical* data description should *not* specify addressing, indexing, or searching techniques or specify the placement of data on the storage units, because these topics are in the domain of physical, not logical, organization. It may give an indication of how the data will be used or of searching requirements so that physical techniques can be selected optimally.

VARIATIONS BETWEEN SCHEMA AND SUBSCHEMA DESCRIPTIONS

The subschema data description may differ from the schema data description in the following ways:

1. The subschema may omit descriptions of certain data that are in the schema. It may omit data items, data aggregates, records, or entire files.

2. The characteristics of data items may be changed. For example, a numeric data item may be in binary-coded decimal (BCD) code in the subschema data description but binary in the schema data description.

3. The sequence of data items in a data aggregate, segment, or record may be different.

4. The sequence of records in a file may be different.

5. Vectors may be redefined as multidimensional arrays.

6. The schema may define relationships different from those in the subschema.

7. Different record types may be described which are composed from data items in other record types.

8. Different data aggregate may be described which are composed from data items in other data aggregates or record types.

9. The privacy locks may be changed.

THE VITAL NEED FOR STANDARDIZATION

It is highly desirable that data description languages should be standardized and independent of specific machines. The data description languages in use today take a variety of forms.

In the early 1970s new data-base management systems came onto the market at a fast and furious rate, and almost all of them had different ways of describing data.

Programming languages, such as COBOL and FORTRAN, have long since been standardized. It is the stated intent of the CODASYL DBTG that their data description language should form the basis of an industry standard for a data language and that all common programming languages will interface with it [1]. This data description language is independent of any programming language but in many ways is similar to COBOL.

Some major authorities have protested that the CODASYL language in its present form is not a suitable standard, and much controversy has raged over this.

Very important benefits would accrue from having a standard data description language. Data would be more easily portable or transmittable from one computer to another. Conversion problems would be eased. One programmer or data administrator would more easily be able to understand and discuss another's data descriptions. Separate data bases could be merged. It would lessen the need to describe data twice in different languages, as often happens today.

The *disadvantage* of standardizing a data description language at this time is that it may restrict the industry to certain classes of data structures and inhibit the development of new forms of structure. As we discussed in Chaper 9 there are major advantages to *normalized* data structures, yet the standards proposed so far are not for normalized structures. Premature standardization has an inhibiting effect on development.

The disadvantage may not be too harmful. The standardization of COBOL was of great benefit to the industry and did not prevent the development of new languages. Standardization of a schema description language will perhaps have similar benefits.

INDEPENDENCE   We have stressed how important it is that the schemas used are independent of the physical storage and organization of data. Both the layout of data and the machines for storing data are likely to change. In some computer installations the physical organization of data is changed frequently as the system is "tuned." For this reason a standardized schema description language should be independent of the physical organization of data. There should be *no* statements in the schema description language which relate to physical storage organization because such statements would destroy the data independence and would make it necessary to change the logical data descriptions when the physical organization is changed.

Similarly, the subschema description language should be independent of the schema description language. The data base administrator should be free to serve the data users as efficiently as possible by modifying schemas and access methods when the change can give an improvement, but such changes should not necessitate any reprogramming of application programs or modification of subschemas.

The CODASYL Data Description Language is intended to be a language for defining schemas. It would provide a data structure suitable for multiple host languages and multiple data manipulation languages. However, CODASYL has also proposed its own data manipulation language [1].

The wide acceptance of a common data description language should lay the foundation for common subschema languages, device/media control languages, and data manipulation languages. In the words of the CODASYL DBTG, *"It is expected that the schema Data Description Language will have a significant impact on the development of functionally compatible data base management systems and will increase the portability of programs between different computer systems."*

CORPORATE   Whether or not a generally accepted industry standard
STANDARDS   exists, it is important that a corporation should have its
                       own internal standards for data description languages.

The standardization of schema descriptions within a corporation is more important than the standardization of programming languages because the schema descriptions become the foundations of an organization's data processing, steadily increasing in complexity and scope. An organization which builds them so that they will have to be changed when data-base software or hardware changes, or when different programming languages are used, is like a man who builds his house upon the sand.

Over the next ten years many corporations will be carrying out the lengthy job of defining the thousands of data-item types they use and constructing, step by step, suitable schemas from which their data bases will be built. The description of this large quantity of data will be an arduous task involving much argument among different interested parties. Stage by stage, separate data bases will be merged logically (and often physically). Eventually the massive data bases that develop will become one of the corporation's major assets. The task of defining the data and agreeing upon suitable schemas that can later be merged or linked requires a standard schema description language throughout the corporation.

If the data base for **purchasing** and the data base for **accounts receivable** are built with separate and incompatible methods for describing data, then it will not be possible to use a data-base management system to answer queries or produce reports using both sets of data. It is highly likely that the **purchasing** and **accounts receivable** data bases will eventually be merged, but to do so will require the conversion of one of them, with consequent rewriting and retesting of the application programs—an expensive and time-consuming operation.

To permit the stage-by-stage growth that data-base software makes possible, a corporate-wide agreement on a data description language is needed. The choice should be a language that is likely to survive. And the death rate among data-base management software has been formidable.

14 DATA-BASE MANAGEMENT SYSTEMS

The schema and the subschemas are both used by the data-base management system, the primary function of which is to serve each application program by executing its data operations.

The main events that occur when an application program reads a record by means of a data-base management system are shown in Fig. 14.1. A number of other events also occur depending on the details of the software, and we will discuss them later. The 11 events below are the essential ones and are numbered in Fig. 14.1:

1. Application program 1 issues a call to the data-base management system to read a record. The program states the name of the record type and gives the value of the key of the required record.

2. The data-base management system obtains the subschema that is used by application program 1 and looks up the record type in question.

3. The data-base management system obtains the schema and determines what record type or types are needed.

4. The data-base management system examines the physical data-base description and determines what physical record or records to read.

5. The data-base management system issues a command to the computer operating system, instructing it to read the requisite record(s).

6. The operating system interacts with the storage media containing the data base.

7. The required data are transferred between the data base and the system buffers.

8. Comparing the subschema and schema, the data-base management system derives from the data the logical record needed by the application program. Any data trans-

formations between the data as declared in the subschema and the data as declared in the schema are made by the data-base management system. The data-base management system thus assembles the logical records which the programmer wants, in the system buffers.

9. The data-base management system transfers the data from the system buffers to the work area of application program 1.

10. The data-base management system provides status information to the application program on the outcome of its call, including any error indications.

11. The application program can then operate with the data in its work area.

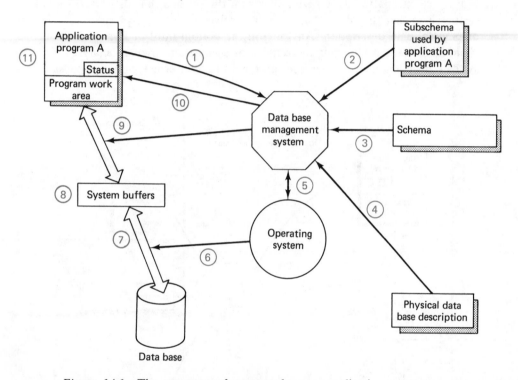

Figure 14.1 The sequence of events when an application program reads a record, using a data-base management system.

If the application program *updates* a record, the sequence of events is similar. The program will normally read it first, modify it in the program work area, and then issue an instruction to the data-base management system to write back the modified data. The data-base management system will make any necessary conversions in the system buffers—the converse of the conversions made when the data were read. The data-base management system then issues the appropriate WRITE command to the operating system.

**VIEWS OF
THE SYSTEM**   A data-base management system will usually be handling multiple data calls concurrently. It must organize its system buffers so that different data operations can be in process together. Multiple application programs may be in operation, and they may use many different subschemas (Fig. 14.2).

The system should be organized so that the view of the application programmer is restricted to the application program, its work area, and subschema—the top third of Fig. 14.2. Anything in the bottom two-thirds of Fig. 14.2 should be changeable *without changing the application programs or their subschema*. Many systems analysts may be familiar with the schema, but their view should be restricted so that they do not concern themselves with the physical storage layout or physical data description. Anything in the bottom third of Fig. 14.2 should be changeable without changing the schema or application-oriented analyst's view. A systems programmer or other specialist may be concerned with the physical or-

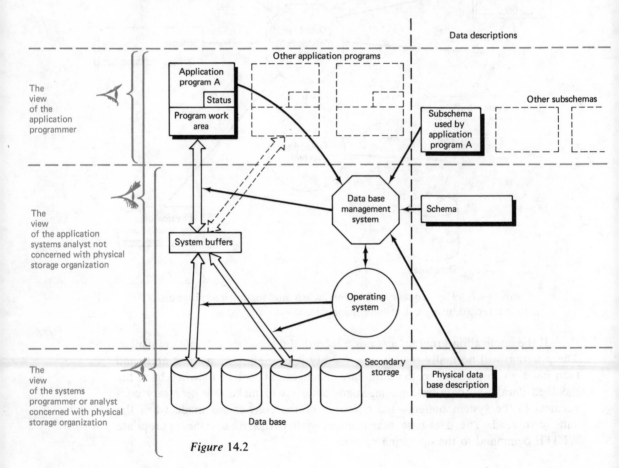

Figure 14.2

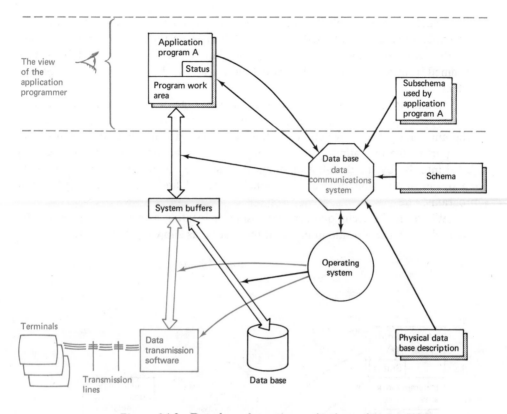

Figure 14.3   Data-base data-communication software.

ganization of data. His view may be restricted so that he is unaffected by those changes in the top third of Fig. 14.2—the application programs and subschemas —which do not require a new schema.

Figures 14.1 and 14.2 are generic diagrams which could apply to a variety of data-base management systems using widely different techniques for accomplishing the steps described. Some of the systems in use do not distinguish in a clear-cut fashion between the subschema, schema, and physical data-base descriptions. Such systems do not achieve full data independence.

Some systems handle data transmission as well as data-base operations. They are referred to as *data-base data-communications* (DBDC) systems. (See Fig. 14.3.)

ADDRESSING
AND SEARCHING
The events we have described are complicated by the fact that the required record usually cannot be located directly from the *key* that is provided by the application program. The record address must be obtained before the input/output routines of the operating system can read or write the record.

Many ways in which the record might be found are discussed in Part II of this book. In one type of method a calculation is performed to convert the key into the requisite record address. This calculation may be performed by a programmed routine which can be called into use by the data-base management system.

In another type of method an index is used. One or more index records must be read or inspected to find the address of the record required by the application program. The program which reads the index records and finds the address may be a part of the operating system. It may be a programmed routine which can be called into use by the data-base management system. Or it may be a routine written by an application programmer which is called and used by the application programs.

Whatever the technique for addressing or locating a record, the program for accomplishing it can reside in one of three places, as shown in Fig. 14.4:

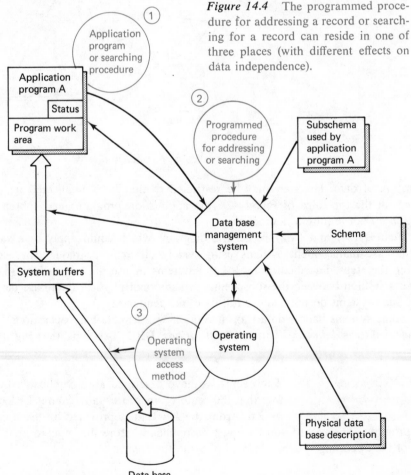

Figure 14.4 The programmed procedure for addressing a record or searching for a record can reside in one of three places (with different effects on data independence).

1. It may be a routine called into use by application programs.

2. It may be a routine called into use by the data-base management system.

3. It may be a facility of the operating system commonly called an operating system *access method.*

If it is an application program routine, this loses some measure of data independence because when the data base is reorganized the program will have to be changed. It is better to make the application programmer's view impervious to data-base reorganizations. If an operating system access method is relied upon exclusively, this limits the range of options possible to the data administrator in optimizing his physical data organization. In many cases the options offered by the access methods are quite adequate. They may be inadequate, however, where secondary keys are used, inverted lists or inverted files are needed, or some elaborate searching operation is required. In such cases it is desirable that the addressing or searching routines be available to the data-base management system.

In some cases the data-base management system may have to examine many records before it obtains the one which the application program requested. It will read such records into its system buffers (8 in Fig. 14.1). The application program will not see them. Control will be passed back to the application program only when the record it requested has been found and transferred to that application program's work area, or alternatively when the data-base management system has determined that the request cannot be satisfactorily complied with. In the latter case the data-base management system will set an indicator in the STATUS area of that application program (10 in Fig. 14.1).

**PRIVACY
CONTROLS**
In the multi-user environment of a data base, privacy controls are necessary to ensure that an unauthorized person or program does not read, modify, or damage data that belongs to someone else. The privacy controls range from being very simple, such as passwords on files, to highly elaborate programmed procedures, such as controls on the use of a statistical data base.

Like addressing and searching techniques, privacy controls may be incorporated into an *application program routine,* into a *data-base management system routine,* or into privacy lock mechanisms of the *operating system* if it has them (Fig. 14.4). Any combination of these three may be used. Often it will be desirable to supplement the operating system security facilities with procedures incorporated either into the application programs or the data-base management system. In most installations it is highly desirable that security should be controlled centrally either by the data base administrator or by a security officer, and hence the security procedures should be in the province of the data-base management system, not the province of the application program.

In one common technique (by no means the only or best technique) the application program must provide the *privacy key* that is required before it can read or modify any data. The data-base management system (or operating system) will check that the key is correct before giving the application program the data it requests or executing any modifications to the data base. To make the check, the key will be compared with a *privacy lock*—a data-item type which should be declared in the schema. The privacy lock may have a constant value, a variable value which is stored in the record, a value which is computed from other data-item values in the record, or a value which is computed from other values such as a terminal user's sign-on code, the time of day, or values in a record relating to the terminal user.

The privacy lock and key may relate to data at the level of data item, data aggregate or segment, record, group of related records, file, or entire data base.

OTHER PROGRAMMED PROCESSES   Just as programmed processes for addressing, searching, or security can reside in the three places shown in Figs. 14.4 and 14.5, so other programmed processes which are used in data-base operations can reside in one of these three positions.

Four categories of program all of which are most likely to be routines accessible to the data-base management system are

1. Programs for monitoring data-base activity, or other forms of "systems instrumentation."

2. Programs for compressing data so that it can be stored more economically.

3. Programs for computing the values of data items in a subschema from other data items in a schema, or for computing schema data items from different physical representations.

4. Programs for checking that data are valid (which may be application programs or data-base management programs).

THE DATA MANIPULATION LANGUAGE   The interface between the application program and data-base management system, referred to as the *data manipulation language*, is embedded in a *host language* such as COBOL. It is desirable that it should have a syntax compatible with the host language because the application program has host language and data manipulation language statements intimately mixed. In fact it should appear to the programmer as though he were using a single language. There should be no *enter* or *exit* requirements from one language to the other.

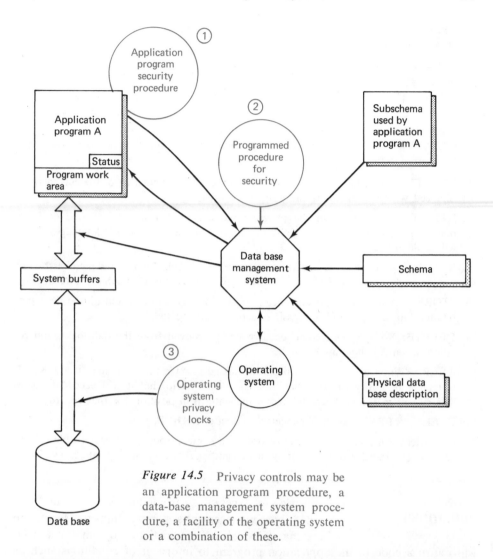

Figure 14.5 Privacy controls may be an application program procedure, a data-base management system procedure, a facility of the operating system or a combination of these.

When the data manipulation language requests a given record, this record is delivered to the work area of the application program from which the application program can manipulate it. Similarly, when a record is to be inserted into the data base, the application program places it in a work area and gives the appropriate command in the data manipulation language.

Typical commands in a data manipulation language are the following (which are taken from the CODASYL DML language):

1. OPEN: A file or set of records is opened, i.e., made available for an application program to use.

2. CLOSE: A file or set of records is closed, i.e., made unavailable to that application program.

3. FIND: The data-base management system locates a specified occurrence of a named record type. It may have to search through several records to find it. The record becomes the "current" record of the application program in question.

4. GET: The contents of specified data items of a specified record occurrence are transferred to the program work area.

5. MODIFY: The values of specified data items of a specified record occurrence are replaced with values in the program work area.

6. INSERT: The record in the program work area is inserted into one or more named groups of records. ("Sets" of records in the CODASYL language—a set will be described later.)

7. REMOVE: A specified record occurrence is canceled from the membership of one or more named groups of records (sets again in the CODASYL language).

8. STORE: A new record occurrence is stored in the data base, and all the necessary relationship linkages and addressing facilities are created.

9. DELETE: A specified record occurrence is removed from the data base, and relationships involving it are deleted.

10. KEEP: When an application program has accessed a record it may use a KEEP statement to notify the data-base management system that it will access it again. The system may then keep the access mechanism in position for that record.

11. FREE: A FREE statement cancels the effect of a KEEP.

12. ORDER: All specified member records in a named group of records (a file or set) are logically reordered in ascending or descending sequence of a specified key.

ERROR CONDITIONS

A variety of types of error conditions can occur when a data-base management system attempts to execute the commands which an application program gives it. It will return a code to the application program to inform it of conditions such as illegal requests, invalid data-item names, records which cannot be found, or infringement of privacy controls.

15 THE CODASYL DATA DESCRIPTION LANGUAGE

This and the following chapter summarize the main features of two of the most important data description languages: the CODASYL Data Description Language, and the IBM data description language, DL/I.

A reader not directly involved with data processing may skip these two chapters if he wishes. It is important to understand, however, that the choice of data description language affects more than merely the way data are described; it determines what form of data structures *can be* described. *A data base designed using the CODASYL language will be structured differently from the same data base described with DL/I. The two are incompatible. Data bases can be merged and interlinked only if they are constructed with the same type of structure.* A CODASYL data base cannot be converted to a DL/I data base, or vice versa, without restructuring the data and hence doing much application program rewriting.

For this reason it is highly desirable for a corporation to standardize its use of data description languages, preferably using the same data description language for all applications throughout the corporation. In this way the corporate data bases can steadily evolve, forming the foundation of the corporation's data processing.

An industry-wide standard language for describing data is therefore needed. There has been bitter argument concerning whether the language we describe in this chapter would form an appropriate standard.

Another way to describe data is in a normalized form (*relational data base*), as discussed in Chapter 9. Normalized data descriptions may eventually become preferable to either CODASYL or DL/I data descriptions when data-base management software which uses them becomes available.

FOUR TYPES   Since 1969 the Conference on Data Description Lan-
OF ENTRIES   guages (CODASYL) has been active in the develop-
                              ment of a common Data Description Language (DDL)
for defining schemas. The current activity within CODASYL on the development
of the DDL is being conducted by the Data Description Language Committee
(DDLC) composed of voluntary representatives from computer manufacturers and
users in industry and Federal Government.

In this chapter we will summarize the main features of the CODASYL Data
Description Language. For a complete description of it the reader should obtain
the original CODASYL specification in Reference 1.

A schema written in the CODASYL Data Description Language contains
four types of entries:

1. *One schema entry* which identifies the schema.

2. *One or more area entries* which define the grouping of records into areas, as we will
   discuss below.

3. *Record entries* which define record types specifying details of their data items and
   data aggregates.

4. *Set entries* which define the grouping of record types into set types (which will be
   described shortly).

The entries are written in the above sequence. Figure 15.2 gives an example
of the resulting code showing the four types of entries used to define the schema
in Fig. 15.1.

The entries consist of English-like statements similar in their form to the Data
Division of the COBOL programming language. Certain words, such as NAME,
PICTURE, RECORD, PRIVACY, and so forth, are reserved, as in COBOL, for
language use. A typical statement is that giving the name of the schema at the
top of Fig. 15.2: SCHEMA NAME IS ORGDATA.

RECORD ENTRIES   A record entry states the name of the record and then
                             lists all the data items in a record. The record type
PERSON at the bottom of Fig. 15.2 contains two data-aggregate types: BIRTH
and SKILLS. SKILLS can occur multiple times in the record. This record type
can be described in the language as follows:

```
RECORD NAME IS PERSON
   01      EMPNO PICTURE "9(5)"
   01      EMPNAME TYPE CHARACTER 20
   01      SEX PICTURE "A"
   01      EMPJCODE PICTURE "9999"
   01      LEVEL PICTURE "X(4)"
   01      SALARY PICTURE "9(5)V99"
   01      BIRTH
      02      MONTH PICTURE "99"
      02      DAY
      02      YEAR PICTURE "99"
   01      NOSKILLS TYPE BINARY
   01      SKILLS OCCURS NOSKILLS TIMES
      02      SKILCODE PICTURE "9999"
      02      SKYLYRS PICTURE "99"
```

The data items and data aggregates are described in a fashion similar to COBOL. The first data item is EMPNO. The PICTURE clause gives the format of the item, indicating, for example, that EMPNO consists of five digits (a "9" in the PICTURE statement means a digit; "9(5)" means five digits). The second data item is EMPNAME, and the TYPE clause indicates that this item consists of 20 characters. A data item can be specified as a bit string, a character string, or arithmetic data which is decimal or binary, fixed-point or floating-point, and real or complex. It can be specified with a PICTURE clause showing the numbers and types of characters, as in COBOL. In the above example, "9999" means four decimal digits; "9(5)V99" means seven decimal digits, five before and two after the decimal point; "A" means one alphabetic character; and "X(4)" means four alphanumeric characters. The data item can also be specified to be of a type to be declared by the implementor. It can be declared to be a data-base *key* with which the record is uniquely identified.

DATA AGGREGATES   The *subentry* which describes a data item can be given a level number; the level number is higher for data items which are components of a data aggregate. The first six data items in the above example have a level number 01. The next subentry, also level 01, is the name of a data aggregate. The subentries following, of level 02, are the data

Schema name: ORGDATA

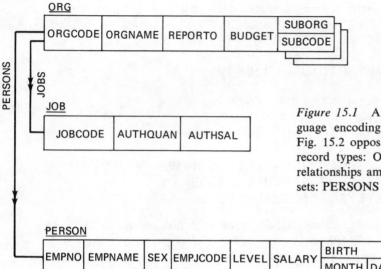

Figure 15.1 A DBTG Data Description Language encoding of this schema is shown in Fig. 15.2 opposite. The schema contains three record types: ORG, JOB and PERSON. The relationships among them are expressed in two sets: PERSONS and JOBS.

items which compose the data aggregate. As with group items in COBOL, the data aggregates can themselves contain data aggregates, and this would be indicated by higher-level numbers. A data aggregate can be a group of single data items, a vector (i.e., a one-dimensional sequence of data items of identical format), or a repeating group (a group of data items which is repeated a specified number of times).

CODASYL SETS

The basic construct of the language is a *set*. A CODASYL set is a new but simple concept. It is, in essence, a named two-level tree as shown in Figs. 15.3 and 15.4. Multilevel trees and certain plex structures can be built up from multiple two-level trees. A CODASYL data base is thus composed of multiple sets. A

Schema ─────────→ SCHEMA NAME IS ORGDATA
entry

Area ─────────→ AREA NAME IS ORGPART
entry

RECORD NAME IS ORG

PRIVACY LOCK IS SESAME

```
          01      ORGCODE   PICTURE IS "9(4)"
          01      ORGNAME   TYPE IS CHARACTER 25
          01      REPORTO   PICTURE IS "9999"
          01      BUDGET    TYPE DECIMAL FLOAT ; IS ACTUAL RESULT OF SALSUM
                      ON MEMBERS OF PERSONS
          01      NOSUBORG   TYPE BINARY
          01      SUBORG OCCURS NOSUBORG TIMES
            02        SUBCODE PICTURE "9999"
RECORD NAME IS JOB
          01      JOBCODE   PICTURE "9999"
          01      AUTHQUAN  PICTURE "99"
          01      AUTHSAL   TYPE FLOAT
RECORD NAME IS PERSON
          01      EMPNO  PICTURE "9(5)"
          01      EMPNAME   TYPE CHARACTER 20
          01      SEX  PICTURE "A"
          01      EMPJCODE  PICTURE "9999"
          01      LEVEL  PICTURE "X(4)"
          01      SALARY  PICTURE "9(5)V99" ; PRIVACY LOCK FOR GET IS
                      PROCEDURE AUTHENT
          01      BIRTH
            02        MONTH  PICTURE "99"
            02        DAY  PICTURE "99"
            02        YEAR  PICTURE "99"
          01      NOSKILLS  TYPE BINARY
          01      SKILLS OCCURS NOSKILLS TIMES
            02        SKILCODE  PICTURE "9999"
            02        SKLYRS  PICTURE "99"
SET NAME IS JOBS; ORDER IS SORTED
     OWNER IS ORG
     MEMBER IS JOB OPTIONAL AUTOMATIC; ASCENDING KEY IS
          JOBCODE DUPLICATES NOT ALLOWED
SET NAME IS PERSONS; ORDER IS SORTED
     OWNER IS ORG
     MEMBER IS PERSON OPTIONAL AUTOMATIC ; ASCENDING KEY IS
          EMPJCODE,EMPNO DUPLICATES NOT ALLOWED
```

Record
entries

Set
entries

Figure 15.2   A description of the schema shown in Fig. 15.1 written
in the **CODASYL DBTG** Data Description Language. Reproduced
with permission from Reference 1.

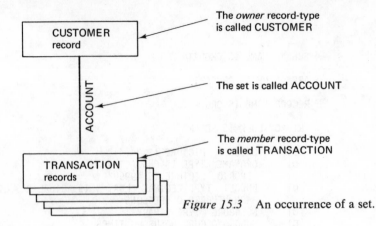

Figure 15.3 An occurrence of a set.

systems analyst can design highly complex structures from many of these two-level linkages, like building bridges with a toy erector kit.

Note: The reader is cautioned not to confuse the CODASYL use of the word set with the use in conventional set theory, which is employed in other data-base literature.

A CODASYL *set* is an occurrence of a named collection of records, and each set type can represent a relationship between two or more record types. Each set type can have one record type declared as its *owner* and one or more other record types declared as its *members*. Each set *must* contain one occurrence of its owner record type and may contain any number of occurrences of its member record types.

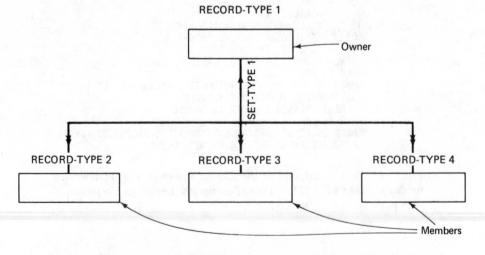

Figure 15.4 A set type can have only one owner record type but multiple member record-types.

For example, a set may be used for customer transaction records. The set type may be called ACCOUNT and its owner record type called CUSTOMER (see Fig. 15.3). The CUSTOMER records may contain details of a customer's name, address, and account balance. The member record type may be called TRANSAC-TION. There would be an arbitrary number of TRANSACTION records in one ACCOUNT set giving details of the transactions that have occurred since that customer was last billed. There could be zero transactions in which case the set occurrence would contain only one record occurrence—that of the owner, CUS-TOMER, record.

The set type may contain multiple member record types as shown in Fig. 15.4. There is a one-to-many relationship between the owner record and the member records, as shown by the double and single arrows in Fig. 15.4. A set thus represents a two-level tree.

In a data base, new record types may be added to a set at a time after the set was originally established. Thus, HISTORY records might be added to the AC-COUNT set in Fig. 15.3 showing a summary of customer purchases. This addition is shown in Fig. 15.5. Although here a new record type was described as becoming a member of an existing set type, alternatively a new set type could have been formed. Figure 15.1 has two set types called JOBS and PERSONS in a two-level tree.

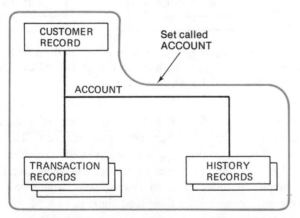

Figure 15.5   A new member record type added to the set in Fig. 15.3.

MULTILEVEL TREES   To represent a multilevel tree, more than one set is necessary. A record type which is declared an *owner* at a lower level in the tree is also declared as a *member* of a higher set.

Figure 15.6 shows a three-level tree. Any N-level tree requires at least $N-1$ sets to describe it. Two sets are used in Fig. 15.6: SALES and ACCOUNT. In this manner, complex multilevel tree structures can be described.

SIMPLE FILES   A *singular set* is a special type of set for which the
                           owner is described as SYSTEM. There can be only one
occurrence of a singular set. A singular set is used to create traditional files in
which all records are of the same type. A data base can have many singular sets,
or files, and they are frequently used.

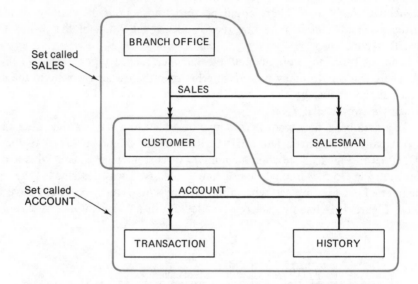

Figure 15.6   A three-level tree requires two sets to describe it. CUS-
TOMER record type is here both an owner of the ACCOUNT set
and a member of the SALES set.

   Any record type can be described as being a member of a singular set at the
same time as being a member of other more complex sets. The CUSTOMER
record type in Fig. 15.6, for example, could be declared a member of a singular
set, as shown in Fig. 15.7. The sequence of the records in a singular set may be
defined to be a sequence different from that of the same records when they
form part of a different set, as will be described shortly.

PLEX STRUCTURES   Every *member* record type has one and only one parent
                           in the same set—its *owner* record type. A member can,
however, have more than one parent if each parent is in a different set. A record
type can be a member of any number of sets. Consquently, a *simple plex structure* with a one-to-many relationship between parent and child can be described
straightforwardly in the language.

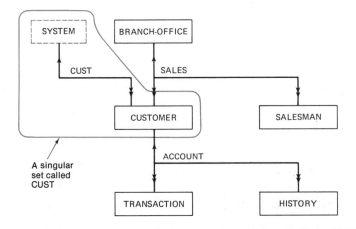

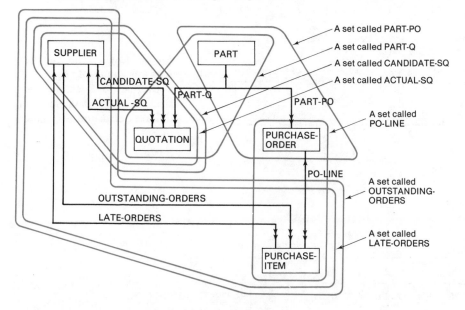

Figure 15.7 The CUSTOMER record type is declared a member of a singular set called CUST. This declaration enables the CUSTOMER records to be treated as a single simple file.

Figure 15.8 A plex structure can be described in using multiple sets in the DBTG Data Description Language.

The plex structure of Fig. 7.8, for example, is redrawn in Fig. 15.8 showing the seven relationships as seven sets. The seven sets have the names CANDI-DATE-SQ, ACTUAL-SQ, PART-Q, PART-PO, OUTSTANDING-ORDERS, LATE-ORDERS, and PO-LINE.

183

While the Data Description Language has no difficulty describing a simple plex structure, a *complex plex structure* (with complex mapping from child to parent) cannot be described without converting it to a simple form. The schema in Fig. 15.9 cannot be described in the form shown. (An instance of this schema is shown in Fig. 8.7.) Instead it must be converted to the form in Figs. 15.10 and 15.11.

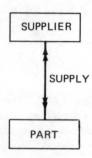

Figure 15.9 A complex structure such as this cannot be represented by the Data Description Language without converting it to the form shown in Fig. 15.10.

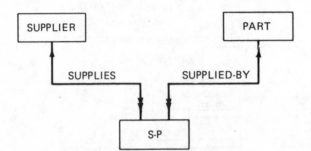

Figure 15.10 The complex plex structure of Fig. 15.9 converted to a simple plex structure. The data items of this plex structure are shown in Fig. 15.11.

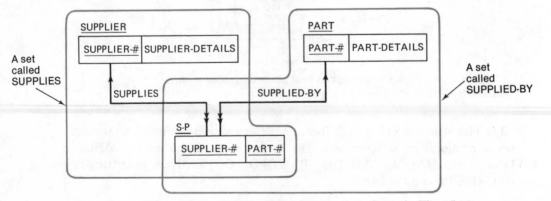
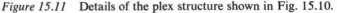

Figure 15.11 Details of the plex structure shown in Fig. 15.10.

Figure 15.9 shows a schema of a plex structure intended to show which suppliers supply which parts. One supplier can supply many parts, and one part can be supplied by more than one supplier. To convert this plex structure so that no child has more than one parent of the same record type, an intermediate record type may be created containing pairs of data items—a part number and a supplier number. There are then two *sets* which in Fig. 15.11 are called SUPPLIES and SUPPLIED-BY.

LOOPS

Loops such as that in Fig. 8.9 are not permitted because no record can be both a member and owner of the same set. Cycles composed of more than one set, such as that in Fig. 8.8, are permitted.

DYNAMIC SETS

A dynamic set differs from an ordinary set in that it does not have any member record types declared for it. Instead, any record can be made a member of it, or removed from it, by executing an appropriate data manipulation function in an application program.

THE ORDERING OF SETS

Each set declared to be part of the data base must have an ORDER specified for its member records stating in what sequence they are to be maintained—although this order may be specified as "IMMATERIAL". The data-base management system will then insert member records into the set in such a way that the *logical* order is maintained. The logical sequence of records (the sequence in which the programmer thinks they are stored) may be quite different from the physical sequence in which they are actually stored. Indeed the same records may be members of more than one set and may be declared to be in a different order in each set.

There are many ways in which a set can be represented physically. The designers of the schema should not be concerned with the question. One way of representing the sequence of records is by means of a chain which links them. In an earlier version of the Data Description Language the user could state that he wanted records to be ordered by means of chaining. He could write ORDER IS CHAIN. It was pointed out that such a statement destroys data independence. The physical methods of ordering might be changed, and the change should not cause the schema or subschemas to have to be changed. In the current version of the language the user cannot specify a *technique* such as chaining. The specification of physical techniques is carried out independently of the schema definition. The word CHAIN and similar technique-oriented words are no longer in the DDL vocabulary of reserved words.

Only *member* records can have an order specified for them. *Owner* records cannot be ordered unless they are member records of another set.

The member records can be ordered in one of several different ways, as follows:

1. The order may be immaterial, and the records can be in whatever sequence is convenient for the data-base management system. The user writes ORDER IS IMMATERIAL or ORDER IMMATERIAL.

2. The order may result from inserting new member records into the set. They may be inserted last in the sequence of member records; the user writes ORDER IS LAST. They may be inserted first in the sequence—ORDER IS FIRST. They may be inserted prior to or after another record selected by the application program—ORDER IS PRIOR or ORDER IS NEXT.

3. A key may be specified, and the records are inserted in ascending or descending sequence of the key value. The user writes ORDER IS SORTED and specifies the key. For example, the bottom two lines of Fig. 15.2 say ASCENDING KEY IS EMPJCODE, EMPNO and then DUPLICATES NOT ALLOWED, stating that no two member records are permitted to have the same values for these two data items which together form the key.

SUMMARY OF SET CHARACTERISTICS   Set characteristics are summarized in Box 15.1.

PLACEMENT CONTROLS   One of the potential disadvantages of making the schema description entirely independent of the physical organization and placement of data is that it may not be possible to use the schema description for optimizing the physical organization. On most systems it is highly desirable that some optimization of physical positioning should occur in order to minimize the response times, maximize throughput, and shorten the time needed to search the data base. On systems which have not been concerned with data independence (almost all systems during the 1960s and many small, specialized, or ill-designed systems during the 1970s) the physical layout of data has often been carefully tailored to sizes of disk tracks and patterns of accessing the records. It is precisely such tailoring that causes the programs to have to be rewritten when the hardware or record content is changed.

Among the types of optimization that are desirable are the following:

1. Records which are commonly accessed together should be placed in close proximity so that there is as little *seek* time as possible between accessing the first and the subsequent ones.

BOX 15.1 Summary of CODASYL Set Characteristics

The following passage from the CODASYL *Data Description Language Journal of Development* summarizes the characteristics and restrictions of sets [17]:

- A set type is a named relationship between record types.
- An arbitrary number of set types may be declared in a schema.
- Each set type must be named and must have one owner record type. However, a special type of set which has exactly one occurrence and for which the system is the owner may be declared. For convenience, this is known as a singular set.
- Each set type must have one or more member record types declared for it in the schema. This does not apply to set types specified to be dynamic.
- Each set type must have an order specified for it in the schema.
- Any record type may be declared in the schema as the owner of one or more set types.
- Any record type may be declared in the schema as a member of one or more set types.
- Any record type may be specified as both an owner of one or more set types and a member in one or more different set types.
- The capability for a record type to participate as both owner and member in the same set type is not supported by the Data Description Language.
- A set consists of an owner record and its member records if any.
- A record cannot be in more than one occurrence of the same set type.
- A set includes exactly one occurrence of its owner. In fact, the existence of the owner record in the data base establishes the set.
- A set which contains only an occurrence of its owner record is known as an empty set.
- A set may have an arbitrary number of occurrences of each of the member record types declared for it in the schema.

2. Where paging is used, records which are commonly referred to together should be placed in the same page to minimize the amount of page switching (thrashing).

3. In a storage device which operates by loading cartridges or other storage cells, records which are accessed together should be placed in the same cell to minimize the time spent changing cells.

4. Frequently referenced items should be stored in an area of the file which can be accessed quickly, whereas infrequently referenced items may be stored in areas needing longer seek times.

AREAS   It may be desirable to make some statements in the schema description which can indicate requirements for physical optimization, but these statements should not presume any knowledge of device characteristics or physical organization techniques; otherwise independence is lost. The schemas should not have to be changed when device characteristics or physical organization techniques change.

To achieve this compromise objective, the Data Base Task Group introduced the concept of *areas*. An area in the CODASYL Data Description Language is a named subdivision of a data base, to which records may be assigned independently of their membership of sets. There may be any number of areas in a schema. The schema described in Fig. 4.4 has only one area, and that area is named ORGPART. It is described with the area entry

AREA NAME IS ORGPART

No record may be assigned to more than one area, and once assigned the record may not change areas. A record type or set type may, however, have occurrences in multiple areas. A set may span many areas.

An area may be either permanent or temporary. If it is temporary, it is associated with the execution of one particular program.

The concept of areas allows the data base administrator to subdivide a data base in ways that may be used to enhance system efficiency without introducing any statements which are device-dependent or technique-dependent. A data-base management system or a physical data-base designer may control the placement of an entire area so as to minimize seek times or confine the area to a given page or hardware zone. Infrequently referenced or archival portions of the data may be suitably placed. A program (task, run unit) may open certain areas and thus indicate that it is confining its attention to a relatively small portion of the data base. This action may permit the optimization of accesses for that program.

Areas may also be used as a convenient unit for fallback. Certain areas may be stored in duplicate or periodically copied.

To indicate that a record is within an area previously named as ORGPART, a WITHIN clause is written in the record description:

WITHIN AREA ORGPART

or simply WITHIN ORGPART.

If the record is to be in the same area of its owner, the description says

WITHIN AREA OF OWNER

or simply WITHIN OWNER.

The area name may be defined as a variable or established by a procedure.

SUMMARY OF AREA   Box 15.2 summarizes CODASYL area characteristics:
CHARACTERISTICS

BOX 15.2   Summary of CODASYL Area Characteristics

The following passage from the DDLC Journal of Development summarizes the characteristics of areas [17].

- An area is a named subdivision of a data base.

- An arbitrary number of areas may be declared in a schema.

- Each area must be named.

- An area may be either permanent, or temporary and local to a run-unit (task).

- Records may be assigned to areas independently of their set associations. A given record type or set type may have occurrences in multiple areas, and a set may span areas.

- Each record must be associated with one and only one area. This association is permanent, and in that a record may not change areas.

The concept of area is one of the most controversial of the current Data Description Language. There is a strong case to be made out that all physical positioning and optimization of data should be carried out quite separately from the description of data by a group who utilize knowledge of how the data is employed. How the data is employed may change frequently, but the logical data description should be independent of such changes.

SEARCHING AND INDEXING   The word SEARCH in the data description declares that a search must be made for certain occurrences of a given record type. The search may or may not employ an index. There are many ways of searching a data base. The word INDEX is used in the CODASYL language to mean *any possible* means of searching the records of a set that does not employ a serial scan of them. The implementor is free to choose and to change the searching techniques. The use of the word INDEX does not conform with the conventional narrower concept of an index.

The user may name an index and could thus write SEARCH USING INDEX NAME DIRECTORY1. He could also name a programmed search procedure: SEARCH USING PROCEDURE S12. If the search is carried out using a secondary key he could write, for example, SEARCH KEY IS JONES. He might write SEARCH KEY JONES USING INDEX NAME DIRECTORY1.

SET SELECTION   Usually there will be many occurrences of a given set type in a data base. It is necessary to provide a means of identifying and locating the required set when it is to be retrieved, and determining where to place it when it is to be stored. Techniques for addressing records are discussed in Chapter 10. The schema should not be concerned with details of these techniques because they relate to *physical* data-base organization. The schema may, however, specify the general form of set addressing, indicating whether an application program routine is used, whether a key is used, or whether the technique involves the use of another set. Addressing is referred to as *set selection*, and the following types of set selection may be specified:

1. The selection may be performed by means of a named program procedure. This is specified by writing a clause such as SET SELECTION IS BY PROCEDURE Z18 or simply SELECTION PROCEDURE Z18.

2. The selection may be performed using a *key*. The application program provides the key of the required owner record, and the data-base management system uses this key to locate the owner record of the set. This type of addressing may be specified by a clause such as SET SELECTION IS THRU OWNER IDENTIFIED BY DATA-BASE-KEY EQUAL TO JONES, or simply SELECTION THRU DATA-BASE-KEY JONES.

3. The address of the required set is found by means of a calculation using a given data base key, for example, SET SELECTION IS THRU CALC-KEY EQUAL TO JONES or simply SELECTION THRU CALC-KEY JONES.

4. The selection may be by means of another set, for example, SET SELECTION IS THRU EMPLOYEE, where EMPLOYEE is a set type used for addressing the required set. In some cases, the set selection will be by means of multiple other sets: SET SELECTION IS THRU DEPARTMENT OWNER IDENTIFIED BY DATA-BASE-KEY IS MAIL-ORDER THEN THRU EMPLOYEE.

16 IBM'S DATA LANGUAGE/I

The data description language on which IBM is basing its main data-base products is DL/I (Data Language/I) [19]. This language is used in the data-base management system IMS (Information Management System) [20, 21, 22], and CICS (Customer Information Control System) can be used with a DL/I data base. The data-base interrogation languages IQF [23] and GIS/VS (discussed in Chapter 17) work with a DL/I data base. Some products of independent software houses can also work with DL/I-structured data, for example, the Informatics MARK IV data-base management system.

Unlike the CODASYL Data Description Language, DL/I is used to specify both the logical representation of the data base (schema) and the physical representation. The physical representation is described in terms of a number of standard techniques for physical storage layout, each with their own addressing techniques, and they are referred to as *access methods*. The logical data description is written separately from the physical description. Nevertheless, it is dependent on the physical description and does not describe the data completely unless the physical description also exists. Changes can be made to the physical description (and hence the physical storage layout) without changing the logical description. Secondary indices designed for searching the data can be specified and implemented with some DL/I systems.

DL/I VOCABULARY When discussing specific data-base software it is often necessary to modify our vocabulary to conform to that used with the software. Figure 16.1 compares the terms used in DL/I with those used in the CODASYL language.

191

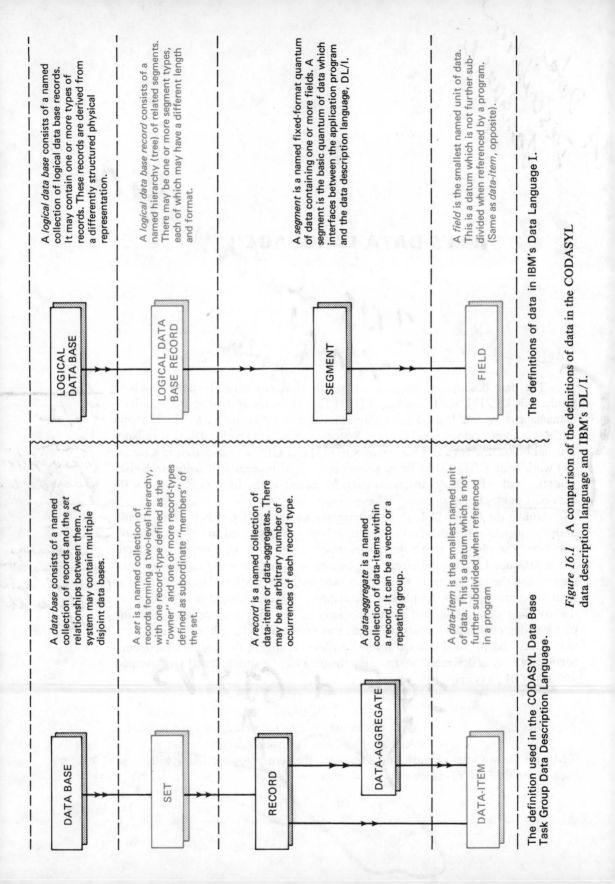

A *logical data base* consists of a named collection of logical data base records. It may contain one or more types of records. These records are derived from a differently structured physical representation.

A *logical data base record* consists of a named hierarchy (tree) of related segments. There may be one or more segment types, each of which may have a different length and format.

A *segment* is a named fixed-format quantum of data containing one or more fields. A segment is the basic quantum of data which interfaces between the application program and the data description language, DL/I.

A *field* is the smallest named unit of data. This is a datum which is not further subdivided when referenced by a program. (Same as *data-item*, opposite).

LOGICAL DATA BASE

LOGICAL DATA BASE RECORD

SEGMENT

FIELD

The definitions of data in IBM's Data Language I.

A *data base* consists of a named collection of records and the *set* relationships between them. A system may contain multiple disjoint data bases.

A *set* is a named collection of records forming a two-level hierarchy, with one record-type defined as the "owner" and one or more record-types defined as subordinate "members" of the set.

A *record* is a named collection of data-items or data-aggregates. There may be an arbitrary number of occurrences of each record type.

A *data-aggregate* is a named collection of data-items within a record. It can be a vector or a repeating group.

A *data-item* is the smallest named unit of data. This is a datum which is not further subdivided when referenced in a program

DATA BASE

SET

RECORD

DATA-AGGREGATE

DATA-ITEM

The definition used in the CODASYL Data Base Task Group Data Description Language.

Figure 16.1 A comparison of the definitions of data in the CODASYL data description language and IBM's DL/I.

CODASYL construct is a set:
DL/1 construct is a TREE.

A *field* in DL/I is equivalent to a *data item* in the CODASYL language. A *segment* in DL/I is a named collection of data items. The data are stored and addressed in segments. DL/I has no need to distinguish between a data aggregate and a record; both are segments.

A *logical data-base record* in DL/I is a hierarchically related collection of segments. *A logical data base* is a collection of logical data-base records. A logical data-base record might be thought of as corresponding to a *set* in the CODASYL language, but, as we will see, the differences are more fundamental than the similarities.

A COLLECTION OF TREES

Whereas the basic construct of the CODASYL language is a *set* and complicated structures can be built from sets, the basic construct of DL/I is a tree. A DL/I data base consists of a collection of trees of segments such as that in Fig. 8.3. Each tree is laid out physically on the file units, the details of the layout being governed by one of the standard DL/I access methods. There can be *logical* linkages between trees. Two of the access methods (HSAM and HISAM) lay out the tree of segments serially, as on tape, for example. Two of the access methods (HDAM and HIDAM) lay out the tree so that there can be direct access to any segments, as on disk or other direct-access storage devices. The letter I in the abbreviation for the access method means that an index is used. The letter H means that the structure is hierarchical or in the form of a tree. The four methods of laying out the trees physically are as follows:

tree is basic construct in DL/1.

    HSAM: Hierarchical Sequential Access Method

    HISAM: Hierarchical Index Sequential Access Method   *} segments serially — tape*

    HDAM: Hierarchical Direct Access Method

    HIDAM: Hierarchical Indexed Direct Access Method   *} segments for disk access.*

DL/I systems are designed so that new access methods can be used in the future without application programs or the global logical schema having to be changed.

A tree can have up to 15 levels. Each level can have multiple segment types. Sometimes only one level, i.e., a solitary root segment, exists. A data base may consist of many of these physical trees, with (logical) linkages between them.

LOGICAL CHILDREN

In constructing the trees, pointers are used to avoid duplicating the same segment in different trees. In Fig. 16.2, for example, an EMPLOYEE segment appears in two separate trees. If the trees were constructed in this form, there would be redundancy between them in

JOBCAT:

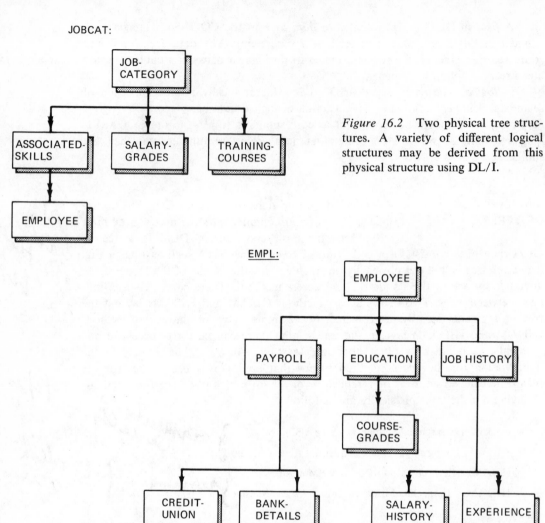

Figure 16.2 Two physical tree structures. A variety of different logical structures may be derived from this physical structure using DL/I.

the EMPLOYEE segment. The EMPLOYEE segment in the JOBCAT tree is therefore replaced by the pointer segment shown in Fig. 16.3. The pointer segment gives the addresses of the relevant EMPLOYEE segments.

The EMPLOYEE segment in the EMPL tree then becomes, *in effect*, a child of the ASSOCIATED SKILLS segment in the JOBCAT tree. It is referred to as a *logical child* because the trees still remain separate physically. The pointers are referred to as *logical child pointers*. In a DL/I data base, many logical child pointers may be used. Used to avoid physical redundancy, they also make it possible to derive multiple logical structures from the physical trees.

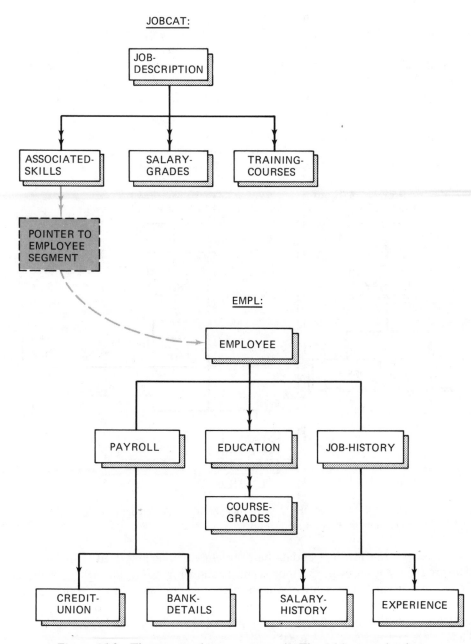

Figure 16.3 The two employee segments in Fig. 16.2 are redundant. One of them is therefore replaced with a pointer segment.

THE LOGICAL
DATA-BASE RECORD
The organization perceived by an application programmer is also a *tree* of segments. However, it may be different from any tree that exists physically. The tree which the application programmer perceives is referred to as a *logical data-base structure.*

Figure 16.4 shows a logical data base. This tree will be derived from the physical tree, EMPL, in Fig. 16.3.

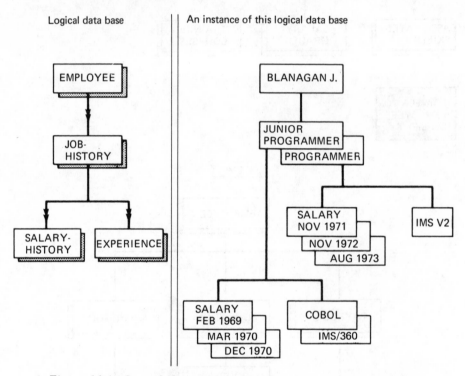

Figure 16.4 One of the many logical data base structures derived from the physical structure in Fig. 16.3.

The segments in a logical data-base structure will be presented to the application program starting with the root segment and progressing through its subtrees from left to right. Each subtree will be presented starting with *its* root segment and progressing through *its* subtrees from left to right. Thus the logical data-base structure shown in Fig. 16.4 would be presented in the sequence shown in Fig. 16.5.

The programmer may read the segments in a logical data base with the following types of call statements:

• GET UNIQUE (GU) to retrieve a named segment within the data base.

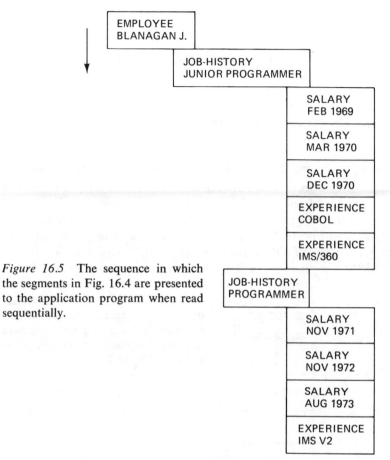

Figure 16.5 The sequence in which the segments in Fig. 16.4 are presented to the application program when read sequentially.

Next record

- GET NEXT (GN) to retrieve the next segment in the sequence shown in Fig. 16.5.

- GET NEXT WITHIN PARENT (GNP) to retrieve the next segments in sequence of a parent segment which is established by looking back to the previous GET UNIQUE or GET NEXT call which was successfully completed. If no further segment exists with that parentage, a NOT FOUND status code is returned.

- GET HOLD UNIQUE (GHU)

- GET HOLD NEXT (GHN)

- GET HOLD NEXT WITHIN PARENT (GHNP)

  These three calls are the same as the previous three except that they indicate that the segment is to be updated or deleted. No other operation may proceed on the segment until the HOLD condition is cleared.

- REPLACE (REPL): This call is used after one of the previous three GET HOLD calls, to update a segment.

• DELETE (DLET): This call is used after one of the three GET HOLD calls, to delete a segment. The segment may not be *physically* deleted until the data base is reorganized; it may be flagged merely to indicate deletion.

• INSERT (ISRT): This call is used to insert new occurrences of a segment type into a data base.

When any of these operations are performed on a logical data base, appropriate status or error messages are returned to the application program.

POINTERS BETWEEN TREES   The logical data-base structure in Fig. 16.4 is derived from one physical tree. Sometimes they are derived from multiple physical trees by means of pointers connecting the trees. Figure 16.6 shows a logical data base which contains segments from both of the trees in Fig. 16.3. To construct it a *logical child* pointer segment is added under the EDUCATION segment in the EMPL tree pointing to the TRAINING-COURSES segment in the JOBCAT tree, as shown in Fig. 16.7.

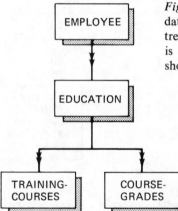

Figure 16.6 To derive the logical data-base structure from the physical trees in Fig. 16.3, a pointer segment is needed connecting the trees as shown in Fig. 16.7.

Logical parent or *logical twin* pointers may be used similarly, either within a physical tree or spanning different trees. For example, if each of the TRAINING-COURSES is part of a particular EDUCATION program, the EDUCATION segment in the EMPL tree could be made the *logical parent* of the TRAINING-COURSES segment in the JOBCAT tree. The pointers between the EDUCATION and TRAINING-COURSES segments could then be declared as *bidirectional* pointers.

Again, segments relating to similar entities may exist in different data bases. For example, both a factory data base and a research data base may contain EMPLOYEE segments. A *logical data base* may combine these separate segments if they are interconnected with *logical twin* pointers.

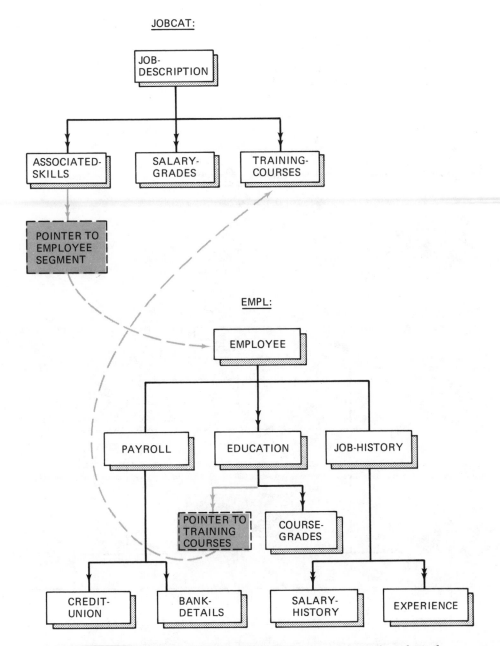

Figure 16.7 The TRAINING-COURSES segment is made a *logical child* of the EDUCATION segment in order to produce the logical data base shown in Fig. 16.6.

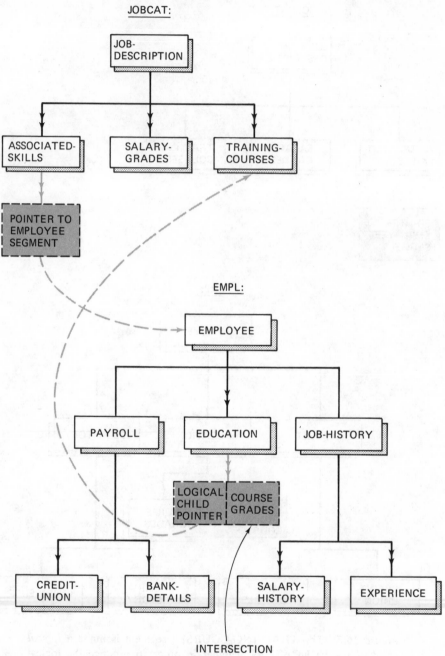

JOBCAT:

JOB-DESCRIPTION

ASSOCIATED-SKILLS   SALARY-GRADES   TRAINING-COURSES

POINTER TO EMPLOYEE SEGMENT

EMPL:

EMPLOYEE

PAYROLL   EDUCATION   JOB-HISTORY

LOGICAL CHILD POINTER   COURSE GRADES

CREDIT-UNION   BANK-DETAILS   SALARY-HISTORY   EXPERIENCE

INTERSECTION DATA

Figure 16.8

INTERSECTION DATA   In some cases when a relationship exists between two segments there can be data which are relevant *to the relationship* but not relevant to either segment by itself. In DL/I terms such data are called *intersection data*.

Consider, for example, a MAN segment and a WOMAN segment. The relationship between them could be called "Married," "Engaged," "Divorced," or possibly other things in this day and age. The nature of the relationship could be stored as *intersection data* in a DL/I representation. The information is incomplete without the data associated with the relationship.

Again, in a manufacturing system there may be a segment describing each subassembly and each product. The intersection data between subassembly and product segments may show how many of that subassembly the product contains. This number is meaningless if attached by itself to one segment. It has meaning only when it relates to the pair of segments.

The COURSE-GRADES in Fig. 16.7 might be better represented as intersection data if they are dependent on the relationship between the employee and his training courses. Figure 16.8 shows them represented as intersection data.

PLEX STRUCTURES   As discussed in previous chapters, not all data structures are in the form of trees. DL/I can handle any form of plex structure (at least in principle); but it has to do so by establishing logical relationships between the physical tree structures. Many DL/I data bases do this in practice. Usually there is more than one method of representing a plex structure. The designer should choose which method he prefers on the basis of such factors as which access paths are the most frequently used, which need fast response times, which data need efficient disk space utilization, which need frequent reorganization, and so forth.

Figure 16.9 redraws the plex structure of Fig. 7.7 again, as in Fig. 15.8. Two logical child segments are needed in order to represent this structure, and intersection data are used to indicate whether a LINE-ITEM or a purchase order is OUTSTANDING or LATE. In the upper version intersection data indicate whether the SUPPLIER related to a QUOTATION is ACTUAL or CANDIDATE.

A complex plex structure can be represented with no more difficulty than a simple plex structure. Figure 16.10 shows the complex-complex mapping between SUPPLIER and PART which was illustrated in Fig. 8.7. Through logical relationships the PART segment may relate to the SUPPLIER segment and vice versa. An instance of the structure is illustrated. The reader might compare this representation with the CODASYL one in Fig. 15.11.

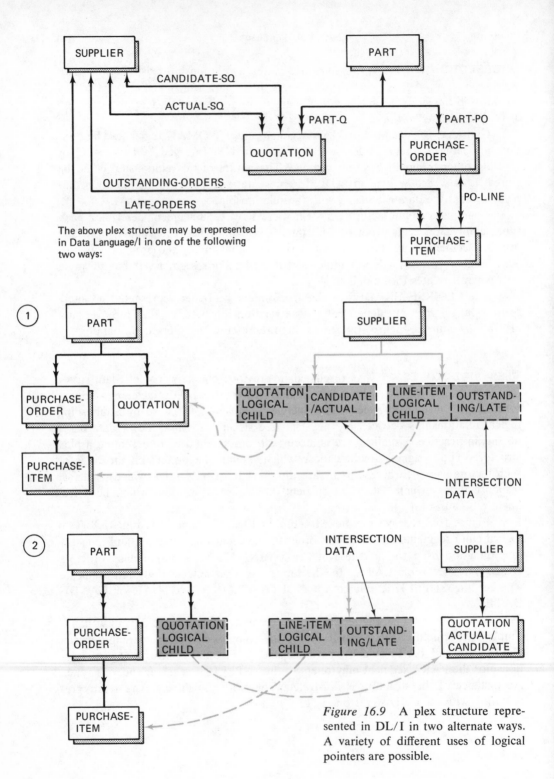

The above plex structure may be represented in Data Language/I in one of the following two ways:

Figure 16.9 A plex structure represented in DL/I in two alternate ways. A variety of different uses of logical pointers are possible.

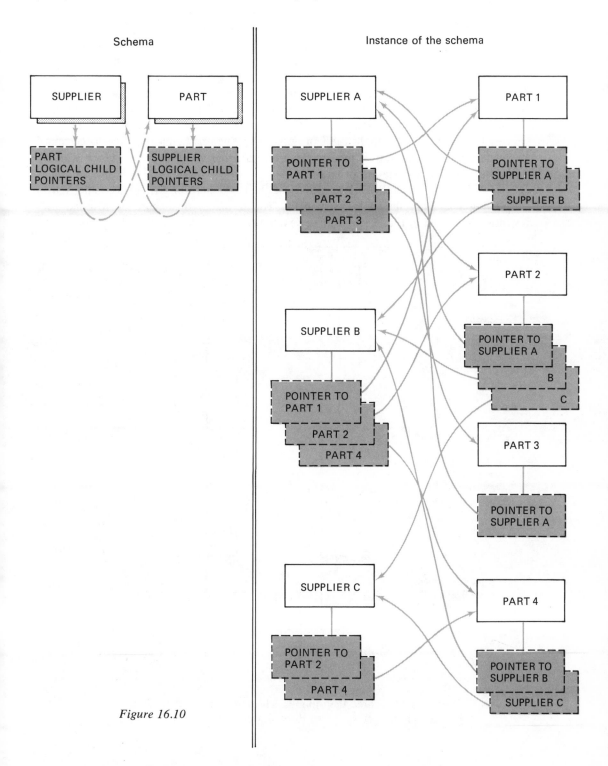

Figure 16.10

APPLICATION
PROGRAM
SENSITIVITY

One application program may see one or more types of logical data-base records. For example, an application program using the data base in Fig. 16.3 may perceive only segments of the type in Fig. 16.4. It cannot read the other segments in the data base. Another application program may perceive quite different segments in the same data base. This concept of separation of viewpoints, an essential step toward data independence, is referred to in DL/I circles as *sensitivity*. An application program is defined as being *sensitive* to certain segments. This definition is incorporated into a *program specification block* which is used by each application program.

There are thus three descriptions of data which form part of a system employing DL/I, as shown in Fig. 16.11. The terms in this figure correspond to those illustrated in Fig. 5.1. All three descriptions are coded in DL/I language.

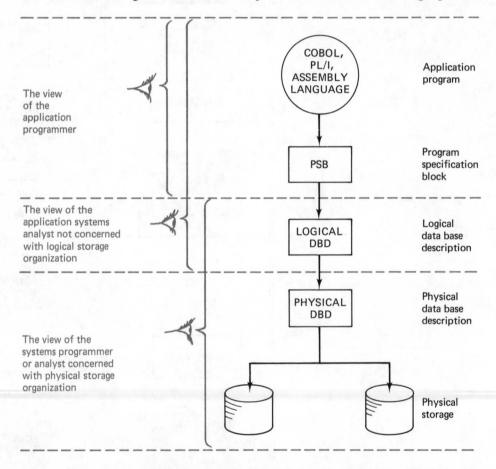

Figure 16.11 Three descriptions which define the data when DL/I is used. These correspond to three descriptions illustrated in Fig. 5.1.

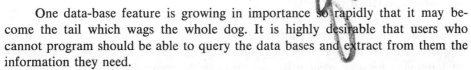

17 QUERY LANGUAGES

One data-base feature is growing in importance so rapidly that it may become the tail which wags the whole dog. It is highly desirable that users who cannot program should be able to query the data bases and extract from them the information they need.

For this purpose a wide variety of data-base query languages exist. Some are simple so that an unskilled user such as a clerk can compose a query. Some can carry out more complex searching and report generating functions, but more skill and training is needed in order to use them.

ON-LINE?
INTERACTIVE?

Some are designed essentially for off-line use. The user composes a query and perhaps a report format, submits it to the computer center, and expects a reply in a few hours or on the following day. Some are designed for on-line use in which the user composes his query at a terminal and expects a reply in seconds or, at most, minutes. On-line use places severe constraints on the data-base organization in that it must be designed to give suitably fast response times. Off-line data-base interrogation can be very valuable. In one corporation with a DL/I data base the capability to interrogate that data base (using GIS, described below) was introduced as a supplementary off-line facility. To the amazement of the data base owners, the users of the data base generated 28,000 reports using the interrogation language in one year of operation. Nevertheless, on-line use can be far more effective than off-line use when the user has the capability to carry on a dialogue with the system. The system can help him to specify complex queries, and he can narrow down his search step by step until he finds the information he is looking for.

HEURISTIC   It is often the case that the answer to a single off-line
SEARCHING   query does not provide the information that was sought.
                      The user needs to try a new query or adjust the pre-
vious one. Often an initial query is too broad and would result in hundreds of
responses or an entire file search. Interactive operation allows the query to be
modified so that it is more reasonable before the full search is executed. On some
systems the user may adjust his query twenty or thirty times before he finds the
information he wants.

The successive modification of queries to home in on information which is
sought is sometimes referred to as *heuristic searching* of a data base.

SPONTANEITY   Executives who understand that data-base information
                      is available to them sometimes develop many sponta-
neous ideas for using it. To put the data base to good use for decision making,
however, they usually need to receive the information *quickly*—tomorrow they
will have a different problem.

As Fig. 17.1 indicates, a vice-president may have to wait weeks or months if
a program written in a conventional language is needed to process his information
request. With a data-base interrogation language usable by the information staff
at terminals, he may receive the information he wants in minutes. Spontaneous
ideas involving information usage are encouraged.

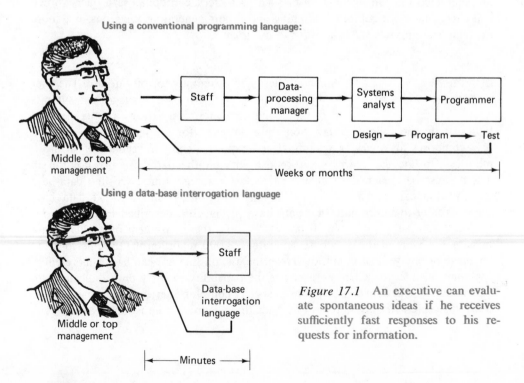

Using a conventional programming language:

Staff → Data-processing manager → Systems analyst → Programmer

Design → Program → Test

Middle or top management — Weeks or months

Using a data-base interrogation language

Staff

Data-base interrogation language

Middle or top management

— Minutes —

Figure 17.1 An executive can evalu-
ate spontaneous ideas if he receives
sufficiently fast responses to his requests for information.

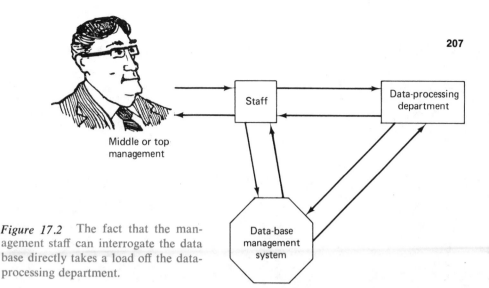

Figure 17.2 The fact that the management staff can interrogate the data base directly takes a load off the data-processing department.

As indicated in Fig. 17.2, the fact that the data base can be interrogated directly by the information staff takes a load off the data-processing department.

STANDARD DATA-BASE STRUCTURE?

We have stressed the importance of data independence and standardized data description languages for most applications. Some data-base query software is designed to operate with data bases constructed from standardized data description languages having the desirable properties we have discussed. Some, on the other hand, have to have their own special data structures, and the advantages of data independence are lost.

In some cases a data base is built solely for the purpose of being searched so that queries can be answered. This would be the case, for example, with a library data base or a store of legal or technical documents. In these data bases the capability to find the required documents is the dominant consideration. The data are not likely to be used for other purposes, and so data independence and flexibility matter little compared with a structure which permits fast and versatile searching. The same may be true of an *information* data base which is separated from a processing data base, as in Fig. 6.2.

FORMS-ORIENTED LANGUAGE

One of the easiest-to-use types of query language is that in which the inquirer fills in a form.

One of the query languages used with the MARK IV data-base management system [24] employs forms for query specification. Informatics Inc., who produce MARK IV, advertise: "Learn to write computer programs in five minutes!"

Box 17.1 gives a simple example of a MARK IV query. The form that it shows can be filled in very simply and quickly and then keypunched and processed.

BOX 17.1   The MARK IV Information Request Form

MARK IV, produced by Informatics Inc., is a data-base management system which permits information requests to be specified very quickly by filling in forms. MARK IV can handle complex data bases using the DL/I language, and process complex information requests. The following is a simple illustration.

An accountant has received a request from his boss for the total year-to-date activity on one vendor's account. Taking an Information Request form, the accountant writes in a Request Name. Any name that fits ① . He writes TODAY in the Report Date box (to get *today's* date on the report) ② .

No other information is required in the heading area of the form. MARK IV provides automatic default conditions for everything left blank. In this example, MARK IV will produce a detail report, single spaced, on standard 8½" by 11" paper.

To be able to request information from a file of data, the file has been defined previously to MARK IV. The file definition provides the accountant with the names of the pieces of data which make up the file. Other qualities of the data, such as size, are also provided. MARK IV stores this definition, and a printed glossary of the names is available any time for any users of the file.

Therefore, when the accountant wants to refer to the data in the file, he just looks at the glossary for the Accounts Payable file and uses the names that were assigned to the pieces of data in the file. For instance, the piece of data which is the vendor number is called VENDOR, and since the vendor in which he is in-

terested is ABC Manufacturing (vendor number 2386), he "selects" that vendor by writing VENDOR EQ (equal) D (for Decimal) 2386 in the Record Selection area of the form. When looking at the Accounts Payable file, MARK IV will pick out only the data about vendor number 2386 ③ .

And, since only activity for 1972 is of concern, the accountant writes A (for And) INVYEAR EQ D 72 to select only the activity concerning ABC Manufacturing Company that has taken place in 1972 ④ .

If no such special selection criteria are required, then the Record Selection portion of the form is left blank. The default condition for this is that MARK IV will report on the total contents of the file.

Now that the accountant has specified the selection criteria, he can specify the data he wants to see on the report itself. He wants to see the vendor's invoice number, invoice date, invoice amount, check number, check date and amount paid. He writes the names for those pieces of data, one to a line and in the sequence he wants them to appear across the report, in the Report Specification section of the form ⑤ .

To get a total of the activity being reported, the accountant simply enters a G (for Grand) in the column marked Total on the same lines as INV-AMT and AMT-PAID. MARK IV will provide a grand total of all the INV-AMTs and AMT-PAIDs in the report ⑥ .

Finally, to give a meaningful title to his report, the accountant writes his own title in the section of the form labeled TITLE ⑦ .

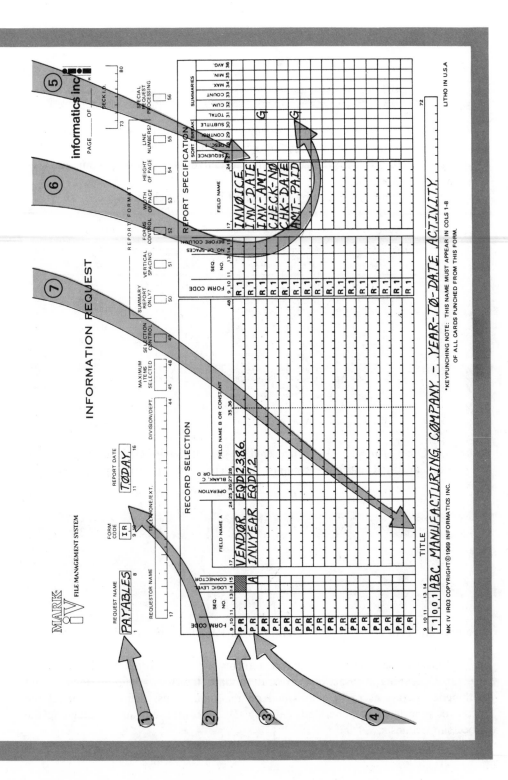

BOX 17.1—*Cont.*

The accountant will give his filled out Information Request form to someone in the data processing organization who will have the form keypunched, put it on the computer, and deliver the resulting report as soon as it is available.

The report produced by this request is shown below:

```
04/28/72    ABC MANUFACTURING COMPANY - YEAR-TO-DATE ACTIVITY      PAGE 1

------------------------------------------------------------------------
            INVOICE    INVOICE    INVOICE    CHECK     CHECK     AMOUNT
            NUMBER     DATE       AMOUNT     NUMBER    DATE      PAID
------------------------------------------------------------------------
            51-03917   01/12/72        3.47   002571   02/15/72      3.47
            51-07242   01/14/72       60.43   002571   02/15/72     60.43
            51-11275   01/21/72      152.40   002571   02/15/72    152.40
            51-12336   01/27/72      104.53   002571   02/15/72    104.53
            51-14514   02/03/72       14.44   002819   03/15/72     14.44
            51-17180   02/14/72      102.42   002819   03/15/72    102.42
            51-20992   02/29/72       63.00   002819   03/15/72     63.00
            51-21541   03/02/72      189.12   002819   03/15/72    189.12
            51-23730   03/07/72       19.72   003093   04/17/72     19.72
            51-24226   03/10/72    1,092.46   003093   04/17/72  1,092.46
            51-28859   03/27/72      605.00   003093   04/17/72    605.00
            51-29331   03/31/72    5,486.00   003093   04/17/72  5,486.00
            51-31155   04/11/72       19.09
            51-33126   04/21/72      187.55
            51-34568   04/25/72       28.90

                                                                7,892.99
```

Other MARK IV forms enable the professional analyst programmer to execute more complex processing and reporting operations.

Courtesy of Informatics Inc., Canoga Park, Calif.

The user employs a simple data dictionary to tell the names of the data items he can list on his form.

MARK IV employs many different forms including forms for defining data structures, defining transactions used to update the files, defining logical and arithmetic operations to be performed on the data items, defining in detail the layout of reports to be generated, defining tables to be used, and cataloguing the processing requests.

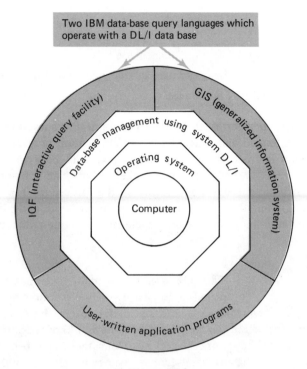

Figure 17.3

QUERY LANGUAGES   MARK IV can operate with a DL/I data base. There
FOR USE WITH DL/I   are two query languages provided by IBM for use with
a DL/I data base. One is called IQF (Interactive
Query Facility) and makes provisions for relatively straightforward interactive
queries from a terminal. The other, GIS/2 (Generalized Information System/2)
permits more elaborate searches and manipulation of the data and is intended
primarily for off-line queries. Whereas IQF is simple to learn so that a clerk would
have no difficulty using it, GIS is more complex. GIS is, in effect, a high-level
programming language and can accomplish more than IQF [25].

Both IQF and GIS are software packages which reside in the computer system along with a data-base management system such as IMS. They operate as application programs using the data-base management system (see Fig. 17.3). IQF
provides its user with three capabilities:

1. Access to the data from remote terminals.

2. Data manipulation capabilities such as sorting, counting, or totaling items.

3. Report formatting capabilities.

GIS also provides these capabilities and in addition gives the user

4. The ability to resequence data for permanent use.
5. Computational ability involving addition, subtraction, multiplication, and division.
6. The ability to create files for future use.

Where a user at a terminal enters a GIS or IQF transaction the query language software is loaded and scheduled as an application program. The user then enters statements instructing the software which data base to examine, which portion of it to read, and how to present the output. The software analyzes the user's statements, determines an efficient search procedure for data selection, gathers the data, manipulates and formats them as required, and prints or displays the results. The user may then refine or clarify his request and enter follow-up queries.

IQF   The IQF user enters at his terminal statements composed of English words. The following is a typical example [26]. A vice-president asks a personnel officer the following question: "What engineers located in the New York area have a knowledge of German? Tell me what department they work in and how long they have been with the company." The personnel officer or his secretary types into the terminal

FROM THE SKILLS INVENTORY PLEASE LIST THE NAME, MAN NUMBER, DEPARTMENT, AND YEARS IN SERVICE OF ENGINEERS WITH A KNOWLEDGE OF GERMAN LOCATED IN THE NEW YORK AREA

Each of the words the terminal operator uses must have been previously defined to the system. They fall in to one of the following categories:

1. Data-base name, for example, SKILLS INVENTORY.
2. Data-item (field) names, for example, MAN NUMBER.
3. Commands, such as LIST, SORT, COUNT, or TOTAL.
4. Arithmetic operators, +, −, /, and * (for addition, subtraction, division, and multiplication).
5. Relational operators:

   EQ is equal to
   NE is not equal to
   LT is less than
   GT is greater than

LE is less than or equal to
GE is greater than or equal to

6. Connectors, for example, AND, OR.

7. Numeric constants, for example, 10, $+37415$, or -17.

8. Literal constants which consist of a fixed string of characters. They are typed enclosed between apostrophes: 'FRED', '32A', or 'CDC'.

9. Null words which have no meaning to the system but which may be included to make the English more natural-sounding, for example, A, THE, OF, CAN YOU, and PLEASE.

IQF maintains its own data base of the words and phrases which can be used in queries and has a data base containing all the data names which may be used. The data names are taken from the DL/I *Data Base Description* (DBD) and *Program Specification Block* (PSB) generation decks (see Fig. 16.11).

The software package initially has a small vocabulary of words which the user can employ. The ease of use of the language derives from the fact that each installation can define its own vocabulary, consisting of as many words and phrases as it wants. The phrases that are employed can be selected to fit the dialect and phraseology of the users in question. The languages can thus be tailored to any application.

Words and phrases are defined to the system by means of a DEFINE command. By means of this a user-defined name and phrase can be made equivalent to any previously defined words. For example, *man number* may be in a data item called MANNO in the DL/I data-base description. Secretaries or other users will not refer to it by this name, so the following DEFINE command is given: DEFINE MAN NUMBER AS MANNO ENDD. ENDD is a command meaning "end definition."

The predefined words and phrases can be used in several different ways. First they can convert the code names of data bases and data items into words which the users normally employ. As users might employ several different words to have some meaning, synonyms can be defined. MANNO, for example, might be defined as MAN NUMBER, MAN NO, MAN #, EMPLOYEE NUMBER, and so forth. If the system is used in non-English-speaking countries, foreign-language equivalents may be defined. Second, abbreviations may be defined so as to reduce typing by employees who make the same types of inquiries frequently. DEPARTMENT could be made equivalent to DEP, for example. Third, English phrases may be defined for clarity or to make a user dialogue easy to learn. For example, SKILCODE EQ 'GERMAN' could be made equivalent to KNOWLEDGE OF GERMAN. Last, null words can be defined to permit flexibility of typing style. In the above illustration, FROM, THE, PLEASE, and WITH A may have been defined as *null phrases*.

If the above query used the basic vocabulary of IQF, with the data names used by the programmers and no words defined for users, it might read as follows:

SKILFILE

JOBCODE EQ 'ENG' SKILCODE EQ 'GERMAN' LOC EQ 'NY'

LIST EMPLOYEE MANNO DEPT SVCYRS

To make the earlier version equivalent to this version, the following DEFINE statements could be employed:

DEFINE FROM AS ENDD   (This defines FROM to be *null* word. THE is already defined as *null*.)

DEFINE SKILLS INVENTORY AS SKILFILE ENDD

DEFINE PLEASE AS ENDD   (This defines PLEASE as *null*.)

DEFINE NAME AS EMPLOYEE ENDD

DEFINE MAN NUMBER AS MANNO ENDD

DEFINE DEPARTMENT AS DEPT ENDD

DEFINE YEARS IN SERVICE AS SVCYRS ENDD

DEFINE ENGINEER AS JOBCODE EQ 'ENG' ENDD

DEFINE WITH KNOWLEDGE OF AS SKILCODE EQ ENDD

DEFINE GERMAN AS 'GERMAN' ENDD

DEFINE LOCATED IN AS LOC EQ ENDD

DEFINE NEW YORK AREA AS 'NY' ENDD

Defined phrases can be removed from the IQF vocabulary with a DELETE command.

A SORT command specifies that the output should be sorted by given data items. Thus, SORT DEPT would cause the output to be in ascending sequence of department number. SORT DEPT, SALARY would give output in ascending SALARY sequence with DEPT sequence. SORT DES SALARY would give output in descending SALARY sequence (i.e., the largest salaries first).

A TOTAL command names data items whose values are to be totaled for output. Thus, TOTAL SALARY ON DEPT would give the sum of all salaries and a subtotal of salaries by department.

Arithmetic expressions can be used: SALARY GE 2700/12 or ITEM 1* ITEM 2 + ITEM 3 GE 100.

Conditional expressions can be used, such as WHEN ITEM 1 GE ITEM 2 or ITEM 1 EQ 'RED' AND ITEM 2 GE 500 or ITEM 1 EQ (ITEM 2/57) AND (ITEM 3 EQ 100 or ITEM 4 EQ 100)

The following are further examples of the use of IQF [26].

1. A production manager wants to know what purchase orders are open for part number 274XYA12 and who is the vendor supplying the part:

    IN THE PURCHASE FILE WHAT ARE THE ORDER NUMBERS
    AND VENDOR NAMES WHEN STATUS IS 'OPEN' AND PART
    NUMBER IS '274XYA12'

2. A production manager frequently wants to know what operations are performed by a particular work center and what parts are affected by the operations:

    DEFINE CTR AS FROM THE FABRICATION FILE,

    LIST THE OPERATION NUMBER AND THE PART

    NUMBERS FOR WORK CENTER ENDD

    CTR '2441'

    CTR '3560'

    CTR '1198'

3. A sales manager makes a query about customers with overdue balances:

    IN THE CUSTOMER FILE, LOOK FOR OVERDUE BALANCES
    GREATER THAN OR EQUAL TO 20000 WITH LAST PAYMENTS
    MADE IN MAY; ORDER THE OUTPUT BY SALES DISTRICT,
    LIST THE ACCOUNT NUMBER, OVERDUE BALANCES, NAME
    OF SALESMAN, SALES DISTRICT AND TOTAL THE OVERDUE
    BALANCES FOR EACH SALES DISTRICT

GIS   GIS is much more powerful than IQF. The GIS user can modify the data in the data base. He can create his own files and manipulate them. He can carry out quite complex logical operations on the data and has a versatile facility for structuring reports.

However, whereas IQF was intended to be used by secretaries or persons with no programming experience, GIS is, in effect, a high-level programming language. Far fewer statements are needed to carry out a set of operations than in, for example, COBOL, but the language is restricted to operations on an existing suitably structured data base.

The following example consists of 14 lines of GIS code. To produce the same report in COBOL would require about 250 lines of code [27].

Figure 17.4 shows a DL/I data base and a GIS query using that data base. Suppose that a marketing manager has been conducting a new advertising campaign. He is concerned after an intensive burst of advertising that certain warehouses may be running out of stock of product number 75438.

From the data base in Fig. 17.4 he receives monthly reports of sales and advertising expenditure. These do not tell him about the sales of the 13 days of the current month which may have been critical. He can obtain a stock status report on any product when he wants it, using a previously written inquiry program. This confirms his fear that certain warehouses may be running short. He can also check the replenishment schedule for the warehouses, and he sees that the next delivery to some warehouses is not until late next week. His staff assistant asks the data-processing manager for an urgent report showing how many days of stock are left at the current rate of sale.

A DL/I schema (data-base description):   *Figure 17.4*   Use of GIS.

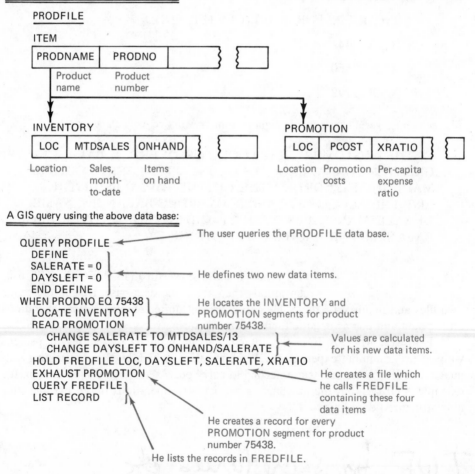

The results could not be obtained sufficiently quickly using COBOL or any other conventional programming language. The GIS specialist enters the query shown in Fig. 17.4. He creates a new file, which he calls FREDFILE, and creates two new data items in it. The first, called SALERATE, shows the average rate of sale of product number 75438 over the past 13 days. The second, called DAYSLEFT, shows how many days stock are left if the item continues to sell at that rate. The printout which results from the query in Fig. 17.4 is as follows:

LOC	DAYSLEFT	SALERATE	XRATIO
ATLANTA	3	805	4.0
BOSTON	10	512	2.7
CHICAGO	15	441	1.0
HOUSTON	20	325	0.8
MILWAUKEE	12	622	2.1
NEW YORK	3	2113	4.1
SAN FRANCISCO	25	401	0.7
ST. LOUIS	4	407	3.7

On seeing the result the GIS specialist decides to add a title to the report and sort the output to show the warehouses that are running out fastest at the top of the list. He enters

> QUERY PRODFILE 'DEPLETION REPORT FOR PRODUCT
>   NUMBER 75438,' PRODNAME
>
> SORT FREDFILE DAYSLEFT
>
> QUERY FREDFILE
>
> LIST RECORD

This time he obtains the following:

DEPLETION REPORT FOR PRODUCT NUMBER 75438, BEDWARMER

LOC	DAYSLEFT	SALERATE	XRATIO
ATLANTA	3	805	4.0
NEW YORK	3	2113	4.1
ST. LOUIS	4	407	3.7
BOSTON	10	512	2.7
MILWAUKEE	12	622	2.1
CHICAGO	15	441	1.0
HOUSTON	20	325	0.8
SAN FRANCISCO	25	401	0.7

The marketing manager holds a conference and decides that some of the product should be moved from the Houston warehouse to the Atlanta warehouse, from Boston to New York, and from Chicago to St. Louis. The advertising expenditure in San Francisco is stepped up.

The GIS specialist improves his routine and his report format in anticipation of its being used again and stores it. Most decision making is rarely a one-step process. The decision maker is likely to come back with a series of refinements, a progressive reexamination of successive results. The ability to store GIS routines, report formats, and interim files and to modify them later is therefore important.

GIS has facilities for more elaborate logical and arithmetical operations. Its output can be edited and formatted as required. The user can query many segments at once, taking different data items from each, and can create many temporary or permanent files. These files, unlike that in the example, could be very large files. It does, however, need a specialist to use it, not a casual terminal user without training.

RESTRICTIONS ON QUERIES
When a person uses a query language it is possible for him to create a query that would require an excessive amount of computing or an exceedingly long file search. In practice, such queries are frequently formulated, especially by users who do not understand the file structure and indices. The system may be designed to caution the user when this happens and give him an opportunity to recast his query.

It is especially important with a terminal-based system that one user should not enter queries which commandeer an excessive amount of the system's processing capability. If an IQF user, for example, enters a query based on a data-item type for which no secondary index has been created, then the computer has no option other than to search all the segments containing that data item. If such a time-consuming search is needed, IQF notifies the user and gives him a chance to confirm the request before continuing the search. Such searches may be postponed by the installation, to be carried out at more suitable time, for example, at night.

MAN-MACHINE PSYCHOLOGY
The computer industry has much to learn about the psychology of communication between terminals and their users. The art of devising dialogues between men and machines should be regarded as a new form of literacy. As yet the majority of practitioners of this art are unquestionably illiterate.

The author has discussed this subject in his book *Design of Man-Computer Dialogues* [28]. A few comments are made here about psychological requirements in data-base interrogation dialogues.

An untrained user should be able to explore a data base, carrying out heuristic searches, without having to remember mnemonics and without being bewildered by some or many of the responses he receives. As the data base is likely to be complex, the dialogue should enable him to see what data items are available to him. Security controls should restrict his view to those data items which he is permitted to see. If he desires, he should be able to display the definitions of the data items.

A man-computer dialogue is built from pairs of transactions, each being a statement or question followed by a response to it. At his first approach to a man terminal interaction a systems analyst may think of the *man* as originating each pair: The man says something to the computer, and the computer replies. Frequently, however, the other possibility gives the better design: The computer originates each interchange, and the man responds. We refer to the former as an *operator-initiated dialogue* and the latter as a *computer-initiated dialogue*.

A dialogue for an operator who has learned a programming-like language is generally *operator-initiated*. A dialogue for an untrained or nonprogramming operator is usually better psychologically if it is *computer-initiated*. Sometimes the conversation consists of both computer-initiated and operator-initiated interchanges, but usually, after the operator has "signed on," the dialogue is of one type or the other.

A computer-initiated dialogue usually results in far more characters being transmitted than an operator-initiated dialogue. To give the operator a generous choice of alternatives at each step a visual display unit is desirable for computer-initiated dialogues rather than a typewriter-like terminal.

In our daily work we are familiar with dealing with two-dimensional representations of information: tables, forms, charts, etc. Many terminal messages are spatially one-dimensional: program statements, character strings, sentences. A computer-initiated dialogue can generally be more effective if the computer presents information and choices to the operator two-dimensionally. The operator should then respond in a two-dimensional plane: pointing to an item, filling in a form, drawing a line. A two-dimensional response is often made more easily with a light-pen than with a keyboard. Where verbal or numeric input is needed a keyboard may be used along with the light-pen or a set of keys may appear temporarily on the screen so that the operator can point to them.

Fast, fluent, and highly effective data-base interrogation techniques can be designed using computer-initiated dialogues with responses in a two-dimensional plane. The operator need learn no mnemonics. The data structures can be explained if necessary as the dialogue proceeds. The untrained operator need never be bewildered by the dialogue.

Such dialogues are the exception rather than the rule at the time of writing. However, to extract the true value from the data bases that are growing in corporations, such dialogues will become vitally necessary.

Figure 17.5 summarizes the categories of data-base interrogation languages.

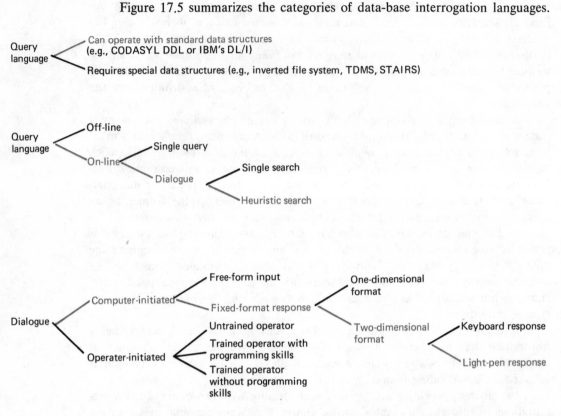

Figure 17.5 A summary of categories of data-base interrogation languages. The red lines indicate what the author considers are desirable paths.

18 DATA DICTIONARIES

As the number of data types in a corporation grows it becomes increasingly necessary to have a catalogue or dictionary of the data. The dictionary contains the name of each data type and a description of what it is and where it is used. Not all data-base systems employ data dictionaries yet. However, their importance is great.

Data are an increasingly valuable corporate resource which should be utilized throughout the corporation, and a data dictionary is an inventory of that resource which can assist in both the utilization and the management of the resource. It is desirable that there should be centralized control over the data and their structuring, but nevertheless that usage of the data should develop freely by the using departments. A data dictionary helps to achieve both ends.

TWO TYPES The data dictionary can be used in two types of ways.
OF USES It can be used by *people*, and it can be used by the
data-base *software*. Most data dictionaries in use today
are application packages intended to aid the data-base administrator, data-
processing staff, and data users.

The data dictionary is used in different ways by different types of people.
The data-base administrator needs a dictionary to help ensure consistency among
the data items, to educate users about the data-base content, and to help ensure
that different departments define the same data in the same way. The systems
analysts may use it to see what data are available when they are designing applications. The programmers may use it to ensure that they have the name and
coding of data items or segments correct in their programs. Terminal users may
employ it to guide their interrogation of the data base. Management may use it as
a guide to what data could be made available to them.

If the dictionary is integrated into the structure of the data-base management
system, then it may also be used for software functions such as maintaining the
three data descriptions (in Fig. 5.1 and 3.1) and compiling or interpreting program
references which use these descriptions.

A DATA BASE A data dictionary is a repository of data about data. It
OF DATA BASES is sufficiently complex that a data-base system may
have the data dictionary as one of its own customers—
one of its own data bases. The programs which operate the dictionary will be a set
of application programs employing the data-base management system.

The dictionary data base will include data types such as the following:

- Data item (field)
- Data aggregate (group)
- Segment
- Subschema record (programmer's record)
- Schema record (stored logical data-base record)
- Subschema (program specification block) (program data declaration)
- Schema (logical data-base description)
- Physical data base
- System

- Source of data (data input)
- Document or dialogue in which data are used (data output)
- Program using data
- User department or person

Not all data dictionaries catalogue all the above data. They differ considerably in their facilities.

The reader might like to try sketching a schema (such as those in Chapters 8, 15, or 16) which contains the above types of data and the relations between them.

The information in IBM's IMS data dictionary is structured as five physical IMS data bases with logical linkages between them, as shown in Fig. 18.1.

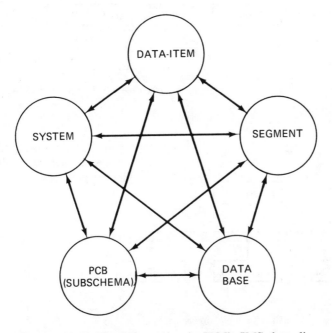

Figure 18.1 The information in IBM's IMS data dictionary is structured as five physical data bases with logical linkages between them as shown here. (Redrawn with permission from Reference 29.)

A variety of subschemas of dictionary data bases will be needed for different uses. Figure 18.2 shows some examples. The first two examples are for programs which show where a given data is used and what data a given program uses. The third example relates to the origination and use of the data and might be employed by the systems analysts in examining the flow of data in a data-processing organization.

(1) Where is a given data item used?

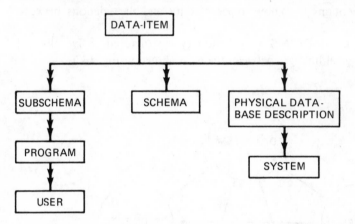

(2) What data does a given program use?

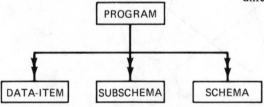

Figure 18.2   A variety of subschemas of the data dictionary will be used for different purposes.

3) Produce a matrix of data-item origination and usage.

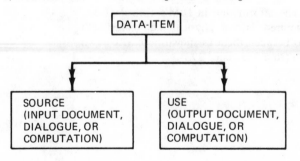

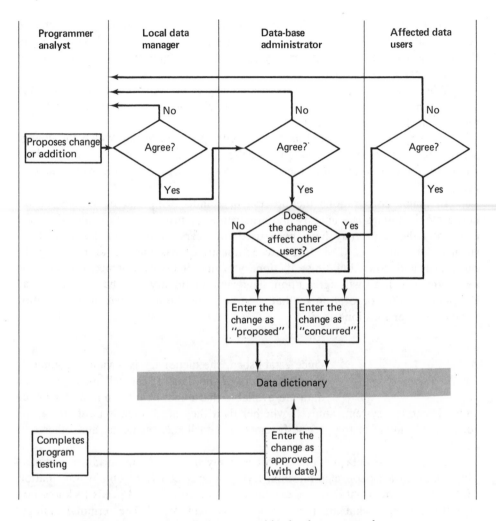

Figure 18.3   A data dictionary used in the data approval process.

STANDARDIZATION   As we have commented, a corporation with advanced data processing often has several thousand data items. They must be defined in an agreed upon manner so that different programmers and users can employ them.

When a programmer wants to add a new data item or change an existing one, he requests permission. The request may be forwarded by the local manager with responsibility for data, if he agrees, to the central data-base administrator. The data-base administrator will decide whether he concurs with the change, examining the data to ensure that they do not duplicate or conflict with existing data. If the change appears to be acceptable, he will determine whether it affects other data users (Fig. 18.3). If not, he will enter the change in the dictionary as a change "concurred" with. If the proposed change affects other users, it will be passed to the affected users to see whether they agree, and the change will be entered into the dictionary as "proposed."

Where there is argument or the users disagree with the proposed change, the data-base administrator must help resolve the situation—a process not shown in the lines at the top of Fig. 18.3.

Once a change is entered as "concurred," program testing which the change necessitates will commence. Once the change is tested and proven, the data-base administrator will enter it into the dictionary as "approved," along with a date of acceptance.

In major corporations the process of standardizing the definitions of the corporate data items is a lengthy and argumentative process. Data items which are essentially the same may have been used for years by different departments in slightly different ways. The data-base administrator has the job of resolving the differences and slowly building a dictionary of data items with names, formats, and definitions which all will agree upon. The same dictionary may be used across all the plants in the corporation so that programs may be developed in one location for use in other locations.

A GUIDE TO DATA USERS

Once established, the dictionary is a valuable guide to would-be users of the data. It can tell managers what data are available that might help them in making decisions. It can tell systems analysts whether data they need already exist. It can inform programmers of the precise formats of data items, segments, and other data constructs.

A use of the data dictionary that is likely to grow in importance is that of giving help to a person at a terminal trying spontaneously to obtain information. He needs to know what data are available in a given area and needs to know how to refer to them—what are the names of the data items? The terminal dialogue should enable him to navigate through the mass of data until he finds what he wants. The design of the interrogation software discussed in Chapter 17 should be linked to the dictionary.

REDUNDANCY,
SYNONYMS, AND
INCONSISTENCY

Listings available from the dictionary system will enable the data base administrator to spot redundant data. Sometimes there are many redundant copies of the same data item created by different programmers. The dictionary can help the data-base administrator to detect and eliminate them.

Again, as a data base is being built up there are likely to be inconsistencies in the data. Essentially the same data item may have different formats in different files. The inconsistencies will be steadily cleared up when it is advantageous to do so, so that the same data item has the same format wherever it is used. There may be many versions of the same data item in different stages of updating. To the users of the data base these differently updated versions appear as inconsistencies, and in some cases users have become very concerned, believing that the inconsistencies really represent inaccuracies in the data.

Another problem is synonyms. Different data items, segments, and records have been named in the past by different programmers, and sometimes by chance two separate data types have been given the same name. As with redundancies and inconsistencies, the synonyms will be steadily cleared up. Often it is not economically justifiable to put them right immediately; the cleaning up may be deferred until new versions of the programs are written. The dictionary system must highlight the redundancies and synonyms but permit them to exist.

SUMMARY

Figure 18.4 summarizes the uses of a data dictionary.

	People								Software		
	General management	Auditors	Spontaneous users at terminals	Application planners	DP management	Data administrator	Systems analysts	Programmers	Compiler or interpreter	Data-base management system	Dialogue software
Basic documentation of data and relationships	✓	✓	✓	✓	✓	✓	✓	✓			
Standardization of definitions of data items			✓	✓	✓	✓	✓				
Helps provide knowledge of what data are available	✓	✓	✓	✓	✓	✓	✓	✓			✓
Guide to spontaneous users	✓	✓	✓								✓
Check for inconsistencies				✓		✓	✓	✓			
Control of synonyms (two data types with the same name)				✓		✓	✓	✓			
Control of redundancy (unnecessary multiple copies of the same data)				✓	✓	✓					
Control of multiple versions of data						✓	✓	✓			
Guidance to programmers and designers				✓			✓	✓			
Design aids showing the data flow				✓			✓				
Assistance in auditing and security checks		✓			✓	✓	✓				
Generation of data definitions for programs									✓		
Generation of data-base description for data-base management system										✓	

Figure 18.4　Uses of a data dictionary.

PART **IV**   **MANAGEMENT CONSIDERATIONS**

Initiation:

From the moment when I first drew the preliminary sketches, I felt it to be a gigantic and necessary task. It was not merely a professional opportunity, though this was an aspect of major importance; it was an exceptional undertaking which demanded and elicited loyalty and enthusiasm, a genuine crusade which united all who took part in an effort to surmount obstacles, opposition, incomprehension, and stubborn and unforeseen resistance.

Implementation:

I wanted to create a discipline which would guarantee the unity of the various groups by establishing the norms and principles for all. . . . We later set up a special service for the approval of plans, ruthlessly applying the above criteria and rejecting all solutions which might have compromised the architecture.

    Looking back, I recall certain details which shook my faith in many things. I saw for the first time how brazenly professional men can jockey for position, how many people are prone to rivalry, and how often unbridled ambition can obliterate the memory of friendships and agreements.

After Inauguration:

The old enthusiasm vanished, the bureaucrats moved in, the bourgeoisie settled down with their ambitions, their conventions and privileges. The moment of creation through which we had lived gave way to routine tasks which proceeded slowly.

   Oscar Niemeyer, the chief architect of Brasilia,
   on the building of that city [30]

19 INFRASTRUCTURE

For many corporations the development of data bases so far has been a struggle. Although some of the problems are becoming solved with better data-base software, the struggle is far from over. The data-base administrators have a tough road ahead. In this last part of the book we will explore the implementation problems.

Hardware storage capacities are increasing by leaps and bounds, and the cost per bit stored is dropping rapidly. The very powerful new storage technologies that are now in the development laboratories make it clear that a major task for corporations for the rest of this decade is to set in place the data-base structures that will become an essential part of the operation of indusry.

Confronted with this realization, it is alarming to observe the spectacular lack of success met with by some of the attempts to build corporate data bases so far. *EDP Analyzer*, in an issue on the building of corporate data bases, began with the following list of the seven phases of a typical project [31]:

1. Uncritical acceptance
2. Wild enthusiasm
3. Dejected disillusionment
4. Total confusion
5. Search for the guilty
6. Punishment of the innocent
7. Promotion of nonparticipants

This cynical commentary has more than a grain of truth in it. There have been some monumental failures among would-be data-base builders. Some of the overenthusiastic and inadequately perceived projects have cost their corporations appalling sums of money and have seriously set back the needed evolution of corporate data bases.

The job of designing data bases will become increasingly professional, especially if they are to perform in an optimal fashion. The software is becoming much more elaborate, and its capabilities are often misunderstood, misused, or not taken advantage of.

There are many different ways in which data can be structured, and they have different advantages and disadvantages. Not least of the complicating factors is that different data have different characteristics which ought to affect the data organization, and different users have fundamentally different requirements. The needs are sufficiently diverse that, often, no one data organization can satisfy all of them—at least with the hardware of the 1970s. Hence, the designer must steer a delicate course through compromises.

A first essential, however, on the road to data-base glory is to select appropriate projects. Many organizations which had the right software, brilliant implementors, and a big budget met with disaster because they were charging windmills.

DELUSIONS   There are several common misconceptions about data-base systems which need clarifying.

First, a data base, or data-base management system, does *not* imply a "management information system." There is no direct relationship between the terms. In their initial use, most data bases should be thought of merely as a way of storing data for conventional applications. Data-base techniques are justified only if *in the long run* they are cheaper, give better performance and better security, or, most important, lower the cost of maintenance and facilitate evolution. The main justification is often that they lower the cost of future application development and make the production of new reports or new programs quicker and easier. They permit the data-processing department to be responsive.

A second delusion is that a data-base system is sometimes described as containing *all* the data items in a corporation or a division. Typical comments on the subject from journals such as the *Harvard Business Review* include the following misconception: "If the company had maintained all its computer-readable data in a single pool or bank—in a so-called 'data base'—and if the company had structured this base of data so that a program for virtually any feasible use could have been run from this data base, then it would have been a matter of sheer expertise and flair for a good, experienced programmer to concoct a program that pulled the desired information together" [32]. And "The data-base concept structures EDP activity in such a way that *all* of a company's computer-readable data are merged in a single pool, which is used to run both routine programs and programs written in response to ad hoc requests" [33].

Any attempt to implement so grand a notion is doomed to disaster before it begins. One of the major reasons for data-base techniques is that files or data bases that were separate can later be combined. In this way larger collections of data can be built up with a subsequent drop in data redundancy and increase in data-base interrogation capability. However, to begin with the notion that the data base will serve everyone who uses data is asking for trouble.

Related to the above delusion is the notion that an organization will have *one* data base. In reality it is likely to have many data bases, eventually perhaps hundreds. Many different data bases may be used on the same data-base system, but they will be both physically and logically separate. They should be built with a common schema language and common design policies because linkages between them will be forged in the future. The data-base management system should be common to all, but the data bases themselves entirely separate.

INFRASTRUCTURE   A better way to think of data-base management systems is that they form an infrastructure which will allow the corporation's various schemas to grow and interlink over the years, becoming more useful as they do so. Furthermore, the schemas can grow without the prohibitive costs of rewriting application programs, and schemas do not have to be changed when the hardware is changed.

If schemas across the corporation are to be interlinkable and transferable from one plant to another or from one data-processing system to another, they should all be written in the same data description language. At today's state of the art, then, most corporations should not talk about a corporate-wide data base but rather a *corporate-wide organizing principle* which forms the structure for database development. An essential of this principle is that the schema description language and data dictionary be standardized throughout the corporation.

INCREMENTAL GROWTH   The growth which the infrastructure permits should have two characteristics. First, it should be *planned,* insofar as is possible. Although planning is desirable it must be recognized that a data base will inevitably be used in ways which were not anticipated when it was designed. Second, the plan should involve small incremental steps, one application or one improvement to be implemented at a time on each data base.

The first applications selected for use with a data base should involve three characteristics. First, the data base should not be too complicated. Second, the application should be one which is clearly cost-justifiable. And third, the operating managements of the user departments should give full support and cooperation. Separate relatively simple data bases on the same system may be used.

When these applications are working the data base may, if appropriate, be extended stage by stage, with the schemas being permitted to grow a step at a time.

Another popular misconception about data bases is that they need to be real-time. Data-base techniques are very worthwhile in the batch-processing world. The stage-by-stage approach may implement a system without on-line inquiry facilities to begin with and add the capabilities for full on-line operation later. If this second step is planned, the data organization for the first step should be designed in such a way that the second step will not cause a major restructuring.

A succession of relatively short projects may be undertaken ranging from a few months to a year in duration. Several such projects may go on at the same time. When a new system is smoothly operating in its initial, relatively simple, form, additional features may be added to it. Some of the incremental steps may be very short to implement, such as the production of a new type of report from an existing data base.

As the projects are implemented the data-base experience of the staff will grow. The projects should be planned so that this necessary experience can develop and be disseminated. Intelligent systems analysts should be placed with data-base projects to learn the techniques and then moved into leadership positions on subsequent projects. The first project attempted by an organization should be regarded as a *seed project*, deliberately planned and used to train a nucleus of data-base staff who will lead the way on other projects. Well thought-out training activities need to accompany the step-by-step build-up to steadily spread the data-base knowledge and experience. Data-base software is designed to facilitate this incremental growth.

The difficult stage comes at the start in determining the data-base strategy and plan, and persuading contending parties that it is the correct approach. The first event should be the appointment of a data administrator with enough knowledge and at a high enough level to develop the data-base strategy and select an organization-wide data description language and data dictionary.

After several years of stage-by-stage buildup the overall data-base systems will begin to look impressive if they were appropriately directed toward overall goals. To be successful the data-base management system used must provide a high level of data independence, so that schema growth can continue without rewriting programs.

Unfortunately, although this stage-by-stage buildup is the best formula for success, an organization-wide all-embracing implementation sometimes appears more attractive to systems analysts or to management. Few projects for a grandiose data-base-to-end-all-data-bases have met with other than bitter disappointment. If grandiose plans are needed, they should be for a standardized corporate-wide framework within which data bases evolve and interlink a stage at a time.

Great cities are not built in one monolithic implementation. They grow and evolve and are the sum of many smaller pieces of work. If their structure can be planned so that the piecemeal implementations fit into an overall design, then they will be more workable cities. However, circumstances change and the best-laid plans of an earlier era go astray so that new plans must be made. The growth of a corporate data base is a little like the growth of a city. Some are more like Brasilia than Paris. In a decade or so's time many corporate data bases will be complex, and expensive to maintain like New York. But like New York they will have to go on working.

20 EVOLUTION

A corporation setting out to build a comprehensive set of data bases has a long journey ahead of it. However, it has to be done sooner or later.

The early stages of the journey should be individual systems for well-defined purposes. It is generally better to start with *operations systems* than *information systems* and to select those operations systems which appear to offer tangible reward. The information systems may arise, in part, as a by-product of the operations systems.

There is a *major* difference however, between a route which gives the best short-term results irrespective of the final goal and a route which is planned to eventually lead to a comprehensive goal while being profitable, insofar as possible, in the short term.

Different systems and applications in a corporation will necessarily evolve separately because of the high complexity involved and the limited span of the minds of implementors. It is essential to ensure that they *can* evolve separately, implemented by teams with localized knowledge, because only in that way can they be closely tailored to the needs of the persons who will use the systems; only in that way can the high level of initiative and inventiveness of the local implementors be fully utilized. Nevertheless, it is desirable that, insofar as possible, the data-processing designers have a *master plan* for the future evolution of data bases in their organization. Centralized control is necessary to ensure an adequate measure of compatibility between the systems. Without such advanced planning the systems become more difficult (and in many cases have proved virtually impossible) to link together. They incur high costs for program or data conversion. They are often more difficult for the terminal operators to use because different terminal dialogue structures are used for different systems. They are much more cumbersome in the data-base planning, and more expensive in application of resources and in telecommunication costs. The linking together of separately designed and incompatible systems has proven to be *extremely* expensive in practice. In many cases the magnitude of the programming effort has been comparable to that when the systems were first installed.

Unfortunately the adherence to a neatly conceived master plan has rarely been achieved in reality. The state of the art is moved by unpredictable tides, and their pressures are strong enough to distort the best-laid plans. A certain machine or software package suddenly becomes available. One approach works and another fails. Natural selection takes over, and we have a process of evolution dominated by the survival of whatever is the most practical.

The master plan, then, must not be too rigid; indeed, *it is absolutely essential to plan for uncertainty*. It must be permissible for different systems to evolve in their own ways. The separate systems should each be of a level of complexity which is well within the implementation capability of the current staff, although the master plan may look forward to more complex systems.

**SUBJECT
DATA BASES**

To obtain the maximum future benefit from the data bases, they should be related to organizational *subjects* rather than to conventional computer *applications*. There should, for example, be a *product* data base rather than separate *inventory, order entry*, and *quality control* data bases relating to that product. Many applications may then use the same data base. The development of new applications relating to that data base becomes easier than if application-oriented data bases had been built.

Typical *subjects* for which data bases are built in a corporation are:

- Products
- Vendors
- Personnel
- Customers
- Orders
- Documents
- Parts
- Accounts
- Engineering descriptions

Some applications use more than one such data base. For example:

Application	Subject data base
Invoicing	Customers
	Products
	Orders
Accounts receivable	Customers
	Orders
	Accounts
Inventory control	Parts
	Products
	Orders

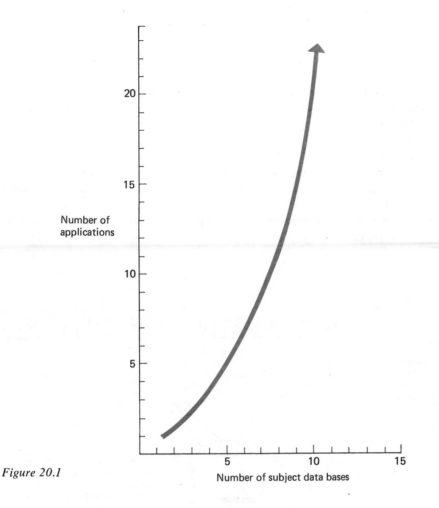

Figure 20.1

Number of applications

Number of subject data bases

By using *subject* data bases rather than *application* data bases the eventual number of data bases is far lower. A corporation builds up a very large number of applications but does not have a large number of operational *subjects*. If *files* are designed for specific applications the number of files grows almost as rapidly as the number of applications, and results in the great proliferation of redundant data found in a typical tape library today. Application-oriented data bases can also proliferate rapidly. Using *subject* data bases, however, the number of applications grows much faster than the number of data bases, as shown in Fig. 20.1. Eventually most new applications can be implemented rapidly because the data is available and the software provides tools to manipulate it. Indeed many of the corporations that have successfully installed subject-oriented data bases have found that the curve in Fig. 20.1 grows so rapidly that they run out of computer power. In some cases they have run out of power on their manufacturer's most powerful processing unit—a highly frustrating state of affairs.

Clearly some data-base systems are going to need very powerful complexes of computers in the future.

CONVERSION

As the first steps into the data-base world succeed, an organization finds itself with a large number of non-data-base programs and files, and a small nucleus of data-base activity. To progress successfully the organization must have an automated means of bridging the gap between the two worlds. A few of the old application programs may be rewritten for data-base operation but the vast majority will not be; they must continue to run without change.

To bridge the gap, conversion programs are needed. Figure 20.2 shows a conversion program which takes the files used before data-base implementation and puts their data into the data base. If all goes well this program may be used once only when the conversion occurs. All updating of the data-base is done by the data-base programs. Many old programs, however, will remain in operation.

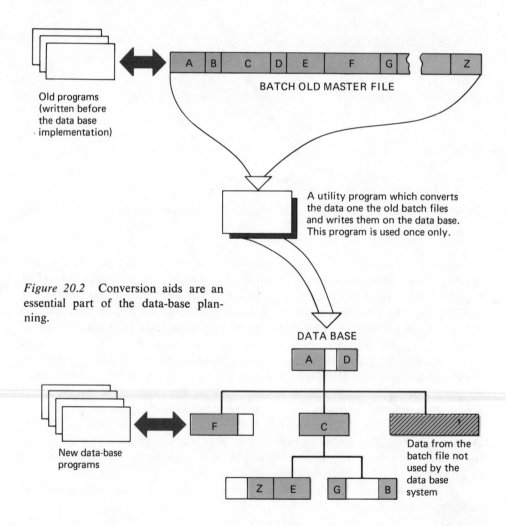

Old programs (written before the data base implementation)

BATCH OLD MASTER FILE

A utility program which converts the data one the old batch files and writes them on the data base. This program is used once only.

Figure 20.2 Conversion aids are an essential part of the data-base planning.

DATA BASE

New data-base programs

Data from the batch file not used by the data base system

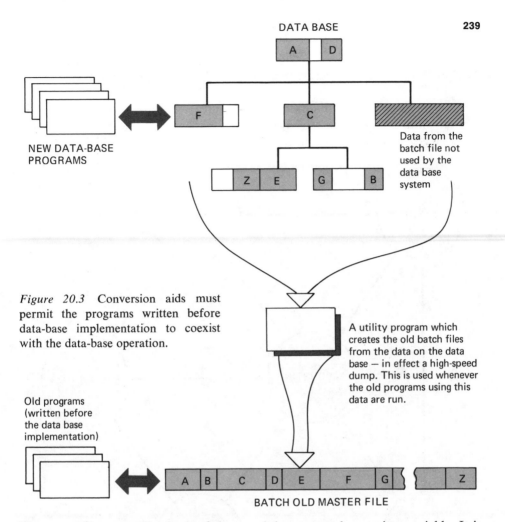

DATA BASE

NEW DATA-BASE
PROGRAMS

Data from the
batch file not
used by the
data base
system

Figure 20.3 Conversion aids must
permit the programs written before
data-base implementation to coexist
with the data-base operation.

A utility program which
creates the old batch files
from the data on the data
base — in effect a high-speed
dump. This is used whenever
the old programs using this
data are run.

Old programs
(written before
the data base
implementation)

BATCH OLD MASTER FILE

There are often many hundreds of them and they cannot be rewritten quickly. It is usually not economical to rewrite them at all except for those which update the data in the data base. Another conversion operation is needed, therefore, which is performed every time the old programs are used. Figure 20.3 shows this conversion. A utility program, which is in effect a high-speed dump, creates the batch files used by the old programs. If a batch program is run once a week, this conversion run will also take place once a week.

The batch programs may use some data items which were not in the original data-base design. They must however be included in the data base so that the files needed by the old programs can be created. The data-base programs will have to update these extraneous data items for the sake of compatibility.

In many cases an input to the data-base system must also be used to create input to the non-data-base operations not yet converted. Such data should be entered into the system only once, and a necessary function of the data-base system is to create the required input for the other operations, as in Fig. 20.3.

DATA-BASE   Figures 20.4 to 20.13 are used to discuss data-
EVOLUTION   base evolution in a relatively small corporation.

Figure 20.5 and the following seven figures relate to a small corporation
with the six functional areas as shown in Fig. 20.4: sales, engineering, production,
stores and purchasing, accounting, and planning.

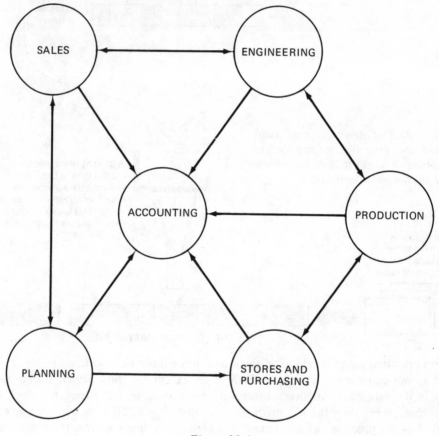

Figure 20.4

A number of data-processing operations take place as shown in Fig. 20.5.
Some of them are daily runs, and some less frequent. Some are rather crude by
modern standards, dating back to an earlier generation of data processing. One
application, the ORDER ENTRY operation, is on-line. The applications were
carried out, with varying degrees of automation, prior to the use of data-base
techniques by the corporation.

SPECIAL
ORDER
PROCESSING
PERIODIC

ORDER
ENTRY
CONTINUOUS
ON—LINE

BILLING
DAILY

SHORT-
ORDER
COSTING
PERIODIC

DEVELOPMENT
OF NEW PRODUCT
SPECIFICATIONS
PERIODIC

QUALITY
CONTROL
PERIODIC

SPECIAL
ORDER
COSTING
DAILY,
WHEN NEEDED

ACCOUNTS
RECEIVABLE
DAILY

PAYROLL
WEEKLY

SHORT-ORDER
PRODUCTION
PLANNING
PERIODIC

PRODUCTION
SCHEDULING
DAILY

SHIPPING
DAILY

GENERAL
LEDGER
AND BUDGET
ACCOUNTING
MONTHLY

LABOR
COSTING
WEEKLY

JOB
DISPATCHING
DAILY

RECEIVING
DAILY

COST
ACCOUNTING
MONTHLY

ACCOUNTS
PAYABLE
DAILY

SHOP FLOOR
CONTROL
DAILY

PURCHASING
DAILY

FORECASTING
MONTHLY

BUDGETING
MONTHLY

INVENTORY
DAILY

GROSS
MATERIAL
REQUIREMENTS
DAILY

ADJUST
CONTROLS
PERIODIC

NET
MATERIAL
REQUIREMENTS
DAILY

EXECUTIVE
ADMINISTRATION
PERIODIC

Figure 20.5

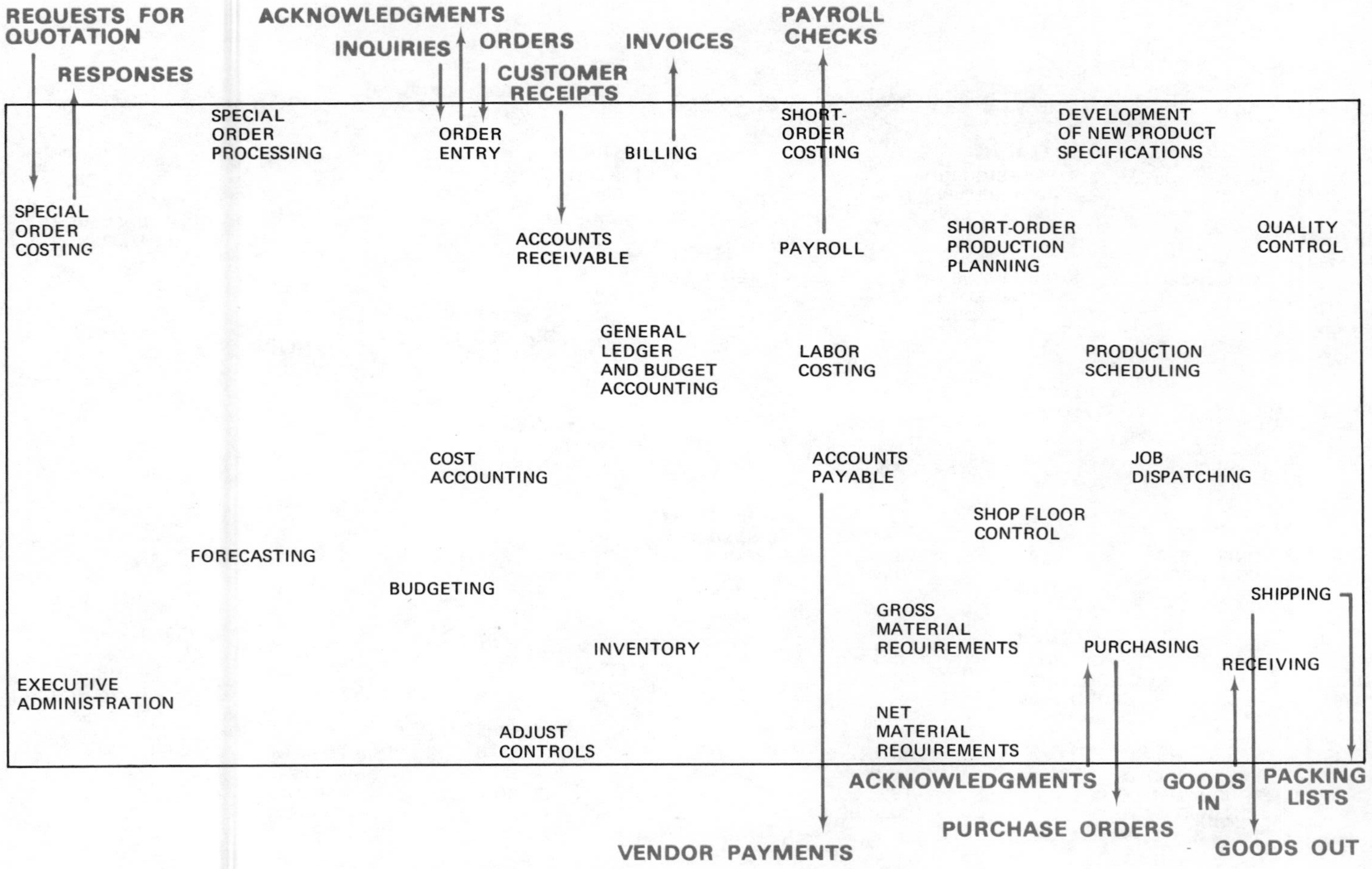

Figure 20.6 Data transfers with the outside world.

There are a number of data transfers between the corporation and the outside world, as shown in Fig. 20.6, but a much larger number of data transfers internally between the separate computer operations, as shown in Fig. 20.7. Most of these internal transfers involve the reading, writing and sorting of batch files.

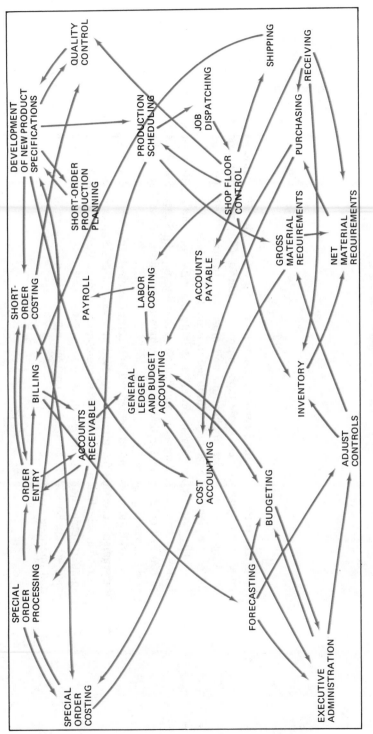

Figure 20.7   Internal data transfers.

The transfers of data between applications, shown in Fig. 20.7, result in a large tape library with elaborate tape control procedures. Corporate data processing in general has more applications and more data transfers than those in Fig. 20.7. The diagrams have been simplified to make them clearer.

The systems analysts, in order to simplify the data flow and clarify the confusion of Fig. 20.7, group the applications according to their functional areas, as shown in Fig. 20.8, and define the data which cross the interfaces between functional areas very precisely.

All data items should be defined in a central data dictionary, and all records or segments crossing the interfaces should be specified in detail along with a brief narrative description. The resulting route map of data flow may be applied to smaller application groupings than those shown. Different application development groups should be brought into agreement and should adhere to the data-item and interface definitions.

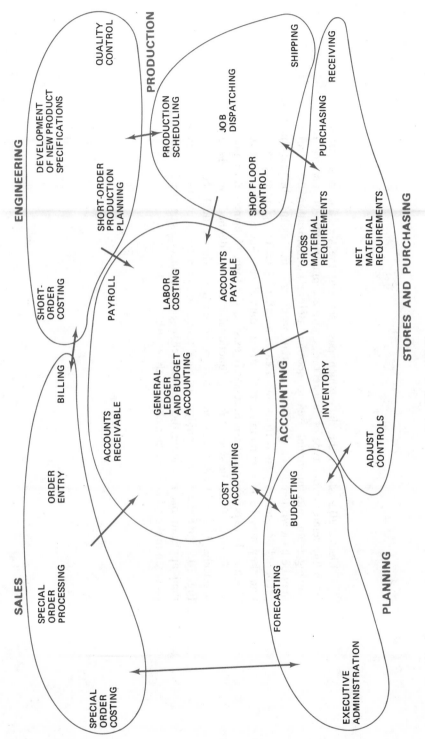

SALES

SPECIAL ORDER PROCESSING

ORDER ENTRY

BILLING

SPECIAL ORDER COSTING

ACCOUNTS RECEIVABLE

SHORT-ORDER COSTING

PAYROLL

ENGINEERING

DEVELOPMENT OF NEW PRODUCT SPECIFICATIONS

QUALITY CONTROL

SHORT-ORDER PRODUCTION PLANNING

PRODUCTION

PRODUCTION SCHEDULING

JOB DISPATCHING

SHIPPING

SHOP FLOOR CONTROL

PURCHASING

RECEIVING

LABOR COSTING

ACCOUNTS PAYABLE

GENERAL LEDGER AND BUDGET ACCOUNTING

GROSS MATERIAL REQUIREMENTS

NET MATERIAL REQUIREMENTS

COST ACCOUNTING

ACCOUNTING

INVENTORY

BUDGETING

ADJUST CONTROLS

FORECASTING

EXECUTIVE ADMINISTRATION

PLANNING

STORES AND PURCHASING

Figure 20.8

245

Figure 20.9 shows the data which pass between the six functional areas. Each line relates to one type of data record, and there may be files of such records passing from one functional area to another. Before mechanization the records may be handwritten documents. After partial mechanization they may be machine-prepared documents passed from one area to another. After complete mechanization they may be in a common set of subject data bases that is shared between functional areas, and need not necessarily exist in the form of printed documents.

The interfaces between the six functional areas are defined formally and precisely. The rigid interface definitions, represented by the vertical red lines in Fig. 20.9, give the systems analysts in each functional area freedom in developing their applications. Providing they do not change the data crossing the interfaces they can make whatever other changes they wish.

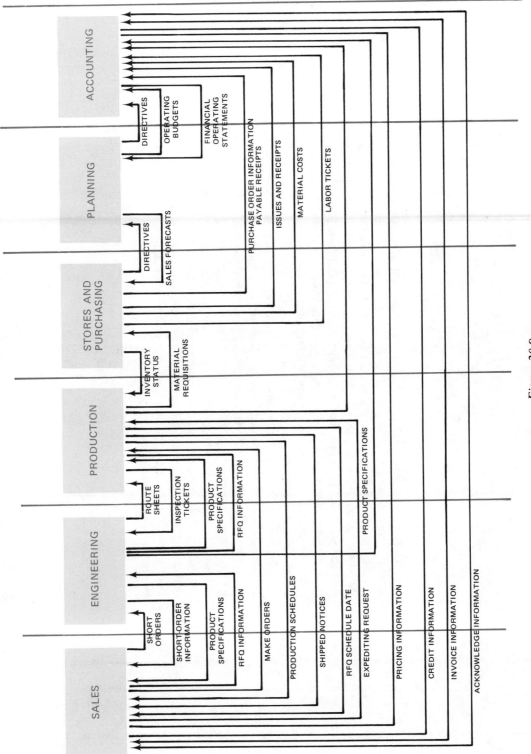

Figure 20.9

In the much-publicized image of a data base, all a corporation's data are stored in on-line storage.

In reality most corporations are a long way from this all-embracing on-line data-base system. Instead they should develop multiple data bases related to *business subjects* and design them to coexist with the older (and proven) non-data-base programs and files. Usually a large non-data-base tape and disk library continues to exist as the first data bases are introduced. Corporations build up their data bases a step at a time, as in the following figures.

Eventually, as the cost of on-line storage drops, the best way to organize a corporation's data may be with one on-line set of subject data bases at each plant or major office location. Most applications would use the storage, sharing a common on-line system, as in Fig. 20.10. The data bases would make data available at terminals to all who can make good use of them. The system would generate documents for communication with the external world and a few *internal* documents would be generated such as work tickets giving instructions to shop floor operatives, but data passing from one computer operation to another would be via the on-line data bases.

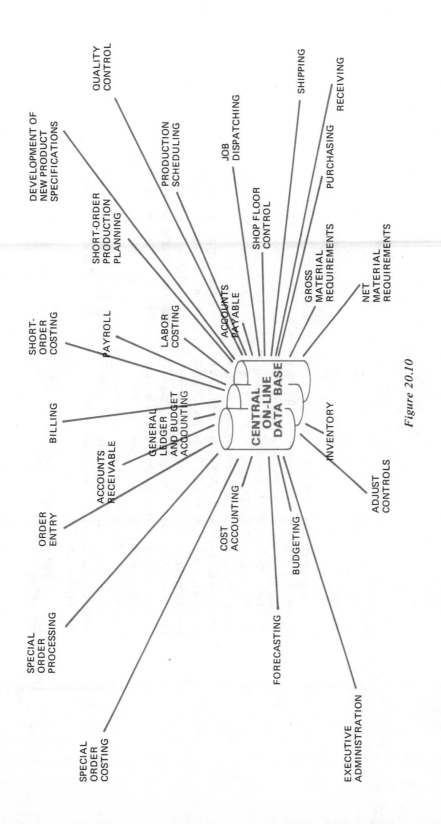

Figure 20.10

A stage-by-stage cutover to data-base techniques should be planned beginning with areas that are not too complex and have a clear payoff. Applications relating to the same business subjects will have their use of data combined a step at a time. In Fig. 20.11, applications relating to customers are linked: ORDER ENTRY and BILLING, then ACCOUNTS RECEIVABLE, then SHIPPING, and so forth. In a second development project, information relating to suppliers may be converted to data-base operation, and then ACCOUNTS PAYABLE. In another development, a data base relating to production schedules may be built, and so forth, as in Fig. 20.12. In this way data bases are built up in easy-to-implement stages. The data bases are not related to specific applications as were the files of earlier systems, but instead are related to business subjects. This results in a much smaller number of data bases which increase in value as more applications are written to use them.

Note that even straightforward "operations" data bases such as these (as opposed to information system data bases) cut across the functional boundaries of the corporation.

250

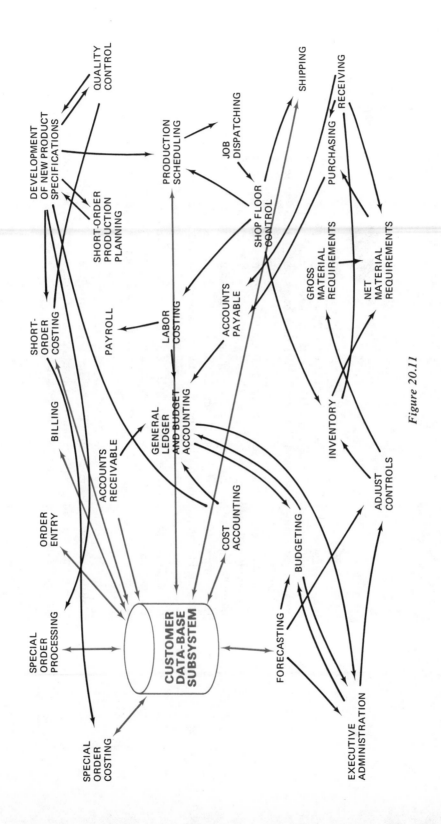

Figure 20.11

A corporation's data processing will probably never reach a state as simple as that suggested by Fig. 20.10. Separate data bases and often separate data-base systems will evolve. As far as possible the separate data bases should be planned from the beginning and planned to be *subject* data bases rather than *application* data bases.

Systems engineers will usually have an irresistible urge to clean up the untidy proliferation of separate systems. The cleaning-up process, while it may result in lower hardware costs, can consume a major amount of manpower that is usually better employed on further development. On the other hand, the early systems often need reimplementing because they incur excessive maintenance costs. In practice, programs which *work* satisfactorily are often left alone to operate with their old-fashioned files. These files contain some of the same data that are on the new data bases. It is essential that the data-base planners plan conversion aids such as those in Figs. 20.2 and 20.3 so that the two types of operation can coexist.

It is imperative that separate subsystem developments can be free to evolve in their way and yet can be linked into the overall structure at a later time. To achieve this, the independence provided by data-base management software and a common data-item dictionary should be used.

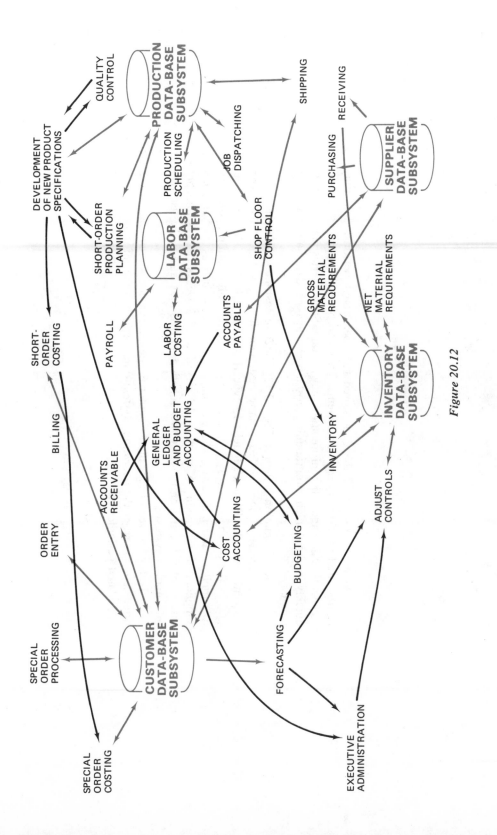

SPECIAL
ORDER
PROCESSING

SPECIAL
ORDER
COSTING

SHORT-
ORDER
COSTING

BILLING

ORDER
ENTRY

ACCOUNTS
RECEIVABLE

DEVELOPMENT
OF NEW PRODUCT
SPECIFICATIONS

QUALITY
CONTROL

SHORT-ORDER
PRODUCTION
PLANNING

PAYROLL

PRODUCTION
SCHEDULING

JOB
DISPATCHING

SHOP FLOOR
CONTROL

LABOR
COSTING

ACCOUNTS
PAYABLE

GENERAL
LEDGER
AND BUDGET
ACCOUNTING

COST
ACCOUNTING

BUDGETING

FORECASTING

INVENTORY

ADJUST
CONTROLS

GROSS
MATERIAL
REQUIREMENTS

NET
MATERIAL
REQUIREMENTS

PURCHASING

RECEIVING

SHIPPING

EXECUTIVE
ADMINISTRATION

PRODUCTION
DATA-BASE
SUBSYSTEM

LABOR
DATA-BASE
SUBSYSTEM

SUPPLIER
DATA-BASE
SUBSYSTEM

INVENTORY
DATA-BASE
SUBSYSTEM

CUSTOMER
DATA-BASE
SUBSYSTEM

Figure 20.12

As a by-product of the data stored for operational reasons, data may be restructured to form information systems. They can be used to process queries of a general nature about the information they contain. Such queries may be answered quickly without high programming costs by means of data-base interrogation languages.

One information system in Fig. 20.13 relates to customers and sales and can answer "queries" such as "How many customers leasing a Model 643 type IV discontinued a lease on a Model 643 type III?" and "List the sales of Item No. 768 in the Chicago area by industry group." Another information system relates to suppliers and purchasing and can answer questions such as "What potential suppliers of commodity X quote a delivery time of 3 weeks or less and have a history of delivering on time?" Other functional areas may also make use of such information systems.

Today, for reasons given in Chapter 6, the *information system* data bases are often separate from the *operations system* data bases and the information in them is updated periodically.

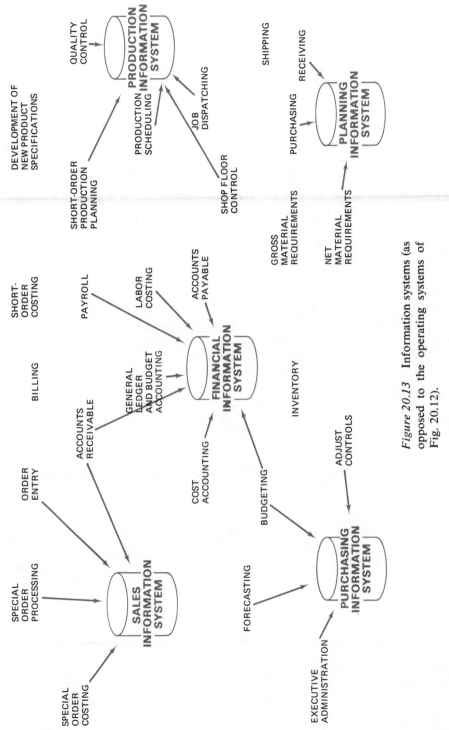

Figure 20.13 Information systems (as opposed to the operating systems of Fig. 20.12).

In a corporation with different divisions and plants in different locations, there will be many computer systems or subsystems. The definitions of the interfaces between separate systems (Fig. 20.9) will be correspondingly complex. As well as the interfaces between functional areas, the interfaces between different factories or operating companies must be specified.

A corporation may develop data-base applications for different functions in different plants, as in Fig. 20.14, with the intention of transferring them to other plants when they are working. "A" in Fig. 20.14, for example, may represent the customer data-base subsystem. "B" may represent the supplier data-base subsystem, and so forth. The development systems analysts will make themselves familiar with the requirements of the plants other than that plant where the subsystem is being developed, so that the subsystem may be transferred without the requirement for difficult modification.

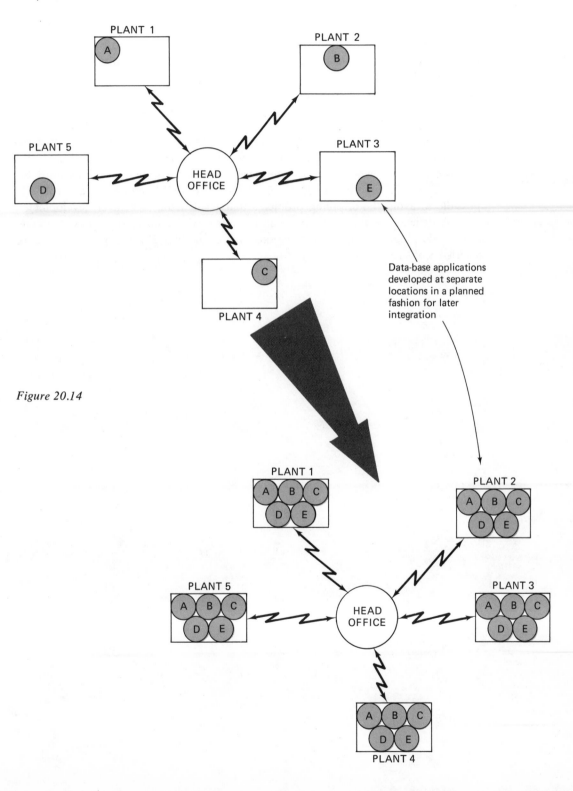

Figure 20.14

Data-base applications developed at separate locations in a planned fashion for later integration

A careful balance between centralization and decentralization is needed in an organization with multiple locations. The applications need to be developed at the plant sites where plant problems are understood. Each system will be modified appropriately for local conditions when it is transferred, and it is important to design the original so as to facilitate this modification.

Centralized control is needed to ensure that the transfer of applications will be possible and can be accomplished without burdensome reprogramming. The data items should be centrally agreed upon and the same data dictionary used by all teams. The same data description language must be used by all and the schemes reviewed centrally. The interfaces between separate subsystems must be agreed upon and vigorously defined, centrally. Only with centralized control is it possible to avoid the crippling problems that result from piecemeal development.

A delicate balance between central control of the infrastructure and decentralized development of the applications is needed. Fig. 20.15 suggests the characteristics of such a balance.

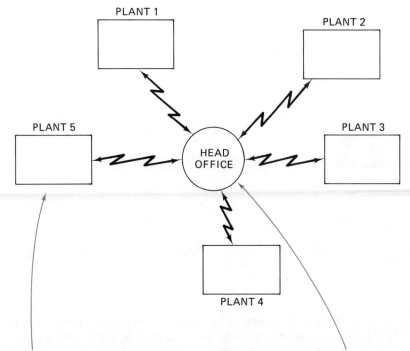

Figure 20.15

Plant DP responsibilities

- Development of applications originating at this location
- Modification of applications received from other locations
- Documentation needed for transfer of applications to other plants
- Liaison with other plants on application development
- Liaison with head office on standardization of data items
- Liaison with head office on schema development

Head office responsibilities

- Project approval and allocation to plants
- Choice of data description language
- Choice of data-base management system
- Standardization of data-item definitions; maintenance of data dictionary
- Review of documentation for transfer between plants
- Guidance on modularization needed to facilitate application transfer
- Integration of schemas between locations
- Agreement of specification of interfaces between subsystems

Figure 20.15

21 THE DATA ADMINISTRATOR AND DATA-BASE ADMINISTRATORS

Because a data base serves many applications and often many departments it needs centralized coordination. This task is performed by the *data-base administrator*. A corporation may have several data bases each having its own *data-base administrator*, or one data-base administrator may take care of several data bases. In addition an overall strategy for the corporation's data resource is needed —top-management planning of the corporation's information facilities. We refer to the man responsible for this vital task as a corporate *data administrator*.

The data administrator has the job of setting up the infrastructure and controlling the evolution of data-base systems in a corporation. The job is likely to become very important. It will be a key to the success of the corporation's future data processing. The data administrator must form a clear view of the corporation's future information requirements, and must steer the evolution of data facilities so that the requirements become realizable.

**CENTRALIZED
CONTROL**
As we have commented, a typical corporation has or will have many thousands of types of data items, all of which must be organized into suitable records, segments, sets, or relations (depending on the preferred terminology and software). A single data item may be used by multiple departments in a corporation and for multiple applications. It therefore needs to be standardized in name, representation, and definition. The groupings of data items need to be organized into schemas which can best serve the widely differing uses, and the schemas must be

mapped into physical organizations. Careful attention must be paid to security, accuracy, and privacy. The data must have suitable controls and must be protected from accidents, acts of God, embezzlers, thieves, and incompetents.

All these functions require centralized control. They should not be scattered to the diverse desires of application programmers, systems analysts, and department heads. Only by centralizing data-base policies can the data base be optimized for the users as a whole; otherwise, parochial, short-sighted, uninformed, or politically biased policies affect the data base. A subordinate group or single application group normally will not understand the *information economics* of the corporation as a whole. To balance the priorities and needs of the various users, and hence employ the most cost-effective techniques, a centralized view is needed. In addition the technical skills of measuring, implementing, and optimizing, data organizations require advanced training. To give such training to subordinate groups would be too expensive and would divert their attentions from their assigned tasks, complicating and delaying the implemention.

Just as one group of specialists in a corporation is responsible for all purchasing, or all shipping, so one group should be responsible for the custody and organization of data. Individual departments do not do their own purchasing, shipping, or data-base design. The centralized control resides in the functions *data administrator* and *data-base administrators*.

DATA-BASE
ADMINISTRATOR
The need for a data-base administrator became apparent at the beginning of the 1970s, and different corporations interpreted it differently. The concept of a data-base administrator ranged from a service function in each installation, something like the installation's systems programmer, to the overall keeper of the corporation's data. In the latter view the function is external to any data-processing department. The corporation's data are such an essential and valuable corporate resource that the custodian of the data may be thought of as being as important as the corporate accountant. Initially, the need for a data administration was perceived largely by data-processing executives rather than by general management, and today the task is usually performed within the data-processing function. The realization of the need for the corporate *data administrator* came later in many firms. Whereas the data-base administrators have technical jobs concerned with the implementation of specific data bases, such as those in Fig. 20.9, the corporate data administrator has a policy-oriented job concerned with corporate strategy and planning. He should be high enough to know the corporate policies and politics, and have strong powers to see that his strategies are implemented.

Figure 21.1 recommends a breakdown of data-base responsibilities between user groups, systems analysts and programmer, the data-base administrators, and the corporate data administrator.

	STAFF			
	USER GROUP	SYSTEMS ANALYSTS AND APPLICATION PROGRAMMERS	DATA-BASE ADMINISTRATOR	CORPORATE DATA ADMINISTRATOR
1. CORPORATE INFORMATION STRATEGY	C	C	P	Prime Responsibility
2. PROJECT SELECTION	P	P	P	Prime Responsibility
3. PROJECT FEASIBILITY STUDY	P	Prime Responsibility	P	P
4. SELECTION OF DATA-BASE SOFTWARE		P	P	Prime Responsibility
5. DATA-BASE DESIGN AND DEVELOPMENT	C	P	Prime Responsibility	P
6. APPLICATION DESIGN	P	Prime Responsibility	P	C
7. APPLICATION PROGRAMMING AND TESTING	P	Prime Responsibility	P	
8. SYSTEM IMPLEMENTATION AND TESTING	P	Prime Responsibility	P	
9. SYSTEM MAINTENANCE	P	Prime Responsibility	P	
10. DATA-BASE MAINTENANCE	C	C	Prime Responsibility	P
11. DATA-BASE ACCURACY AND SECURITY	C	C	Prime Responsibility	P

P = PARTICIPATING RESPONSIBILITY
C = CONSULTING WHEN REQUIRED

Figure 21.1 Recommended breakdown of data-base responsibilities.

**GOVERNMENT
FUNCTIONS**

For complex data bases the functions of the data-base administrator are sometimes carried out not by one man but by a group. A single man is unlikely to combine the technical expertise that is needed, the knowledge of the corporation's data, and the negotiating skills. Concern has been expressed about the growing overhead that such functions represent, but as data processing develops, like the growth of society, it becomes more complex, and more government operations are needed to prevent chaos and to enable further development. Some of the government functions are legislative, making the programmers and systems analysts conform to the rules that are for the benefit of the majority. The early pioneers did not need such rules, but in a data-base world they are essential. Police are needed also, to prevent violations of security and privacy. Where violations occur, or where the data are of exceptional value, data-base systems may need their own FBI.

There are administrative functions in maintaining the data definitions and schemas and in settling differences between groups who want the data defined, represented, or stored differently. The settling of such differences is often the most difficult part of the data-base administrator's job because of the arguments that break out about data that should be shared between departments who have not previously shared it. Department managers are understandably reluctant to relinquish full control over data about their departments. Furthermore, integration of the data base often necessitates the restructuring of earlier files and rewriting programs which use them. Departments may argue vehemently before undertaking this work.

Just as a city government organizes *services* for which its residents pay, such as transportation and sewerage, so the data-base administrator organizes *services* for the application programmers and analysts which relieve them of much of the work they had to do in an earlier era. The data-base administrator plans the file-addressing schemes, the physical data layout, the security procedures, and the means of restart and recovery after failures have occurred. He selects and provides data management software so that application programmers will no longer have to program such functions.

The data-base administrator will be constantly concerned with performance, "tuning" the physical data structures to improve performance. The usage of the data will be monitored so that impending performance problems can be anticipated and adjustments made.

Unlike most governments in society, a good data-base administrator provides valuable counselling and consulting services to the data users. Application programmers can be helped with their data definitions, systems analysts can be helped to understand the structure of the data base, and user departments can be helped to understand what data can be made available to them.

These roles of legislator, diplomat, policeman, consultant, and technician are usually too much for one man—hence the need for a small team to serve the data-base administrator function. Many corporations do, however, employ one man in the role of data-base administrator. Such a job requires that we either omit some of the functions we describe or else regard them as specifications for a superman.

FUNCTIONAL SUBDIVISION   The main functions performed by the data-base administrator or his department thus fall into the following categories:

- Data definition, standardization, and liaison
- Design of data-base organization and techniques
- Performance measurement and improvement
- Software and hardware selection
- Security control
- Daily operational control
- Consultant to programmers, analysts, and users

The biggest and most essential of these is the first—achieving agreement on common data definitions, representations, and structures.

As in most data-processing functions, different talents and temperaments are needed for the *design* of operations and the day-to-day *running* of operations. The design functions in data-base administration should therefore be handled by a different man from the one who handles day-to-day control functions. The design of security procedures should be separated from the day-to-day security administration. The design of integrity procedures should be separated from the day-to-day operations for correcting file errors and ensuring that lost data can be reconstructed. The design of monitoring procedures should be separated from daily monitoring operations.

Security administration is a separate function from data-base administration on many systems in which security is a major concern. The day-to-day security operations may not be the concern of the data-base administrator.

Considering the separation of design functions and day-to-day operations, the data-base administrator's staff may be organized as in Fig. 21.2.

Many data-base installations contain several separate data bases among which, at least for the time being, data are not shared. In such a case separate persons may be responsible for the definition and standardization of the data in the separate data bases, as shown in Fig. 21.3. These persons may carry out their data-base duties part time. Such an arrangement has the advantage that they will be fully familiar with their own application areas. Their schemas will still have to meet with the approval of the overall data base administrator and will have to conform with his policies for data definition. The design expertise in Fig. 21.3 is still centralized and so are the security and integrity functions.

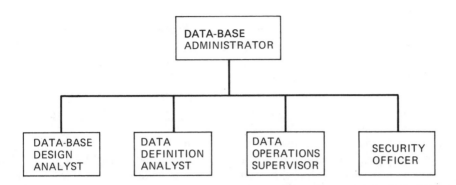

Figure 21.2

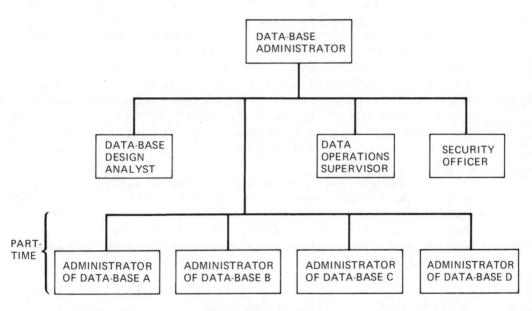

Figure 21.3

RELATION WITH USERS   A particularly delicate and important aspect of the data administration is the relation with the user groups or the groups who program specific applications. Often such groups find it more difficult to use data in a shared data base than to have their own files which they can use in their own way. Data-base administrators must explain to them the advantages of the new methods. This task may require the art of persuasion if the groups in question find the service with a data-base system to be in some way inferior to that when they had their own files.

In a data-base environment it is often not clear who "owns" the data, and so specific rules must be established about who is responsible for their updating. Certain users may "own" certain data items in otherwise common records. The data-base administrator must arbitrate and control the use of the data. Too often the conceptual clarity of shared data bases becomes clouded by political warfare. To resolve the bitter arguments that ensue the data-base administrator must have considerable diplomacy and authority. It is necessary to be able to argue articulately for the right course of action.

The data-base administrator frequently has to turn down a user's or programmer's request for service or for additions to the data base. In a shared data base the request may be in conflict with the needs of other users. He should explain clearly the logic of turning down a request and must have a full understanding of the user's needs. The users must have the feeling that they are talking to an unbiased and impartial authority and that the decisions being made will ultimately benefit the user groups as a whole.

There can be a delicate balance between short-term needs and long-term development. The corporate data administrator should insist that plans for the long-term development of the data bases should be drawn up. He should maneuver the short-term implementations into directions likely to enhance the long-term prospects, or at least ensure that no further short-term decisions are made which seriously impede long-term development. Many of today's short-term data-system implementors are digging graves for themselves by installing systems that will be very difficult to modify or expensive to reprogram as future developments are added.

Other important aspects of the data-base administrator's relation with the users are education and documentation. The users must be educated concerning the principles and policies governing data-base design and usage. They must have available to them detailed information about what the data base contains and how it can be used. The application programmers must have access to a data-base dictionary.

DETAILED LIST OF FUNCTIONS   Box 21.1 details the data-base administrator functions. It divides them into the heading shown in Fig. 21.2. In practice a variety of different organizational structures is used for data administration, and the following functions are allocated to departmental structures in different ways.

BOX 21.1   Data-Base Administrator Functions

A.   Data Definition Analyst

1. All data-item types are named and a standard schema format agreed upon for them. With some data-base management systems data-item synonyms are permitted so that when the same data item has been named or represented differently in different subsystems these different names and representations may be preserved and equated.

2. Details of all data items and their definitions are documented, preferably by means of an automated *data dictionary*. A cross-reference list stating which programs use which data items should be maintained. When any changes are proposed the cross-reference list will show who or what programs are affected.

3. The combining of data items into named groups (data aggregates, records, segments, relations) is agreed upon.

4. The logical relationships among groups is agreed upon and hence the schema definition created. The data-base administrator staff makes any necessary changes to the schema when the data are changed or new data are added.

5. When an application programmer wishes to create a new type of data item, record, or relationship, he must apply to the data definition analyst, who makes the necessary changes to the schema. An application programmer cannot create new data on his own.

6. The data definition analyst may determine what policies govern the retention of data, for example, to comply with government regulations.

7. He gives advice to programmers, systems analysts, and user departments concerning the data and their logical structure.

8. He attempts to maintain a view of the future needs and applications, so that the data base can be made to evolve in an appropriate manner.

9. He defines rules and functions to ensure validity, consistency, and accuracy of data.

Box 21.1—*Cont.*

B. Data-Base Design Analyst

1. The design analyst is responsible for the physical structuring of the data.

2. He employs design tools such as mathematical or simulation models of the physical storage to help determine which methods of physical organization best meet the performance criteria.

3. He recommends which data-base hardware and software should be used, and specifies any additions to data-base software that might be needed.

4. He designs appropriate access methods.

5. He designs the means of restart and recovery after system outages, and the means of backup.

6. He designs the means of reconstructing data in the event of loss of records or of catastrophic destruction of entire files.

7. He assists in logical file design. Certain systems analysts or programmers in the user departments may be competent file designers. The design analyst or the data-base administrator staff will work with these.

8. He specifies the techniques for monitoring the data base performance.

9. Actual data base performance will be correlated to the predictions of the design-tool models in an attempt to react to future performance problems before they arise.

10. Measurements of how full the file spaces are will be checked periodically so that appropriate restructuring can be carried out when necessary.

11. The design analyst determines when and how the physical data base needs tuning to improve its performance.

12. Viewing the data base as a whole, he determines what categories of security techniques should be used. He designs the detailed structures and techniques for maintaining privacy.

13. He designs any data base searching strategies, or plans any use of inverted files or inverted lists.

14. He defines the rules relating to access constraints, including rules to prevent concurrent updates or interlocks, and rules to prevent excessive time-consuming search operations.

15. He determines the policies for deleting or dumping old data, or data migration.

16. He designs compaction techniques.

17. He provides advice to the systems analysts concerning data-base techniques.

Box 21.1—*Cont.*

C. Data Operations Supervisor

The data operations supervisor deals with data problems that arise on a day-to-day basis.

1. He investigates all errors that are found in the data. He flags data that are known to be in error.
2. He supervises all restarts and recovery after failure.
3. He supervises all reorganizations of data bases or indices.
4. He cleans up any data conflicts that are found (such as data items that are different when they should be the same). When existing files are merged into the data base, data conflicts almost always show up.
5. He initiates and controls all periodic dumps of the data, audit trails, vital record procedures, etc.
6. He ensures that the volume library is correctly controlled and maintained.
7. He exerts some control over computer scheduling when necessary for data-base reasons.
8. He supervises the transfer of files to alternative media when necessary.

D. Security Officer

The security officer may not report to the data-base administrator. His functions vary widely, depending on the seriousness of security in the installation.

1. The security officer investigates all known security breaches.
2. He receives a listing each morning of all violations of correct security procedure which could reflect attempts to compromise security.
3. He determines who is authorized to use each locked facility or each locked data item, record, area, or file. He is responsible for the authorization tables which control the locked facilities or records.
4. Nobody can make any changes to the security authorization tables other than the security officer.
5. He modifies the data locks and keys whenever necessary.
6. He ensures that the machine room and volume library security procedures are complied with.
7. He conducts periodic security audits.

TOOLS　　　　　　　　　A variety of tools is becoming available to assist data administration staff.

First, there are languages for describing the schema, as discussed in Part III, and languages for describing the physical data structures, such as DL/I. Associated with these languages are facilities enabling the data-base administrator staff to modify the logical or physical data structures.

Second, there are tools for examining the relationships between data items and how the data items can best be grouped into segments, records, tree-structures and other data-base structures—what groupings best satisfy the diverse output requirements.

Third, there are programs for maintaining a data dictionary, glossary, and cross-references.

Fourth, there will be tools to assist in the design of physical data structures, perhaps automatically mapping the data to physical storage on the basis of specified user requirements.

Fifth, there are design tools which enable a design analyst to simulate or otherwise model the data base, estimating access times, search times, data densities, or number of overflows.

Sixth, there are monitoring aids associated with the hardware and software. Eventually data-base systems will become self-regulating and self-tuning.

To the extent that such tools exist the data-base administrator staff will be able to carry out their functions more efficiently and set wiser policies. The most difficult task will remain, however, that of dealing with the political problems in an organization that must be settled as data processing evolves toward the dream of an all-embracing organization-wide set of data bases.

22 SECURITY AND PRIVACY

Data in data-base systems must be kept secure and private. The information stored is sometimes of great value to a corporation. It must not be lost or stolen. The more vital the information in data bases becomes, the more important it is to protect it from hardware or software failures, from catastrophes, and from criminals, vandals, incompetents, and people who would misuse it.

Data security refers to *protection of data against accidental or intentional disclosure to unauthorized persons or unauthorized modifications or destruction.*

Privacy refers to *the rights of individuals and organizations to determine for themselves when, how, and to what extent information about them is to be transmitted to others.*

Although the technology of privacy is closely related to that of security, privacy is an issue that goes far beyond the computer center. To a large extent it is a problem of society. To preserve the privacy of data about individuals, solutions are needed beyond the technical solutions. Future society, dependent on a massive use of data banks, will need new legal and social controls if the degree of privacy of personal information that is cherished today is to be maintained.

It is more difficult to protect data in a data base than to protect it in the earlier systems of separate files. A file on tape usually has one owner and is accessed by one set of application programs. One man can be made responsible for what happens to it. Data in a data base may be used for many different applications by many different people and may have no one clearly defined owner. The controls to prevent unauthorized access to data are therefore more intricate and are closely bound up with the data-base management software. Nevertheless, those data-base systems for which the security precautions have been designed with care are usually more secure than their separate — file predecessors.

Data can be locked up in a computer data base as securely as it can be locked up in a bank vault. Nevertheless, the data on many systems cannot be regarded as being highly secure because insufficient attention has been paid to the design or implementation of the security procedures.

Security is a highly complex subject because there are so many different aspects to it. A systems analyst responsible for the design of security needs to be familiar with all features of the system because the system can be attacked or security breached in highly diverse ways. Sometimes a great amount of effort is put into one aspect of security and other aspects are neglected. If a moat is seen as the way to make a castle secure, a great amount of security engineering could be applied to the moat. It could be very wide, and full of hungry piranha fish, and could have a fiercely guarded drawbridge. However, this alone would not make the castle secure. A determined intruder could tunnel under the moat. A security designer sometimes becomes so involved with one aspect of security design that he fails to see other ways of breaking into the system. It takes much knowledge and ingenuity to see all the possible ways.

SEVEN ESSENTIALS   Box 22.1 lists seven essentials of data-base security:

BOX 22.1   The Essence of Data-Base Security

A data base should be

- PROTECTED
- RECONSTRUCTABLE
- AUDITABLE
- TAMPERPROOF

Its users should be

- IDENTIFIABLE

Their actions should be

- AUTHORIZED
- MONITORED

1. The data should be *protected* from fire, theft, or other forms of destruction.

2. The data should be *reconstructable* because, however good the precautions, accidents sometimes happen.

3. The data should be *auditable*. Failure to audit computer systems adequately has permitted some of the world's largest crimes.

4. The system should be *tamperproof*. Ingenious programmers should not be able to bypass the controls.

5. No system today is completely tamperproof, but bypassing the controls can be made extremely difficult. Users of the data base must be positively *identified* before they can use it.

6. The system must be able to check that their actions are *authorized*.

7. Their actions should be *monitored* so that if they do something wrong they are likely to be found out.

The appendix lists some of the main means of security protection. Further information can be obtained from Reference 37.

LAYERS OF
PROTECTION

The nucleus of security control lies in the design of the computer system and its programs. Without tight controls in the hardware and software, no other precautions can make the system secure.

Design of a tightly controlled computer system, however, is not enough by itself. As indicated in Fig. 22.1, it must be surrounded by layers of control external to the system design. The layer of technical controls is surrounded by that of physical security. This refers to locks on the doors, guards, alarms, and other means of preventing unauthorized access, fire precautions, protection of stored data files, and so forth. It is not enough to have good hardware and software if disks can be stolen or the tape library destroyed by fire.

The next layer is that of administrative controls to ensure that the system is used correctly. The programmers and data-processing staff must be controlled so that they do not misuse the system. Controlled computer-room and program-testing procedures must be enforced. The administrative controls extend beyond the data-processing section to the user departments, the auditors, and general management.

The layers in Fig. 22.1 are not entirely separate. Physical security is not irrelevant when designing system techniques. The question of what data volumes should be stored off the premises affects both system design and physical security. The administrative procedures are very much related to the system design, especially with a real-time or terminal-based system. The auditors need to be involved in the system design, and the views of general management concerning security very much affect the system design.

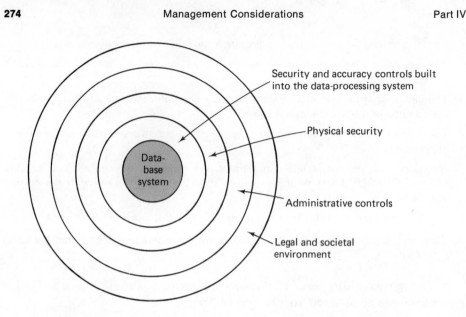

Security and accuracy controls built into the data-processing system

Physical security

Data-base system

Administrative controls

Legal and societal environment

Figure 22.1   Four layers of control needed for data-base security and privacy.

The outermost layer in Fig. 22.1 is by far the most problematical. When the computer and telecommunications revolution has run its full course (and today it is only just beginning), society will be very different. Many controls will no doubt have evolved, seeking to maximize the benefits and minimize the dangers of a technology of which George Orwell never dreamed. A legal framework is beginning to emerge in some countries which will relate to data-base systems.

TYPES OF
SECURITY EXPOSURE
Table 22.1 lists some of the main types of security exposure. The diversity of the list will indicate that many different forms of protection are needed to make data secure.

Catastrophes such as fire and major embezzlements have resulted in dramatic headlines, but by far the most common and most probable causes of computer calamities are human carelessness and accidents. Carelessness has sometimes had spectacular results. One company reported a "$2.8 million deficiency" caused by an error in cutover. Usually, however, failures are less spectacular and more frequent.

A security program must therefore be designed to protect an installation both from calamitous events that rarely occur and from relatively minor events, such as damage to individual records, which occur on some systems several times a week.

Table 22.1 Types of Data-Base Security Exposure

Type of Exposure	Inability to Process	Loss of an Entire File	Loss of Single Records	Modification of Records	Unauthorized Reading or Copying
Acts of God					
Fire	✓	✓			
Flood	✓	✓			
Other catastrophe	✓	✓			
Mechanical failure					
Computer outage	✓				
File unit damages disk track			✓		
Tape unit damages part of tape			✓		
Disk, or other volume, unreadable		✓			
Hardware/software error damages file		✓	✓		
Data transmission error not detected			✓	✓	
Card (or other input) chewed up by machine			✓	✓	
Error in application program damages record			✓	✓	
Human carelessness					
Keypunch error			✓	✓	
Terminal operator input error			✓	✓	
Computer operator error		✓	✓	✓	
Wrong volume mounted and updated		✓	✓	✓	
Wrong version of program used		✓	✓	✓	
Accident during program testing		✓	✓	✓	
Mislaid tape or disk		✓			
Physical damage to tape or disk		✓	✓		
Malicious damage					
Looting	✓	✓			
Violent sabotage	✓	✓			
Nonviolent sabotage (e.g., tape erasure)	✓	✓	✓	✓	
Malicious computer operator		✓	✓	✓	
Malicious programmer		✓	✓	✓	
Malicious tape librarian		✓			
Malicious terminal operator		✓	✓	✓	
Malicious user (e.g., user who punches holes in returnable card)			✓	✓	
Playful malignancy (e.g., misusing terminal for fun)		✓	✓	✓	✓
Crime					
Embezzlement			✓	✓	✓
Industrial espionage					✓
Employees selling commercial secrets					✓
Employees selling data for mailing lists					✓
Data bank information used for bribery or extortion					✓
Invasion of privacy					
Casual curiosity (e.g., looking up employee salaries)					✓
Looking up data of a competing corporation					✓
Obtaining personal information for political or legal reasons					✓
Nondeliberate revealing of private information					✓
Malicious invasion of privacy					✓

THREE-LEVEL ATTACK   Each security exposure must be attacked in three ways:

1. *Minimize the probability of it happening at all.* A major part of fire precautions should be preventive, and this is just as important with all other security breaches. Would-be embezzlers should be discouraged from ever beginning.

2. *Minimize the damage if it does happen.* An intruder who succeeds in bypassing the physical or programmed controls that were intended to keep him out should still be very restricted in what he can accomplish. A fire once started, should be prevented from spreading. A disk that has been dropped and bent should be prevented from damaging a read head, which in turn could damage other disks. If the security procedures are compromised, it must be possible to limit the harm that could result. Some security designers have made the grave error of supposing that their preventive measures will always work.

3. *Design a method of recovering from the damage.* It *must* be possible to reconstruct vital records or whole files if they become accidentally or willfully damaged or lost. It *must* be possible to recover from a disastrous fire sufficiently quickly to keep the business running. If an authorized person obtains a security code or a file of security codes, it must be possible to change these quickly so that they are of no use to him. It is important to attack the security problem *in depth*, and recovery procedures are vital to the overall plan. The designers of the preventive mechanisms must not be allowed to become so infatuated with their schemes that they neglect recovery techniques.

TWO CATEGORIES OF FILE DAMAGE   There are two types of file damage. In one a few fields or records may be harmed; they can be corrected relatively quickly, providing there is some means of knowing what the correct records should be. In the other, an entire file is destroyed or a large segment of a file; the damage is too extensive to be corrected by manual methods. One hopes that the latter massive file damage will never occur. However, it would be folly to assume that it cannot. A reconstruction program must be in existence to deal with the eventuality of massive file damage.

In one installation massive file damage was caused after a program-testing session that continued through the night, because the wrong files were loaded on to the machine. In other cases a disk had been dropped and bent and was unloadable. On one real-time system the wrong files were loaded and contained out-of-date information in what otherwise appeared to be valid records. The wrong records were updated for many hours with an extremely high transaction throughput before the process was stopped. Because it was a real-time system, the run could not be repeated with the same input.

On a well-run installation such eventualities (it will be thought) should never occur. In reality they have occurred, occasionally, on installations that were thought by their managers to be well run. Instances of sabotage to files have occurred on installations where sabotage was thought to be too improbable to consider. The data must be reconstructable.

GRANDFATHER, FATHER, AND SON TAPES

Reconstruction procedures are generally easier on batch systems than real-time systems. A new file is usually created on a different disk or tape. Figure 3.2 gave a typical example. Last week's product master file is run with the tape of new orders and a new product master file is read in the invoicing run, and a new customer master file is written. To give the ability to recover from any errors or unforeseen catastrophes, last week's files are retained. The tapes are sometimes referred to as father and son tapes, the father tape being the input to the run and the son tape being the new output. To be extra safe, the input to the previous run is also kept, and this is called the grandfather tape. Some installations retain earlier members of the family tree, but usually grandfather, father, and son are thought to be sufficient. Because the tapes are retained, entire runs can be repeated if they are found to be faulty or if the new tapes are damaged in some way. As a precaution against fire, theft, incompetent operators, or malicious deeds, the older tapes needed only for reconstruction purposes should be stored away from the computer installation, preferably in a fireproof strong room.

CHECKPOINTS

It is desirable not to have to repeat the whole of a batch run when something goes wrong if it can be avoided. This is especially true when the run is long. For this reason checkpoints are built into the run at appropriately short intervals. If a machine failure occurs or a fault is detected, it is necessary to rerun the work from the last checkpoint, not from the beginning of the entire batch. When a checkpoint is reached, the batch totals up to that point will be recorded along with any other information necessary to restart the run. Any checks which can be performed to test the accuracy of the run up to that point will be completed.

UPDATING FILES IN PLACE

When files are recorded on disk or other direct-access devices rather than tape, they may be updated in place (as with Figs. 3.3 and 3.4). The disadvantage of updating in place is that the grandfather-father-son sequence does not exist. During a run the previous versions of the modified records are lost. The run therefore cannot be reexecuted in the event of trouble. A different means of reconstructing records is needed.

To permit reconstruction, the files that are directly accessed and overwritten must be dumped periodically. The input transactions used since the last file dump must be retained. The files can then be reconstructed by a program that uses the last file dump and the input transaction tapes. Any corrections that may have been made to individual records in the files must be recorded on the input tape so that they can be reconstructed also. Figure 22.2 shows the tapes in question.

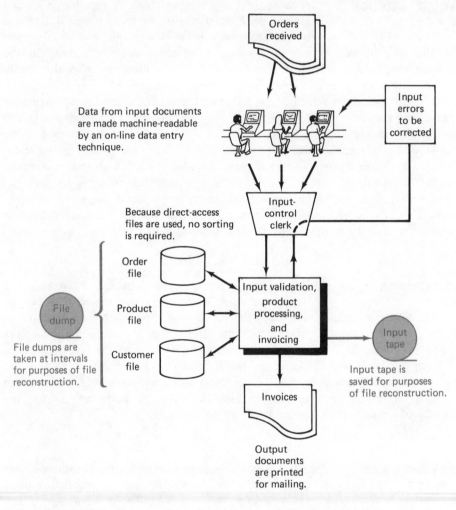

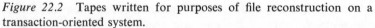

Figure 22.2 Tapes written for purposes of file reconstruction on a transaction-oriented system.

The program for file reconstruction should be written and tested before the installation is first put into operation. It is during the first weeks of operation that file catastrophes are most likely to happen because of unforeseen program bugs or operators unfamiliar with their job.

REMOTE   When modifications to the data are made at remote
TERMINALS   terminals in many different offices, the input controls
                            which are a feature of batch systems cannot be applied.
There is no batch control clerk or input/output control group.

A file-action journal is usually kept which logs, often in an abbreviated fashion, the changes made to the data base. An input transaction journal may also be kept to provide a means of recovery from computer failures. The input journal can help ensure that no transaction is lost or double-processed during the period of recovery from failures.

JOURNALS   System journals are also sometimes referred to as *logs*.
                            Table 22.2 lists types of data that may be stored on
such journals. Along the top of the table the possible functions of the journals are given. In addition to facilitating recovery from data loss, the journals permit auditors to follow the history of a transaction and permit investigation of the causes of errors found in records. Journals can be processed to reveal information about how a system is being used and to highlight procedural violations which may be an indication of possible breaches of security.

DUPLICATE   Some systems keep duplicate copies of critical data on
FILES   the files. When the system updates these data, it up-
                            dates both copies. If one file becomes temporarily un-
available or if one copy of the data becomes damaged, for example, by a read/write head crashing on a track, the second copy is immediately available. Unfortunately, this does not provide protection from program errors, because these will usually damage both file copies. It is not, therefore, a substitute for the transaction and file-action journals. Its advantage is in providing immediate backup where this is important. On most real-time systems it is worthwhile to duplicate a portion of the files, if only the program files. The files that are most critical to continuous operation are usually a small proportion of the total. Conversely, on most systems there is no need to duplicate all the files, although total file duplication does exist on some systems. Figure 22.3 illustrates the journals, dumps and duplicated files used on a real-time system.

Table 22.2 Information which may be recorded on journals (logs) for purposes of system protection and auditing.

KEY: ✔ = Yes
P = Possibly
I = At specified intervals

Functions:	To provide an audit trail for an auditor to follow the history of a transaction	To permit recovery when it is found that a user has incorrectly updated or deleted a record	To investigate the causes when a record is found to be faulty	To assist recovery from massive file destruction	To assist in correcting the file when a program has been damaging data	To correct false information which has been sent to system users	To monitor procedural violations to highlight possible breaches of security	To assist in correct recovery from a system failure	To monitor the way the system is being used (as an aid to design)	To recover from the loss of a file-action journal
Transaction journal										
Incoming inquiry transaction						✓			✓	
Incoming update transaction	✓	✓	✓			✓		✓	✓	✓
Transaction type		P	P			✓	✓		P	
Transaction number	✓	✓	✓			✓		✓		✓
Originating terminal	✓	✓	✓			✓	✓	✓	✓	✓
Originating operator	✓	✓	✓			✓	✓		✓	✓
Time and date	I	I	I			I	✓	I	I	I
Response to inquiry transaction						✓			✓	
Response to update transaction	✓	✓	✓			✓			✓	✓
Indication that response was received correctly	✓	✓	✓			✓		✓		✓
Procedural violations on input							✓			
Record of start and end of file reconstruction									✓	
Note of completion of update									✓	
File-action journal										
Transaction number	✓	✓	✓		✓					
Time and date		I	I	✓	I					
Addresses of items updated	✓	✓	✓	✓	✓					
Contents of items before they are updated										
Contents of items after they are updated	✓	✓	✓	✓	✓			✓		
Note of completion of update	✓	✓	✓	✓	✓			✓		
List of programs used for update			✓		✓					
Full contents of any records created			✓		✓					
Full contents of any records deleted			✓		✓			✓		
Details of any indices opened or closed			✓	✓	✓			✓		
Procedural violations deleted during update or processing							✓			
Contents of items corrected, before correction	✓		✓	✓				✓		
Contents of items corrected, after correction	✓		✓	✓				✓		
Indication of start and end of a correction run	✓		✓	✓				✓		

The above information may be all on the same journal.

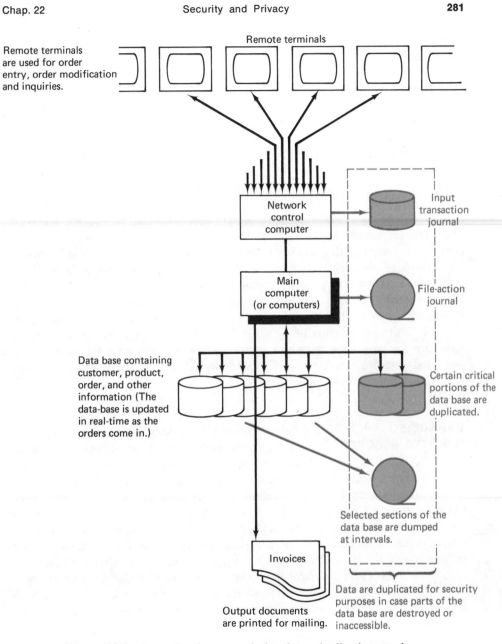

Figure 22.3 Journals, dumps and data-base duplication used for security purposes on a real-time system.

LARGE
DATA BASES
When a system has small direct-access files, there is no difficulty about copying the files periodically onto tape or disk and retaining this for recovery purposes. A long time is needed, however, to copy a large data base, and data bases in use are becoming larger at a rapid rate.

A set of data bases with many billions of characters will probably not be copied in its entirety. The data may be divided into vital and nonvital records, and only the vital ones copied. Different parts of the data will have different copying cycles. At one extreme, some of the data may be unchanging and will only be copied once. Some of the data may never be copied because they will quickly be replaced with new data. Some of the data will change only rarely, such as the addresses of persons and firms, and they will only be copied rarely, if at all. At the other extreme, some files that are vitally important to the day's operations will be copied every night so that a quick recovery can be made if they should be harmed.

Much of the data will change sufficiently infrequently that it is quicker to create the backup copy by updating an earlier copy than by duplicating the files. The file-activity journal may be employed for this purpose in an off-line batch-processing operation that goes on continuously in support of the real-time system.

In future generations of systems, it would seem desirable to construct the hardware for very large data-base systems in such a way that the data in it are protected from fire, flood, and theft, as they would be in a strong, locked, fireproof, waterproof, burglarproof vault.

DAMAGE TO
ISOLATED RECORDS
Whereas massive file reconstruction should be a very rare event, the correction of single data items or records may be needed frequently, because of terminal operator errors, incorrect input documents, or program errors, or possibly because of a reason inherent in the application, such as customers changing their minds. On some installations it has been difficult to tell where the file errors are, but they are certainly present. On some real-time systems, especially those with a high degree of multiprogramming, the programs never become fully debugged. Rarely occurring and almost untraceable coincidences in the data can trigger timing program errors that cause incorrect file updates. The imperfections are rare enough to live with, provided that file errors can easily be corrected when they are found. The correction process itself, however, may be a security loophole and needs to be carefully controlled.

In real-time systems the records directly accessible can be made only too easy to correct from a terminal. The problem is not correcting the record but maintaining adequate control over this process.

Systems will have different reasons for adopting particular procedures for dealing with damaged real-time records. The procedures may permit records to be corrected by one of three groups of persons:

1. The terminal operator who orginally created the record or entered the data. Operators at a branch office may correct the records for that branch if the location has overall responsibility for its own records.
2. The owner of the data. A given man may be designated as being responsible for each data-item type, segment type, file, or other data grouping. He must be notified of any errors that are found in it and must be responsible for correcting them, with appropriate controls.
3. A special group whose function it is to deal with errors in the system. This group will be familiar with all the errors arising and the ways to minimize them. The group may report to the data-base administrator.

On systems in which embezzlement is a danger, the prime concern will be control of any changes. On many real-time systems, however, this is not a concern, and the prime need is to correct wrong records as quickly and easily as possible. On a police system for keeping track of emergency calls and police operations, for example, the sole concern is to keep the files representing the current status as accurately as possible. A history log will be kept, but this will not normally be used for file reconstruction, as events move too rapidly. At the other extreme, if an error is found in a record containing financial data, the record will be flagged to indicate that there is an error and the new value may be recorded elsewhere. The data item in question will be updated later when tight control procedures can be assured.

PRIVACY LOCKS   The question of *who* is authorized to do *what* to a data base is very important. Before each operation involving the data base the computer should check that it is an authorized operation.

Authorization schemes vary from being very simple to highly complex. One of the simplest schemes requires that the user key in a *password* which only he should know. If it is an acceptable password for the program or file in question, he is allowed to proceed. The CODASYL Data Description Language uses *privacy locks* appended to the data. The privacy lock is a single value which is specified in the schema description. Data locked in this way cannot be used by a program unless the program provides a value which matches the privacy lock. It is rather like the user of a bank safe needing to know the combination which will open the safe. Unlike a bank safe, however, different combinations can be used for all different data types. The locking mechanism can be much more intricate than with a bank safe.

The combination that unlocks the data is specified by a clause in the description of each data type. Privacy locks can be declared at data-item, data-aggregate, record, set, member, area, and schema levels for protecting any of them. At each of these levels the locks relate to specific functions such as reading or modifying the data items or inserting new records. A typical clause in the description of data type would be PRIVACY LOCK FOR MODIFY IS 753019. The data type that this clause is appended to can be modified only if the key 753019 is provided.

The lock could be a constant, as with a bank safe combination lock, or it could be the value of a variable or the result of a programmed procedure. The lock clause might say, for example, PRIVACY LOCK FOR GET IS PROCEDURE K24. The key required to read (GET) the data in question must then match the result obtained by executing program procedure K24. The locks which apply to the use of a record type can relate to one or more of the following functions: INSERT, REMOVE, STORE, DELETE, GET, MODIFY, FIND.

AUTHORIZATION SCHEMES

Authorization schemes in general may give permission to use various combinations of data types, as indicated in Fig. 22.4. They may relate these data types to

1. Individual users

2. Groups or categories of users

3. Security levels (top secret, corporate confidential, etc.)

4. Application programs

5. Time of day (like a time lock on a bank vault).

6. Terminal or terminal location

7. Transaction types

8. Combinations of these

A certain type of datum, for example, may be usable only by a certain category of user and only if he is at a certain terminal.

The authorization process may be broken down into stages. The blocks in Fig. 22.5 show a possible sequence of events when a terminal is used. The locks that might be applied need not all be used on the same system; however, a secure system should have more than one lock in the chain, so that if any one lock is bypassed, accidentally or deliberately, the data are still secure.

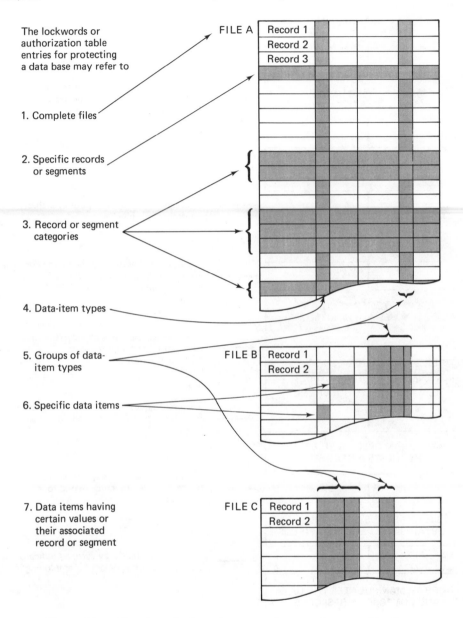

Figure 22.4 Data-base lockwords can apply to various combinations of data.

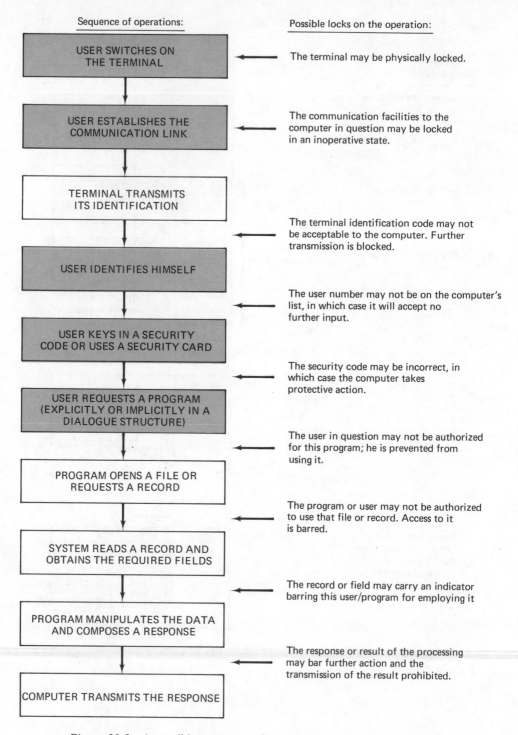

Sequence of operations:	Possible locks on the operation:

USER SWITCHES ON THE TERMINAL — The terminal may be physically locked.

USER ESTABLISHES THE COMMUNICATION LINK — The communication facilities to the computer in question may be locked in an inoperative state.

TERMINAL TRANSMITS ITS IDENTIFICATION — The terminal identification code may not be acceptable to the computer. Further transmission is blocked.

USER IDENTIFIES HIMSELF — The user number may not be on the computer's list, in which case it will accept no further input.

USER KEYS IN A SECURITY CODE OR USES A SECURITY CARD — The security code may be incorrect, in which case the computer takes protective action.

USER REQUESTS A PROGRAM (EXPLICITLY OR IMPLICITLY IN A DIALOGUE STRUCTURE) — The user in question may not be authorized for this program; he is prevented from using it.

PROGRAM OPENS A FILE OR REQUESTS A RECORD — The program or user may not be authorized to use that file or record. Access to it is barred.

SYSTEM READS A RECORD AND OBTAINS THE REQUIRED FIELDS — The record or field may carry an indicator barring this user/program for employing it

PROGRAM MANIPULATES THE DATA AND COMPOSES A RESPONSE — The response or result of the processing may bar further action and the transmission of the result prohibited.

COMPUTER TRANSMITS THE RESPONSE

Figure 22.5 A possible sequence of events when a terminal is used, and the locks that could be applied to each stage.

IDENTIFYING THE TERMINAL USER   On on-line systems operated with terminals, the first step toward making the system secure is to identify the person at the terminal. Until he is identified he should not be permitted to have access to any sensitive data or to make any modifications to the files. On other systems, it is not necessary to identify the terminal user, providing the computer knows which terminal it is, because only security-cleared personnel can use that particular terminal. There are three ways in which a person can be identified:

1. *By personal physical characteristic*: For example, a device can be used for reading and transmitting a person's fingerprints or thumbprint, and the computer can have a program for identifying this. Less expensive, his telephone voice, speaking certain prearranged digits or words, can be transmitted to the computer; the computer will have a program for recognizing his voice by comparing his speech against a stored *voice print*. Such schemes are under development, but they are not commercially available at present. They are likely to be the most expensive of the three ways to recognize a person.

2. *By something carried*: A terminal user can carry a badge, card, or key. He inserts the badge into a terminal badge reader or the key into the terminal itself. Magnetically encoded cards like credit cards are used for this purpose.

3. *By something known or memorized*: He can memorize a password or answer a prearranged set of questions. Techniques of this type require no special hardware. They are least expensive of the three, and under most circumstances they can be made reasonably secure if applied intelligently. The user's identification number, however, must not be a number that might be guessed, such as his birth date or car license number.

Keys, locks, machine-readable badges, and credit cards all have one disadvantage: They can be lost. The user may fail to remove them from the terminal after the transaction is complete. If a sign-on action is used along with a badge or card, the user may forget to sign off. It may be possible to duplicate the key or badge. For these reasons, the use of the key, card, or badge is not necessarily more secure than identification of a terminal operator by a memorized security code or a sequence of questions. Keys on banking system terminals and badges in certain airline systems have been in operation for years, although nobody pretends that they would keep out an ingenious and persistent imposter, any more than an apartment lock would keep out an ingenious and determined burglar. They are better than no lock at all.

On most systems, the computer can be programmed with a time-out mechanism so that it will not react to a terminal for a given period after the operator signs on, in case he has left it unattended. On some military systems the terminal has a small fence around it, and the operator cannot leave the area without opening a gate with the same badge or key that he uses on the terminal.

A password has been used on a number of systems to identify the user. In its simplest form, all the terminal users, or users of a given category or at a given location, know the same password; until this is typed in, the system will take no action. For any reasonable measure of security, however, it is desirable to provide each of the individual terminal users with a different security code. He must type this code into the terminal. The computer will then check what the individual using that code is permitted to do. On some systems, the user keys in his own personal identification number, followed by a security code which has been issued to him. The computer checks that he has entered the correct security code and checks that the transactions he enters are authorized for that individual. A table such as that in Fig. 22.6 may be used. As a result of this check, categories of authorization may

USER'S IDENTIFICATION NUMBER	SECURITY CODE (CHANGEABLE)	PERMISSIBLE TRANSACTION TYPES	CATEGORIES OF AUTHORIZATION
		200 bits, one for each transaction type	

1. The system obtains the user's identification number.
2. The system requests the user's security code.
3. If the security code is correct, the system checks that the user was permitted to enter the transaction type he did enter.
4. The listed categories of authorization are then used to control access to the data base.

Figure 22.6   Use of a simple authorization table.

be established indicating what types of data-base action the individual is permitted to take.

The security code must be changed periodically. On some systems, it is changed once per month. Each terminal user must take care not to let anyone else know his code. For example, the code for a user may be mailed in such a way that the code is on a detachable piece of card with nothing else written on it. The receiver is instructed to detach this piece of card immediately. If the card with the security code on it is lost, anybody finding it is unlikely to associate it with the correct personnel number. It must be possible to issue a user with a new security code whenever he wants it. If he feels that security has been compromised in any way—for example, by someone looking over his shoulder and seeing his security code as he types it in the terminal—then he should be able to ask immediately for a new security code. On some terminals, the security code is automatically prevented from being printed or displayed as it is keyed in.

The disadvantage of the password or security code technique is that the code can be given to another person without any physical loss by the giver and without anything having to be duplicated. There is no physical evidence of the other person's possession of it. This technique must, therefore, be accompanied by rigorous controls and a serious attempt to catch, quickly and automatically, any person who is using another person's code. If the terminal users think that there is a high probability that they will be caught if they attempt to enter the system with another person's code, then they may be deterred psychologically from making an invalid entry.

THE SYSTEM'S   To maintain high security in any building or organiza-
POLICEMEN   tion, policemen are needed. A secure computer system
                          needs a staff responsible for the security of the data
files and the control of the authorization to use these files. A security officer should be appointed who will be the sole person able to change the authorization tables or file lock-word tables in the system. He will have details of what each individual is authorized to read or change on the files. He is responsible for issuing passwords or security codes and for ensuring that they are used correctly. As indicated in Chapter 21 this job is sometimes a function of the data-base administrator.

In a system with terminals in scattered locations, there should be a person responsible for security in each of these locations. A suitable person with another job, such as an office manager, can be a local security officer. He takes instructions from the main security officer. The system sends him listings, which are described later, of all detected violations of correct procedure that occur in his location.

**BURGLAR
ALARMS**
When the system detects a violation of correct security procedures it should immediately take some action.
Most terminal users can be expected to make occasional mistakes. When a user's first violation is detected, the computer should ask him to reenter the data and log the fact that the violation occurred. However, if an operator who made one mistake immediately makes a second, again attempting to enter an invalid code or access an unauthorized file, this may be an indication that he is attempting to do something illegal on the terminal. The system then immediately informs the local security officer in the hope that the culprit will be caught red-handed. This miscreant may be "kept talking" by the system, but locked out of any sensitive files, until he is caught.

Another approach that has been used is to lock the terminal completely the moment the second violation occurs. The application programs are written in such a way that no more information is accepted from that terminal until the condition has been cleared. The only man who can clear it is the security officer for that location.

**AUDIT AND CONTROL
PROCEDURES**
Any persons contemplating an invasion of the files either through curiosity or malicious intent should be deterred by the thought that there is a high probability that the system will detect them and inform the appropriate security officer. The psychological deterrence of knowing that the system has effective burglar alarms is great.

A log should be kept of all violations of correct procedure, for example, when a terminal user types in a security code that is not the one allocated to him or attempts to access a file for which he has no authorization. Details of these violations are printed and sent to the security officers. A branch security officer will receive a listing of all the violations that have occurred within his branch. A file owner will be sent details of all unauthorized attempts to read or change records in his file. This log of violations should be analyzed to detect any unusual activity. Most violations are accidental and caused by a geniune mistake on the part of the terminal operator. The sudden departure from the norm in this activity, however, may indicate that some user is tampering with the system, possibly exploring and trying to find a method of gaining unauthorized access. The list of violations may be printed out once a week; on the other hand, it may pay to do it more frequently on a system containing highly secure and highly sensitive information. The location security officers may be sent a list of any violations that occur each night. Then a would-be intruder will have little time to practice.

It is particularly important to maintain extremely tight security over the authorization records and the file lock words. If an imposter can change them, then most of his problems are solved. No one should be given the authority to read or change these records except the file owners or the security officers. If any change is made, then the appropriate file owner or security officer will be sent details of that change the following day. Such changes may be detected on a nightly run by comparing last night's authorization records and file lock tables with those of tonight. If an unauthorized person has managed to make any changes in them, it will be detected quickly.

It is recommended that a history be kept in which all changes that are made to these security records are logged, indicating who made the change and where it was made.

A SOLVABLE
PROBLEM

There is much more to security than we have described in this chapter, and the reader who would like to read further on the subject should obtain Reference 37.

In general, data-base security should be regarded as a solvable problem. It needs to be solved at an appropriate cost for the data bases in question. The systems analyst responsible for security needs the broadest possible view of the system. Overemphasis on narrow security measures should be avoided.

23 INFORMATION QUALITY

The computer with its growing storage facility is a tool *par excellence* for collecting enormous quantities of otherwise indigestible data. The collection of data, however, has little value unless the data are used to understand the world and prescribe action to improve it. Volumes of disorganized facts and figures are of little use—in industry, in government, or anywhere else. The central problem of much data processing is extracting from a mountain of facts an essence of value to human users.

Some authorities use the word *data* to refer to the mass of undigested facts and figures which computers collect, and information to refer to morsels which have been extracted from this mass and processed for a specific person or persons, for a specific purpose, or to fulfill a specific request. "Information" is digested "data." The same data can be processed in a variety of different ways to produce different pieces of information which are useful in different circumstances. The key to making computers useful to management is learning how to present the right information in the right way, and this is no simple matter.

The same problem exists in all communication media. The newspaper columnist has a mass of facts available to him. He must distill from these facts an essence which captivates and informs his reader. The movie director has an infinity of camera angles and subjects open to him and the film he shoots can be edited in an endless number of ways. He must choose those ways and those subjects which grip his audience. The same is true with computerized information systems, but until recently the computer has not generally been regarded as a communications medium. It is still rare to find systems analysts who think about it in this way. The communication of information is an art. Much has been said about "computer science" but little about the art of communication between machines and men. Like journalism and movies, man-computer communication must develop its own literacy and style. It is far from accomplishing this as yet. Many man-computer dialogues are barely fit for human consumption.

The information that can be successfully communicated, for example, to management, varies greatly with the means and style of communication, with the choice of data, and with the way the data are processed.

CAN YOU JUSTIFY AN INFORMATION SYSTEM? Some computer systems can be cost-justified in tangible terms. It will be increasingly difficult in future systems to find tangible justification. For that matter the telephone systems of a corporation, and many other services, cannot be justified tangibly. The justification of a computer doing payroll depends on the number of clerks it replaces. The justification of an information system depends on the *value of the information it provides*. It becomes necessary to assess this value, rather than merely to assess cost reductions or displacements. The value of the information must exceed the cost of providing it.

Can we measure the value of information?

The answer to that question depends on what the information is used for. If it is used in an "operations system," the value of the information can usually be estimated, at least approximately. If it is a general-purpose information system, the value may be impossible to estimate in any other than the most subjective terms. It would be exceedingly difficult to estimate the value of having your telephone. Information systems will be evaluated equally subjectively.

WHAT QUALITIES ARE NEEDED IN INFORMATION PRESENTATION? To have the maximum likelihood of being valuable to its potential users, computer-provided *information* must have a number of characteristics, which are listed in Box 23.1. A manager who is given information lacking in these qualities should not accept it passively. He should discuss the matter with the data-processing manager or systems analysts.

BOX 23.1   Computer-Provided Information Should Have the Following Qualities; System Designers, Please Note.

1. It must be *accurate*. The worst criticism of some information systems is that the information is inaccurate.

2. It must be *tailored to the needs of the user.*

3. It must be *relevant* to what he requires at that time.

4. It must be *timely*. Often it must be given in response to a user's request. If it is given to him a day late, he may not use it in some cases.

5. It must be *immediately understandable*. Some computer printouts are remarkably unintelligible.

6. Its significance must be immediately *recognizable*. This is often a function of the method or format or presentation.

7. It helps if it is *attractively presented.*

8. It should be *brief*. The lengthy listings characteristic of batch processing often conceal rather than reveal information. Single significant facts should not be camouflaged by the inclusion of other less relevant data.

9. It should be sufficiently *up-to-date* for the purpose for which it will be employed.

10. It should be *trustworthy*. Management is often suspicious of computerized information sources. Management will soon lose confidence in them if occasional errors in the data are found.

11. It should be *complete*. The user should not be left feeling that he has received only part of the information he really needs. To obtain complete information, it may be necessary for the user to browse in the files or ask certain types of questions relating to the information. Man-machine dialogue then becomes a vital part of the information-finding process.

12. It should be *easily accessible*. If a terminal is difficult to use, or confusing, it will not be used.

QUALITY
RATING

Having too much data can be almost as bad as having none at all. Several of my colleagues receive computer-printed listings of technical articles and reports in their fields of interest. The listings are mailed to the users periodically, and the users provide the system with a "profile" of their range of interests. The envelopes in which the listings arrive can be recognized, and many of the users drop the envelopes into wastebins without opening them. The trouble is that the system provides too much data and the items have no quality rating. The user cannot possibly read all the literature that is listed, and he is given no way of telling which is worth reading. He finds out what is worth reading by word of mouth from his colleagues and ignores the computer listing.

What is needed is a quality rating on the input given to the system. If the reports could be classified with codes such as

E:	Excellent	N:	Nothing new
P:	Platitudinous	B:	Badly written
S:	Useful survey	I:	Contains new ideas
M:	Highly mathematical		

or better, a grading under various headings, perhaps being mean and standard deviation of many opinions, then the information would be of value.

The reason why the *Michelin Guide* to food and hotels in France (Chapter 11) is so valuable is that it is full of quality ratings and indications of the best items on menus, and these ratings are trustworthy.

It sometimes seems socially undesirable to make quality judgments about technical reports or men's work. However, because of the information deluge that computers can produce, it must be appreciated that an egalitarian attitude to information systems can be disastrous.

ACCURACY

The worst criticism of some management information systems is that they contain inaccurate data. Inaccuracies can arise in three ways. First, the hardware, software, or transmission lines may introduce data errors. There are various effective technical controls which can prevent this happening [37].

Second, and more serious, the personnel who feed information to the system may have made errors. Human data entry errors are more difficult to control than machine errors and are far more numerous. This is especially so when the data are entered at geographically scattered terminals. There are, however, various checks and controls which can be placed on data input [38].

Third, and still more serious, the input to some information systems becomes methodically distorted. If the system contains schedules, the users may enter deliberately pessimistic estimates. If the system is being used to judge employees in some way, the employees may learn to adjust the figures they give it. Because of complex psychological relationships between the system and its users, the information it contains may in some cases degenerate in quality.

One factor often works against data accuracy. The managers who use the system expect the data it gives them to be accurate and usually feel that the question of data accuracy is a technical problem to be solved by the data-processing department. The data-processing department, on the other hand, sees its job as including the design of technical controls on accuracy but thinks that if users feed wrong information into the system, that is a problem for management. In some major systems, neither side has taken responsibility for preventing input being methodically distorted, and the result has been a misinformation system that has become generally suspect.

Often, lower or middle management feels threatened by a system which makes information about their areas immediately available to their superiors. They may permit the input to the system to become distorted or take little care with its accuracy. T. B. Mancinelli, discussing experience with U.S. military information systems, compares them with corporate information systems as follows:

> The former middle management decision makers lose both authority and responsibility. No matter how much better the decision may be, lower-level management personnel are anti-computer and anti-centralization. This is understandable for they are being stripped, slowly but inexorably, of their authority, responsibility, and former decision-making powers. What are they being given in return to compensate for their loss? Mainly, more requirements to collect and submit data to the new decision makers! Is it any wonder that middle and lower level management personnel show little enthusiasm for data accuracy, completeness, and timeliness? Especially in large organizations, middle and lower level management are being required, more and more, to operate strictly within the system. There is little room left for individual initiative and the important role at this level is becoming more input oriented. This represents a most serious human problem to be overcome in highly centralized automated management information systems [39].

THE SCALE OF PROBABILITY   Information needs can be graded on a basis of how predictable they are. The degree of predictability has a major effect on the design of data-processing systems.

At the bottom of the scale in Fig. 23.1 the information in question is asked for repeatedly, many times a day, like a branch bank officer asking for details of customers' accounts or a factory foreman asking for details of jobs to be done.

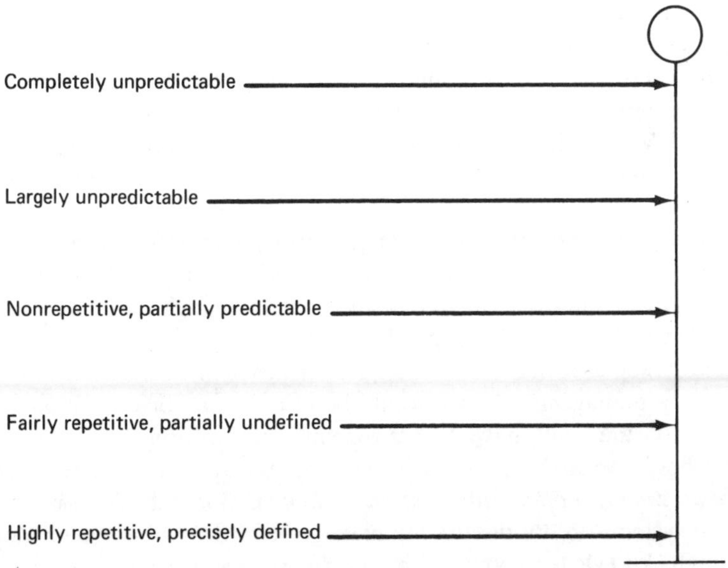

Completely unpredictable

Largely unpredictable

Nonrepetitive, partially predictable

Fairly repetitive, partially undefined

Highly repetitive, precisely defined

Figure 23.1

Furthermore, the nature of the information requested is known precisely, in advance of the request. It is not known which job the foreman will inquire about next, but what he wants to know about it will be anticipated precisely. As the system designers have precise knowledge of the information requests, there is no excuse for the system not responding to them in a manner which is crystal clear. The information should have all the attributes listed in Box 23.1.

Higher up the scale, the requests for information may not come quite so repetitively. There might be one per day. There might be some variation in what is asked for, so that the computer has to compose a reply. If the information is asked for less frequently, the answer has to be more valuable in order to justify the cost of the system.

At the top of the scale the information sought might be highly valuable. It might be information for a top-level corporate decision. However, the request has never occurred before. Considerable foresight would have been needed in order to anticipate it. It is quite likely that all the data needed to respond to the request will be in the data base somewhere, but possibly scattered through different record types. However, to respond, the data must be located and processed. The data can be located quickly only if they are organized in an appropriate fashion, and they can be processed only if a suitable program exists.

The books in a library illustrate the problem of locating data. The catalogue is designed to enable you to find a book of a given title or books by a given author. If, however, you ask the question "Which books have the word 'management' in their title?," the catalogue does not give a direct answer. The catalogue would have to be searched and because "management" may not be the first word in the title, *all* the catalogue entries would have to be inspected—a lengthy operation. The time-consuming search could be avoided by having a different type of catalogue (a KWIC index), but most libraries do not have this. Similar arguments apply to computer files. Certain types of questions can be answered only either by an expensive search through the files or by means of a special index. The question "How many books have been written about hippopotamuses?" needs either a complete search or a special index. If the special index were available, we could say that these *types* of questions had been anticipated, though not their exact nature. We are halfway up the scale of Fig. 23.1.

If the library user had asked the question "Which books discuss information systems for top management?," we would be in a much worse position. The books needed may or may not have "management" or "information systems" in the title. Some books with these words in the title would be quite irrelevant (*Greenhouse Management, Police Information Systems*). Some books on management information systems do not discuss *top* management. Searching the catalogue alone is not enough; knowledge about the books themselves is needed. If good abstracts of the books existed, the question might be answered using them. It might be answered from a set of key words describing the main themes of the book. On the other hand, it might not. It depends on whether the abstract or the set of key words is suitably composed, and many such questions would be answered only incompletely in this way. Furthermore, there is the problem of searching the abstract or key words. If this is to be other than a very long job, specially constructed directories are needed. Considering all the questions that might be asked, the directories would become massive. Already the directories to a data base occupy much more space than the data themselves in some computer systems.

"Information systems for top management" is a fairly major topic. If the user had asked "Which books mention the Westinghouse information system?," a much more detailed search would be necessary. Again, "Information systems for top management" is a fairly well-defined topic. The user could have asked "Which books cast light on the influence of protestantism or the rise of capitalism?"

The trouble with information is that it comes in an almost infinite number of varieties. We could not devise a library computer that could answer every user's question. Similarly, we cannot devise a management information system that can answer every manager's question. Top management asks the most variable and the most important questions—but they, like the questions of the most intelligent library user, are the most difficult to answer.

It is the hallmark of a good manager that he asks the right questions. He constantly varies his questioning in search for the answer which is of the most use to him. He is familiar with doing this with people, not machines. However, the way to extract high-level information from future computer systems is likely to be to interrogate them at a suitably fast terminal with a variety of questions until their capability to provide the needed information is clarified. Fast searching of multiple attributes is necessary.

What can we do about the hard-to-catch nature of information? In a library there is no substitute for a really skilled librarian. If you ask a knowledgeable librarian any of the above questions, she would probably come back with a reasonable answer. Similarly, in a management information system, or any other sort of information system near the top of the scale in Fig. 23.1, there is no substitute for human intelligence. The best solution to many problems results from the combination of human intelligence and computers. To provide top management with information is a formidable problem, and we cannot hope to solve it by machine alone. We need an intelligent management information "librarian" who thoroughly understands the nature of the information sources and can use the computer to process the information.

With the proliferation of corporate data bases a vastly increased amount of data is becoming available for corporate decision making, but it is still difficult to cast into the form of useful information. An important adjunct to corporate information systems is a small staff of intelligent professionals who understand the structure of the various data bases and know how to extract information from them on demand. This pliable human link is needed to bridge the gap between information users and data-base systems.

24 MANAGEMENT INFORMATION SYSTEMS

Probably no term in data processing has caused as much controversy as *management information systems* (MIS). Innumerable corporations claim to have them, universities have departments dedicated to them, MIS budgets run into millions, and yet knowledgeable critics refer to them as "myths" [40] and "mirages" [41].

One article in the *Harvard Business Review* says "unless U.S. industry aggressively seeks greater productivity in this area (MIS) where the potential gains are greatest, we will forfeit our economic lead over Russia and the rest of the world" [42] and another says "of all the ridiculous things that have been foisted on the long-suffering executive in the name of science and progress, the real-time management information system is the silliest . . . a company that pursues an MIS embarks on a wild-goose chase, a search for a will-o'-the-wisp" [41].

Some writers and consultants have described data-base systems as though they were synonymous with management information systems. As we commented earlier, the terms are unrelated. A data base can have value for narrow groups of applications which do not necessarily provide any information to management. The majority of data-base systems are *not* management information systems. On the other hand, to build an information system, data-base techniques and data-base management software are desirable if not essential.

THREE LEVELS OF MANAGEMENT

It is important in thinking about management information to distinguish between the needs of different levels of management. Three levels of activities in an organization are generally distinguished.

BOX 24.1   Three Levels of Operations.
Level 1 operations can be almost completely automated.
Level 2 operations can be partially automated but need management involvement.
Level 3 operations require intelligent human thinking with assistance from computers.

Level 1: Routine operations and reflex actions
Recording of customer orders
Breakdown into parts and subassemblies
Determining net requirements of parts and material
Shop floor data collection
Preparation of work tickets
Maintaining inventory records
Reordering parts and materials
Production of purchase orders
Goods receiving
Payment of suppliers
Accounts payable
Goods shipping
Invoicing
Accounts receivable
General ledger
Budget accounting
Costing
Payroll
Quality control

Level 2: Well-defined management operations
Setting working budgets
Planning working capital
Determining prices
Choosing suppliers
Sales management
Short-term forecasts
Production scheduling
Shop floor expediting
Maintenance management
Routine personnel administration
Formulating rules for routine operations

Level 3: Strategic planning and creative decision making
Determination of markets
Long-range forecasting
Directing research
Choosing new product lines
Setting financial policies
Setting personnel policies

Level 1:   Reflex actions or routine operations. Reflex actions in a living creature can be handled by low-level mechanisms that do not involve thinking in the central brain. In precomputer days, routine corporate operations were done by clerks or junior management. In a computerized corporation they may be completely automated, with human intervention occurring only when something goes wrong or something is recognized by the computers as being an exceptional circumstance needing human intervention.

Level 2:   Operations involving well-defined thinking. Before computers these would have been performed by middle management and their assistants, setting operational budgets, choosing suppliers, or scheduling production, and so forth. With computers they remain a human function but with the machine doing much of the work or providing well-specified information for a human to make decisions.

Level 3:   Operations involving creative thinking or strategic planning. These are the domain of top management and the corporate staff. Even in a highly computerized organization they remain eminently human tasks. The computer will help in many areas, but it is more difficult to provide computerized information or assistance at this level for two reasons. First, the level of thinking is often complex and ill-structured, and, second, the needs are unpredictable.

In striving for automation it is desirable to bring as many of the operations as possible into level 1 and give as much assistance as possible to level 3. Box 24.1 shows a breakdown of some of the main functions of a manufacturing corporation into these levels.

TOP MANAGEMENT Most of the questions that top management asks—
QUESTIONS the questions relating to level 3—cannot be answered directly by today's computer systems. Top management does not tend to ask questions which can be answered by a new juxtaposition of existing data items, such as "What percentage of sales quota did Branch Office 124 make in October?" They are more likely to ask questions like "Why are sales down?" or "What changes should be made to the salesman compensation plan for next year?" A staff seeking to answer these questions may well use computer programs which examine forecasts or simulate the effect of differing compensation plans using data which *are* derived from existing data items.

Much of the criticism of "management information systems" comes from persons who assume that MIS refers to top management only and that top management questions cannot be anticipated or answered in a direct way by computers alone. No matter how useful data base systems are at levels 1 and 2, they only go part of the way needed in providing information at level 3. Part of the way, however, is better than having no computer-searchable data at all. Many of the presentations made to top management by their staff benefit greatly from accessibility to appropriate data bases.

DATA FOR   Data needed for the three levels are likely to differ in
THE THREE LEVELS   their structure. The data for routine processing such as
payroll, and reflex actions such as stock reordering,
may be in files tightly designed for these operations. The data for routing human
operations will be organized for specific forms of human inquiry or dialogue. That
for the corporate staff or top management are likely to omit much of the detail
that is in the lower-level files and will be organized insofar as possible so that
unanticipated types of information requests may be answered.

The data subsystems for reflex operations may feed summary information to
subsystems for routine human operations, and these may feed information to subsystems for top management or corporate staff, as shown in Fig. 24.1. The lower-
level data bases in the diagram may be in many peripheral locations, attached to
plant computers or district office computers. On the other hand, all the operations,
routine and otherwise, could be handled from one central data base. The lowest-
level data contains the mass of detail that is needed for operations such as send-
ing purchase orders to suppliers or preparing work tickets for the shop floor. Some
of this information will be made available for level 2 inquiries, for example, assisting a purchasing officer to select suppliers or a marketing manager to make
decisions about his customer base.

What is much less clear is what is needed for level 3. What information
should be in a data base designed for top management or their staff? It will be

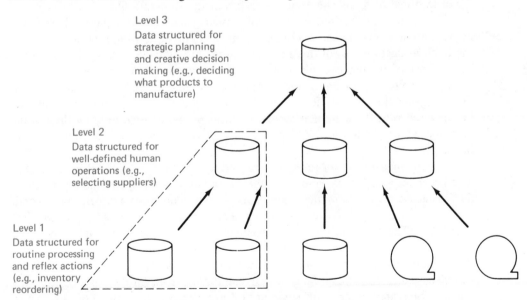

Figure 24.1   Summary information may pass from the lower-level data
bases which are designed for routine operations to the higher-level
data bases which are designed for nonroutine questions. In some functional areas data bases for the different levels may be combined, for
example, those inside the dashed line.

seen that the information systems illustrated in Chapter 20, in Fig. 20.10, do not include a data base for top management. They are information systems for managers of functional areas. In reality most so-called "management information systems" in operation today are of this type. Most attempts to build level 3 data bases have succeeded in answering only a very small proportion of top management's questions. Part of the reason is that there are an almost infinite number of possible questions, and the answering of most of them which are answerable requires complex programs.

It is this inability to define the information needs of top management that has led critics to dismiss the concept of top management information systems as unworkable.

The simpleminded idea of leaving a pool of relevant data items, in which management can go fishing, has proven to be of little value. Top management needs the data processed in some way. They need information, not raw data. Some attempts to provide this have resulted in producing summaries of operational or financial data. Cash flow, profit-and-loss figures, and costing summaries can be maintained automatically on a continuing basis. Financial models of corporations have been programmed, with which the effect of different financial decisions can be tested. Top management and their aides, however, are often not contented with the summary information that has been predigested for them. Sometimes they want to fish in the more detailed data base; they want the fresh fish of the operational files, not the deep-frozen fish of the summary files.

The nature of the information which management may request differs enormously. Some items are easy to obtain from the computing files, such as "Give me the total production cost of this product." Some are difficult, such as "What would be the cost of having two models instead of one model of this product?" The questions which top management is interested in tend to be the difficult ones. In many organizations today the majority of top management questions, if they can be answered with the computer system at all, can be answered only by the writing of a special program for the purpose, possibly using a data-base interrogation language.

Top management can rarely be induced to use its own terminal with success. The lower levels of management, on the other hand, employ terminals very effectively because their information requirements, first, tend to be simpler, and second, tend to be of the type that can be anticipated; hence programs are ready to deal with them. The lower levels of management, such as production managers, store managers, office managers, and so forth, more frequently need operations systems rather than general-purpose management information systems.

Top executives doing the same job can differ greatly in their information demands. Some are content with summary information. Some want to drop down to use level 2 (Fig. 24.2). Some ask for a degree of detail that can be found only in the operational files (level 1 of Fig. 24.2).

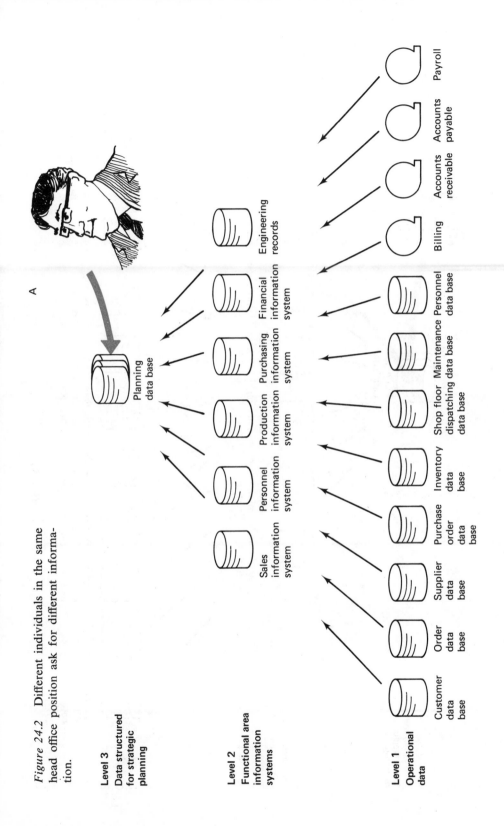

Figure 24.2 Different individuals in the same head office position ask for different information.

Level 3
Data structured for strategic planning

Planning data base

Level 2
Functional area information systems

Sales information system

Personnel information system

Production information system

Purchasing information system

Financial information system

Engineering records

Level 1
Operational data

Customer data base

Order data base

Supplier data base

Purchase order data base

Inventory data base

Shop floor dispatching data base

Maintenance data base

Personnel data base

Billing

Accounts receivable

Accounts payable

Payroll

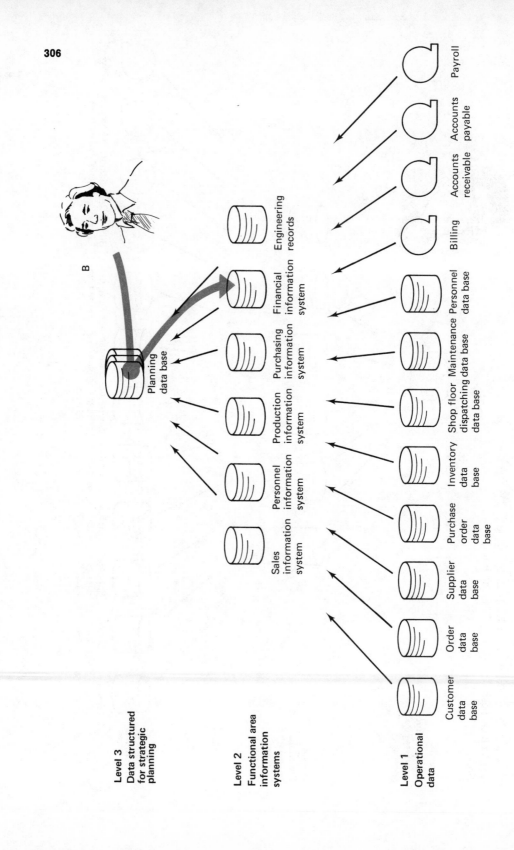

Level 3
Data structured for strategic planning

Level 2
Functional area information systems

Level 1
Operational data

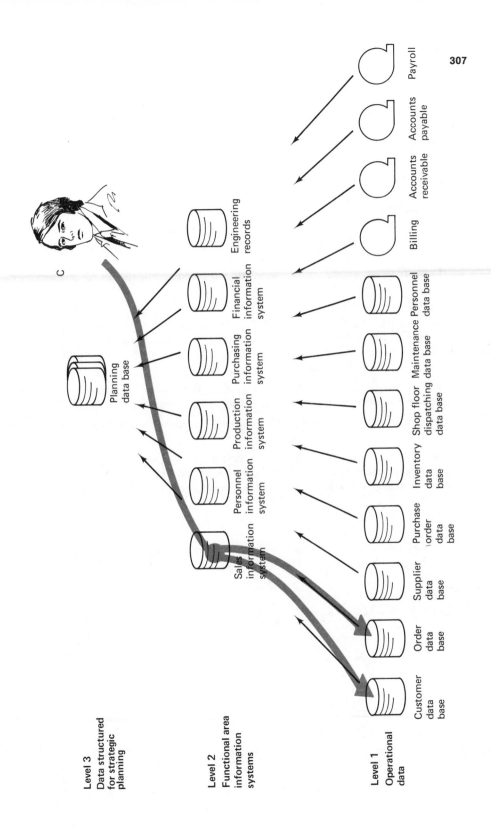

Level 3
Data structured
for strategic
planning

Level 2
Functional area
information
systems

Level 1
Operational
data

Engineering
records

Financial
information
system

Purchasing
information
system

Production
information
system

Personnel
information
system

Sales
information
system

Planning
data base

Personnel
data base

Maintenance
data base

Shop floor
dispatching
data base

Inventory
data
base

Purchase
order
data
base

Supplier
data
base

Order
data
base

Customer
data
base

Billing

Accounts
receivable

Accounts
payable

Payroll

Figure 24.2 shows differences in the style of operating of different executives or head office staff. Individual A is content with the planning data base that has been created. Individual B is concerned almost exclusively with financial information. He uses the financial information in the level 3 data base but usually needs the greater detail of the level 2 financial information system. Individual C is an ex-salesman, and this causes him to ask questions about sales and customers which need level 1 data. He never uses the level 3 data base.

Unfortunately for the systems analysts, when a new man fills a top-level post the demands for information often change completely. Several comments can therefore be made about an information system for top management:

1. The staffs which provide information for top management should have access to all the different data bases. Terminals to all the different systems should be installed in one head office location (Fig. 24.3).

2. That location should be staffed with information specialists who know the nature of the various data-base subsystems and understand how to extract information from them. As we commented in Chapter 23, a high-level information system needs the intelligence of a skilled librarian.

3. Insofar as possible the various terminal dialogues should be similar in their structures so that one person can become expert using all of them.

4. The various data bases should be constructed using the same data description language.

5. The data-base management system or systems used should make available a data-base interrogation language of a comprehensive nature, so that unanticipated but complex requests can be dealt with fairly quickly.

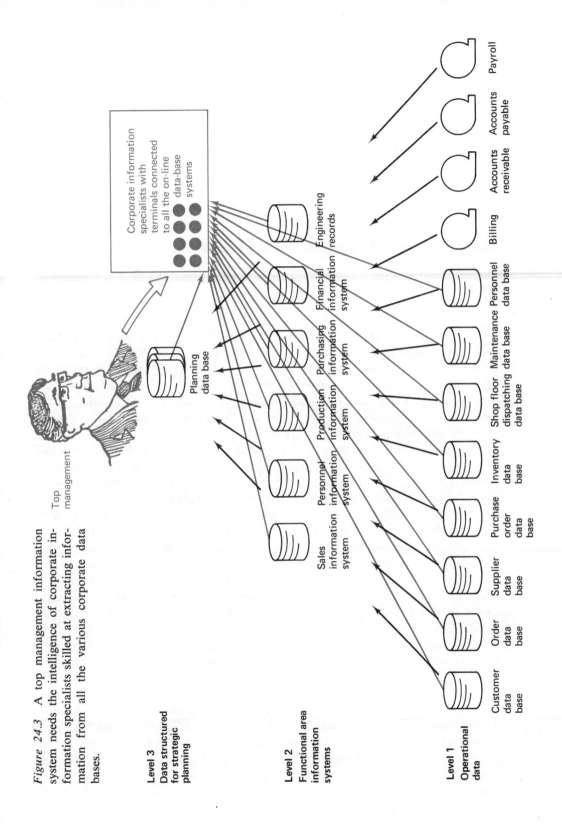

Figure 24.3 A top management information system needs the intelligence of corporate information specialists skilled at extracting information from all the various corporate data bases.

Top management

Level 3
Data structured for strategic planning

Planning data base

Corporate information specialists with terminals connected to all the on-line data-base systems

Level 2
Functional area information systems

Sales information system

Personnel information system

Production information system

Purchasing information system

Financial information system

Engineering records

Level 1
Operational data

Customer data base

Order data base

Supplier data base

Purchase order data base

Inventory data base

Shop floor dispatching data base

Maintenance data base

Personnel data base

Billing

Accounts receivable

Accounts payable

Payroll

25 RESISTANCE TO RATIONAL SYSTEMS

Organizations are designed to be rational. If they were truly rational, then data bases and information systems could fit into them smoothly like parts of a machine. In practice, however, the individuals who comprise an organization do not make their decisions like parts of a rational mechanism. They each have their own ambitions, fears, fantasies, and emotions, and managements in different organizations tend to have their own "style." Consequently, there exist perverse forms of resistance to rationality.

The reaction to computers is often irrational. Sometimes there is overt resistance; sometimes the resistance is hidden but strongly felt, waiting to manifest itself when the opportunity arises—and it arises often in a corporation groping toward information systems for management. Often an individual's resistance is subconscious, with fear of losing a job, being made a fool of, or not being able to adapt. Occasionally, the irrational reaction favors the machine, with computers or MIS being idolized or inappropriately grasped as a magical way out of current dilemmas.

A large number of executives voice objections to computers and to data-processing personnel. There are certainly valid reasons for complaint. Many mistakes have been made, and the horror stories are numerous. However, mistakes can be corrected and do not warrant a blanket condemnation of the future of computing. The executives who condemn computers so emotionally often have deep subconscious reasons for their objections. As with the comments of a patient on a psychiatrist's couch, the reasons a person states verbally are often far from the real reasons. The real reasons are hidden, deep-seated, and powerful; cannot be indefinitely repressed; and will make themselves felt time and time again.

An executive is right to speak up about misuses of computers—it is his duty. In this chapter we are concerned with resistance not to *misuses* of machines but to uses which would in reality improve the functioning of the corporation. It is desirable that systems analysts and managers trying to introduce corporate-wide data bases should appreciate the hidden reasons for resistance.

MODES OF
POLITICAL BEHAVIOR

The first cause of the difficulty is that the relation-ship between managers and departments is far more complex than the organization chart would indicate, and the information which passes between them is not governed by straightforward rules. This is especially so in old or large corporations where managers have long since learned that in order to survive, or be promoted, certain modes of political behavior are necessary and care is needed in handling most types of information. Executives in bureaucratic organizations have a long and successful education in how to protect themselves and their departments. Computerized information systems threaten to wreck the carefully cultivated patterns.

In many organizations the education in bureaucratic survival teaches managers to hide or manipulate much information. It teaches deceit, rivalry, and mistrust. Elaborate cover-ups become a way of life. Much information is prevented from reaching other departments or higher levels of management, and much communication of information is deliberately delayed, distorted, or funneled through certain channels. It is not surprising that the image of a corporate data base or "management information system," making information freely available to higher management, is a cause for alarm. Just as computerized inventory systems revealed the chaotic state of the stores, so advanced data-base systems may reveal to top management how much has been hidden from them.

TOO RAPID
INFORMATION
TRANSFER

With a powerful information system, information can pass very rapidly up the chain of command. In the Viet Nam war the American field commanders reportedly expressed much concern at certain times because the Pentagon and even the President were becoming involved in decisions which should have been theirs. With some corporate systems higher management similarly becomes involved and may not know all the facts. Data which should have been the concern of a department manager have been seen by *his* manager *first*. The data are collected at their source, are processed in real-time, and are then available at the display screens of the system. The department manager does not have the time buffer that he had before, during which he could chew over the situation, find out the reasons for anything that was wrong, put it right, think up excuses, devise policy suggestions, or hide the facts. In other systems a manager's performance has been analyzed by his boss using the computer, and the first view he has seen of the analysis figures was when he was called into the boss's office to justify them.

A shop floor foreman was responsible for scheduling the sequence of work under his control. He knew everything that was taking place in his area, and people outside his area knew only what the foreman chose to tell them. With computers, each worker enters details of the status of his operations into a work station terminal. Such information passes immediately to a computer where it is correlated. The foreman has lost part of his control. When management wants to argue about the scheduling of a certain job, they can go first to the computer terminals or information room staff.

Similar arguments apply from the top to the bottom of a computerized corporation. Managers, who have been used to retaining control over information about the work they are responsible for, lose the ability to withhold, delay, or manipulate the information. It passes into the all-too-accessible data bases far too quickly for them.

FEAR OF FUTURE POTENTIAL   In many cases it is not so much what a computer can do today that causes the fear of computers but the potential, vividly expressed but not yet accomplished, of what a real-time information system will *eventually* do. There will be nowhere to hide. A manager's mistakes will be highly visible. Decisions which are less than optimal may be analyzed and questioned. A manager who has learned the multitude of tricks necessary for making his forecasts and budgets into self-fulfilling prophecies may be confronted with all manner of interference. When he exceeds his quota, or is well within his budget, he cannot save some of the excess for next time like a squirrel. He may have much more difficulty in setting a budget or quota which he knows he can meet because he now has to argue with staffs who have access to the information system. He had many little secrets which he could use in times of difficulty, and he fears that an all-pervading data base might prevent use of these, making everything too precise and too open. Managers who have relied on hiding the full facts in order to increase their chances of political survival fear that a computerized information system will pull the rug out from under them.

INTERDEPARTMENTAL RIVALRY   Many organizations foster a high level of competitiveness between departments and between managers. In many ways this is healthy. It keeps managers on their toes and helps to ensure that they make the best possible demands on *their* management. However, in such an environment managers tend to build walls around their domains to protect them from other departments, and tend to be secretive about information.

Antony Jay, in his book *Management and Machiavelli* [43], compares corporate department heads to the barons of medieval England. England, like other countries, was frequently torn by interbaronial rivalries and jealousies even when there were great dangers threatening, or great opportunities beckoning, from overseas. The internal strife, says Jay, should be no surprise to those familiar with large corporations. Few employees of large corporations would be so naive as to say "After all, we're all part of the same company, aren't we? Why can't we all work together instead of wasting our time on these internal wrangles?" The employees understand the strength of the interbaronial rivalries. The barons, when permitted, would build superbly strong castles. Periodically the kings used to find it necessary to knock down some of the castles. The bricks and mortar that corporate barons build their castles with, in Jay's analogy, are *withheld information* and *unreferred decisions*.

The designer of corporate data bases tries to cut through such internal boundaries and often attempts to do so in a highly naive fashion. Unless he has the full support of the king he is unlikely to succeed. He attempts to combine freely data from different departments in order to give the most efficient or most useful data-base structure. The same data items go to work for different departments. Interdepartmental withholding of data has no place in the designer's scheme for maximizing the value of the data. In his view the maximum *cooperation* is needed. He sees corporate politics as a barrier to efficient systems design, which has to be overcome. In some corporations the barons, who are divided on everything else, have united on the fact that the MIS designer is a menace. Fortunately for them, he needs a long time to bring his plans to fruition, and he is unlikely to survive that long. Top executives who want an information system must be prepared to wield their power over the barons.

FEAR OF PERSONAL
INADEQUACY
Most men feel nervous about the nature of their jobs being changed, but often a new job demands the same types of abilities as the old and they feel reasonably sure that it will only be a matter of time before they have mastered it. A machine tool operator can learn to operate a new machine tool even if it uses a high level of automation. A scientist can learn a new field of research and will probably enjoy doing so. But a manager confronted with the spread of computerized decision making often feels decidedly apprehensive because he simply cannot understand what the operations research staff is talking about. Nobody has explained "integer programming" or "regression analysis" to him; he has forgotten all but the simplest of his mathematics; he simply does not know how to judge the validity of the output of a computer model. He once went to a one-day course on management science, but he cannot relate what was said to his own job and cannot understand the mess of symbols in the notes that were handed out. He doubts whether he will ever understand. He may not even want to understand. When he talks to the accountants or lawyers his management skill enables him to extract the essence from what they are saying, ask the right questions, and make judgments about the value of their advice. Not so with the operations research staff. He tries to ask the right questions but somehow seems to receive responses which are both condescending and as difficult to make judgments about as the pronouncements which triggered the questions.

INCOMPREHENSIBILITY   A high-level manager once asked the author to sit in on a meeting, as a personal favor, in which the senior OR man was going to present the conclusions of a year's work. The manager pleaded, "I know I won't be able to understand what the hell he's talking about. I'd like you to listen to it and explain to me whether it makes sense and how far it would be sensible to go with it." The bearded OR man came in with flip charts. He spent the first half hour explaining in child-like terms how one function of the corporation operated. The manager listened with tactful patience, suppressing his growing irritation at being told information which he thought everybody knew. The OR man then switched his presentation to a mathematical analysis of the operations. His charts had partially unlabeled axes, his symbols were inadequately explained, and the purpose of his mathematics was not made clear. Only a person already familiar with the techniques in question could have followed what he was saying. The lecture ended with no clear proposal for action, and the manager said "Well, what do you want us to do?." This triggered another burst of unclear mathematics which was cut short after 10 minutes by the manager saying he did not understand and the OR man reverting to the child's guide to how the company operates.

It was difficult to be sure whether the OR man had subconscious motives for being obscure, but there was virtually no chance at the end of the afternoon that the manager *could* have made a confident decision about how best to proceed. He appealed for help afterwards: "It's always like that. Did you understand what he was talking about? . . . Why can't he give a straightforward answer to my questions?"

It is not surprising that such managers produce an irrational reaction to rational systems. On the surface their reaction may be annoyance that the management scientist cannot express his views more clearly, but beneath the surface there is a fear of making decisions with the basis for the decisions unclearly understood. Worse—much worse—there is a horror that the management skills they have so arduously acquired may be inadequate in a world of computers and mathematics.

To some extent the executives in a highly computerized corporation do need skills and talents different from those required before computers. The type of person best suited to decision making with computers is often unlikely to have risen through the ranks of conventional management. Conventional managers are often skilled at using intuition for judging situations and make much use of past experience, but experimentation with computer models or dialogue with an information system is foreign to both their temperament and intellect. Instinctively conventional management dislikes and distrusts the machine and seeks more familiar modes of operating.

THINKERS AND
THUMPERS

The majority of decision makers in corporations tend to be at one or the other end of a scale; they tend to be organizers—men of action with little contemplation—or to be creative men with little organizing ability. One colleague refers to them as "thinkers" and "thumpers." The thinker may be found in the research department or on the corporate planning staff. Sometimes he is the brain behind many aspects of the computer systems. He is bored with routine administration and cannot organize anything. His secretary has to organize him. However, his ideas are often brilliant and his knowledge formidable. Sometimes he has a keen vision of the future and how the corporation must change over the years ahead. The thumper, on the other hand, may never have had an idea in his life, but he can give orders and make sure they are obeyed. He can make a department shipshape and efficient and can motivate men to work well. He can see that accounts and documentation are kept efficiently. When men or organizations fail to perform well, he thumps the table. His world is one of routine. Often he has little respect for the intellectual. To him the thinker is a necessary evil, and perhaps not even all that necessary. The thumper finds no satisfaction in contemplation of things that could be done or methods that could be used.

The thumpers form the backbones of corporations because of the vast amount of routine work which has to be done. Put in charge of a department the thinker would be a catastrophe, and the thumper knows it. On the other hand, the thumper is incapable of questioning the need for his own department. He will perpetuate it, make it grow, and fight with other departments for the resources he wants. He has little idea about future directions if they are different from the present. He steers the course he has been given, or if he is not given a course, he charges straight ahead. If there is disaster ahead, he will run straight into it.

Now, with the spread of computing, the thumper fears that his world may be eroded. His actions are being monitored on terminals. He is receiving detailed instructions from computers. He fears that the thinker will be telling him how to thump.

A psychological need of the thumper is his feeling of wielding power. Computerized decision making tends to deemphasize the use of personal power. A decision is implemented because it is the computed optimum, not because it is so-and-so's decision. Many managers fear that computerization will reduce their ability to give orders simply because the computers have been given power. The thumper has become familiar with "shaking the place up," "turning the joint around," "rattling the cage," "tightening the screw." His magical ability to obtain results has often resulted from the sloppiness of current practices or the lack of adequate measurements or data. The more the operation comes under the tight surveillance of on-line data-base systems, the less the scope for the aggressive manager to produce dramatic improvements.

Increasingly what is needed as computer-related methods spread is an effective combination of the thumper and thinker. The person who can organize and motivate men will always be essential, but in an increasing number of situations he will have to understand the capabilities of the computer and carry on terminal dialogues. Few people are pure thinker or pure thumper. Most thumpers have some ability to think, and most thinkers have some ability to thump. However, the person who does both well is rare. Most people tend to be primarily one or the other.

What makes the grafting of the two species especially important is that the thinker and the thumper have serious difficulties in communicating with one another. The thinkers need to be led by other thinkers and have little respect for the leadership of the thumpers. The thumpers need equally strong thumpers to control them. The person who is primarily thumper has an emotional horror of the invasion of his domain by the management scientists and data-base designers. He usually has to make a show of embracing them, but they should not be deluded by the smile with which they are received. They are in hostile territory. They need their wits about them if they are to survive.

POWER AND FREEDOM
In some areas a major effect of computers is likely to be that they can automate those parts of jobs which were easy for man but cannot touch the parts which were difficult. Where this is true they increase the overall difficulty man has in doing his work. This is seen in many walks of life in the steady spread of complexity that the modern world is bringing. Paradoxically it is not necessarily bad for the individual concerned. His job may become more difficult, but it also becomes more interesting, more stimulating, and more fulfilling. The easy parts of his job were the dull parts, and it is now possible to dream of a world in which dull jobs are done by machines and interesting jobs are done by humans. Unfortunately, we are some way from this world as yet.

A less fortunate aspect of computerization occurs where it is possible to automate those parts of a man's job that give him a feeling of power, achievement, or responsibility.

It is interesting to reflect upon the reasons men in corporations seek power. No doubt some of them do it for the sheer enjoyment of exercising naked power. Except in a few extreme cases, however, this is probably not the main reason. Some want power in order to achieve objectives they believe in. Probably the major reason, however, stems from the need for *freedom*. The more power they have, the freer they are to take the actions they want—the freer they are to control their environment. Freedom of action is a basic need of capable men. How many of the younger capable men in a corporation do you hear saying that they want to be their own boss? They would like to leave the organization and work for themselves, or they want to be left free to see a job through in their own way. It has become a cliché of youth that they want to "do their own thing." They are asking for freedom.

Computers used in some of the ways we have described can decrease the freedom of action of junior or middle management, and for some men this can be exceedingly frustrating. Information is collected in real-time and computers are involved in decision making. The data-base system can centralize many of the important decisions. Many decisions are taken out of the hands of the local managers. If a local manager wants to alter a plan, he may not be able to do so. He may make a request for a change and have a new plan given him by the computer. An advanced computer system may create a very unattractive environment for the local decision maker.

Chris Argyris, Professor of Administrative Sciences at Yale, has studied the effects of computers on middle management [44] and concludes that they can be similar to the effects of job specialization on lower-level employees.

> A young man can start working on an assembly line with a rather high degree of commitment. But he learns very soon that if he maintained that commitment, he could go mad. So he begins to withdraw psychologically. And as he withdraws certain things begin to happen: He no longer cares about the quality of the work as he used to; he also begins to see himself as a less responsible human being.

Confronted with computers making the decisions, Argyris claims, many middle managers also lose much of the commitment.

> Daily goals are defined for (the manager), the actions to achieve those goals are specified; his level of aspiration is determined for him; and his performance is evaluated by a system over which he has no influence.
>
> These conditions may lead managers to perform as expected. However, they will also lead to a sense of psychological failure. Those managers who aspire toward challenging work with self-responsibility will be frustrated; those who prefer less challenge will be satisfied. The former may leave, fight, or psychologically withdraw; the latter usually stay and also withdraw. In short, the manager, because of information systems, will experience frustrations that his employees once experienced when quality control engineers first designed their work and monitored their performance.
>
> Middle managers feel increasingly hemmed in. In pschological langauge, they will experience a great restriction of their space of free movement, resulting in feelings of lack of choice, pressure, psychological failure. These feelings in turn can lead to increasing feelings of helplessness and decreasing feelings of responsibility. Result: a tendency to withdraw or to become dependent upon those who created or approved the restriction of space of free movement.

Some managers fear a future when their corporation has the totally comprehensive data-base system they have read about. If a manager does not use the computer terminals, he will be fired. If he does use them, he will be psychologically fired because he will feel useless. There will be no scope for initiative. "If he follows the new rationality, he will succeed as a manager and fail as a human being." It is not surprising that he resists the spread of integrated data-base systems.

MANAGEMENT STYLE Many managers do not think in these terms but instead have the confidence to believe in the natural superiority of their own methods. They have their own *style* of managing, and if any technique comes along which is incompatible with that style, it will be largely ignored. Often the style of managing is cultivated by the corporation. It is a corporate style rather than an individual style, but the individual, in order to succeed, has assimilated the style completely.

If the general manager says "I will not have a boob-tube in my office," then the systems analyst may have no hope of persuading any of top management to have a terminal. If certain types of decisions are made by committees, it may be next to impossible to have them made by computer models. Management may have unshakable faith in the superiority of their own intuitive decisions. This is their style, and woe betide any computer specialist who challenges it.

It can be extremely frustrating, and indeed baffling, for a management scientist to find that after working for five years on a financial model of the corporation, top management ignores it and continues to make financial decisions in the same intuitive way. This has happened and will go on happening because many top managers, especially older ones, have unshakable faith in their own style of decision making (usually borne out by past success).

The specialist in computerized information systems has many problems in environments such as those described. He is often fairly young and a newcomer in the organization. He may enter the organization near the top without being attuned to its social customs and undercurrents. He may not lunch in the executive dining room, or may seem out of place if he does. The older managers usually think he is overpaid. The system designers and management scientists often seem arrogant, naive, and lacking in understanding of the management style. Often they fail to understand the subconscious reasons for resistance to systems which would undoubtedly help the corporation.

A very high level of interpersonal competence is needed if the ways of a large organization are to be changed.

26 EPILOGUE: HOW TO SUCCEED

We have made a variety of comments throughout the book about decisions in data-base implementation that are likely to lead to success or otherwise. Box 26.1 summarizes major requirements for success and lists causes of failure or disappointment.

BOX 26.1 Reasons for Long-Term Data-Base Successes and Failures

Reasons for Success	*Reasons for Failure or Disappointment*
• Top management understanding and support of the objectives, and determination to make the data bases a valuable corporate resource.	• Dissenting political factions who prevent the integration which can maximize the value of data.
• Concentration on well-specified, profitable uses of the data bases.	• Overselling "Management Information Systems" (especially MIS for top management).
• Development of data bases which relate to corporate subjects, rather than computer applications.	
• A planned step-by-step buildup of applications of the subject data bases, with each step being suitably small and easy.	• Plans for the installation of a grandiose all-embracing system.

BOX 26.1—*Cont.*

Reasons for Success	*Reasons for Failure or Disappointment*
• Corporate-wide planning by a high-level competent data administrator.	• Fragmented plans by noncommunicating groups.
• Conversion planning that permits the old non-data-base programs to coexist with the new. This requires well-tested conversion programs which create the data files required by the old programs.	• Inadequate attention to coexistence of the old and new; attempts to rewrite too many old programs.
• All persons are thoroughly educated at a level appropriate to their function.	• Lack of understanding of database principles or implementation requirements.
• Tight technical control by the data-base administrators.	• Inadequate CPU power or main memory. Failure to estimate response times or maximum throughput. Failure to monitor usage and performance. Failure to select appropriate physical data structures.
• Adoption of a corporate-wide data description language. (The software will change while the schema data descriptions remain the same.)	• Use of multiple separate incompatible data-base management systems.
• Adoption of proven state-of-the-art software with both logical and physical data independence.	• Writing your own data-base management facilities or modifying existing software. (In the long run this is usually a disaster.)
• Thorough end-user involvement in the data-base design.	• Ill-defined user requirements.
• Employment by end users of a powerful easy-to-use data-base interrogation language.	

BOX 26.1—*Cont.*

Reasons for Success	*Reasons for Failure or Disappointment*
• Recognition of the vital nature of a data dictionary and system library. —Naming standards —Update control —Version synchronization	• Casual approach to library control.
• Program specifications containing full details of types and sequences of data-base accesses, thoroughly reviewed with structured "walk-throughs" with the data-base administrator present.	
	• Lack of a comprehensive system testing plan including the testing of compatibility with the surviving old applications.
	• Inadequate controls on data accuracy or quality.
	• Inadequate security or embezzlement controls.
• "Keep it simple."	• Excessive complexity. Confused thinking.
• Careful selection of the first data-base project. The first project should be chosen to maximize the chances of success, and to act as a seed project used to develop expertise (see Box 26.2).	
• An appropriate mix of centralized standardization and guidance, and decentralized implementation (e.g., split as in Fig. 20.15).	• Lack of centralized guidance leading to a proliferation of incompatible systems.
• Technical management has a business orientation.	• Excessive centralized control by a group out of touch with the reality of local operations and problems.

A particularly important step is the first data-base project. This needs to be *seen* to be a success if the data-base road is going to be pursued whole-heartedly. The first project should therefore be one that is *likely* to succeed. It needs to be simple, yet profitable in its own right. The early projects should be employed as a training ground for developing the expertise that is required on subsequent projects. Box 26.2 summarizes features of the first project that are likely to lead to success.

Eventually most major corporations will have comprehensive data-base systems. The road to this goal, however, is a long one, illustrated in Fig. 26.1. At the far end of the road, better software and hardware is required than is available today. The computer industry needs to produce a "search engine," powerful data-base interrogation capabilities, and effective software for distributed data bases.

Corporations and other organizations embarking on this road have a long way to travel, and the sooner they put an appropriate infrastructure into place the better.

BOX 26.2   The First Project is Critical to the Acceptance of the Data-Base Route and Needs to be Seen to Succeed

Reasons for Success on the First Project	*Reasons for Failure or Disappointment*
• A worthwhile profitable new project with its own "bottom-line" payoff. Project visibility.	• Replacement of an existing system without adding new function. (All this will prove is that data-base systems are more expensive.)
• A relatively simple project, e.g.; 3 CODASYL sets or 2 DL/I physical data bases 10 programs 2 disk packs 10 terminals No complex data structures	• A complex or grandiose beginning.
• Management commitment to future data-base use.	• The project is approached in a skeptical "evaluation" mode.

BOX 26.2—*Cont.*

Reasons for Success on the First Project	*Reasons for Failure or Disappointment*
• A strong technically competent project leader who is respected above and below.	
• Proven bug-free software likely to be of lasting importance.	• The latest software wonder.
• Very thorough education of the individuals involved.	
• A project without a critical deadline.	• Inadequate manpower or too short a schedule.
• Less than 12 hours on-line per day.	• On-line 24 hours per day.
• Thorough assessment of the hardware requirements.	• Inadequate CPU power, main memory, or access speed.
• Data bases with a high potential for sharing with other applications in the future.	
• Careful design and thorough testing of conversion aids.	• A high degree of interaction with other current applications.
• Thorough attention to detail.	• The solving of problems put off for later.
• Very thorough system testing and training of user groups.	

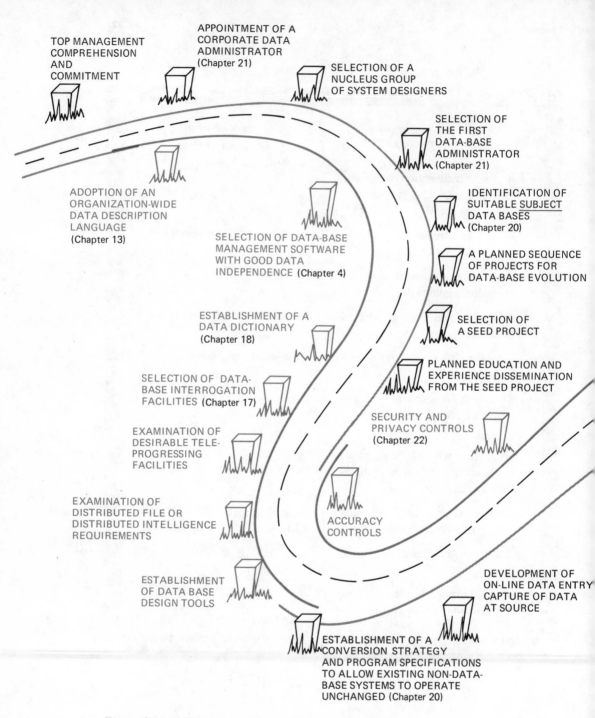

Figure 26.1 Milestones on the road to a comprehensive information system.

INFORMATION
QUALITY
CONTROLS
(Chapter 23)

PLANNED INTERRELATION
OF GEOGRAPHICALLY
SEPARATE DATA BASES
(Chapter 12)

EXTENSION OF
DATA COMMUNICATIONS
NETWORK

PLANNED USE OF
DISTRIBUTED
FACILITIES

ADOPTION BY USER GROUPS
OF DATA-BASE INTERROGATION
LANGUAGES (Chapter 17)

IMPROVEMENT
OF DATA
SEARCHING
CAPABILITIES
(Chapter 11)

DEVELOPMENT
OF FUNCTIONAL
INFORMATION
SYSTEMS
(Chapter 6)

ON-LINE FACILITIES PERMITTING
NON-PROGRAMMERS TO SEARCH
AND MANIPULATE THE DATA
(Chapter 17)

DEVELOPMENT
OF ON-LINE
OPERATIONS
SYSTEMS
(Chapter 6)

USE OF PROGRAM
AND DIALOGUE
GENERATORS TO
AVOID APPLICATION
PROGRAMMING

AIDS FOR DATA-
BASE MONITORING
AND PERFORMANCE
IMPROVEMENT

DEVELOPMENT OF A
SEARCH ENGINE

IMPLEMENTATION OF A
DISTRIBUTED DATA-BASE
NETWORK (Chapter 12)

AUTOMATED
DATA-BASE
ORGANIZATION

GLOSSARY

ACCESS. The operation of seeking, reading, or writing data on a storage unit.

ACCESS MECHANISM. A mechanism for moving one or more reading and writing heads to the position at which certain data are to be read or written. Alternatively the data medium may be moved to the read/write station.

ACCESS METHOD. A technique for moving data between a computer and its peripheral devices, e.g. serial access, random access, remote access, virtual sequential access method (VSAM), hierarchical indexed sequential access method (HISAM).

ACCESS TIME. The time that elapses between an instruction being given to access some data and that data becoming available for use.

ACTIVITY RATIO. The fraction of records in a file or data set, which have activity (are updated or inspected) in a given period or during a given run.

ADDRESS. An identification (number, name, label) for a location in which data is stored.

ADDRESSING. The means of assigning data to storage locations, and subsequently retrieving them, on the basis of the key of the data.

ALGORITHM. A computational procedure.

ALTERNATE TRACK. A track which is automatically substituted for a damaged track on a disk or other storage device.

ANTICIPATORY STAGING. Blocks of data are moved from one storage device to another device with a shorter access time, in anticipation of their being needed by the computer programs. This is to be contrasted with demand staging in which the blocks of data are moved *when* programs request them, not *before*.

AREA (CODASYL). A named sub-division of the addressable storage space in the data base which may contain occurrences of records and sets or parts of sets of various types. Areas may be opened by a run-unit with *usage modes* which permit, or do not permit, concurrent run-units to open the same area. An area may be declared in the schema to be a *temporary area*. The effect of this is to provide a different occurrence of the temporary area to each run-unit opening it and at the termination of the run-unit, the storage space involved becomes available for re-use.

ASSEMBLE To convert a routine coded in non-machine language into actual machine language instructions.
   To perform some or all of the following functions: (1) translation of symbolic operation codes into machine codes; (2) allocation of storage, to the extent at least of assigning storage locations to successive instructions; (3) computation of absolute or relocatable addresses from symbolic addresses; (4) insertion of library routines; (5) generation of sequences of symbolic instructions by the insertion of specific parameters into macro instructions.

ASSOCIATIVE STORAGE (MEMORY). Storage which is addressed by content rather than by location, thus providing a fast way to search for data having certain contents. (Conventional storage had addresses related to the physical location of the data.)

ATTRIBUTE. A field containing information about an entity.

AVAILABILITY. A measure of the capability of a system to be used for performing its intended function, as a result of the system's being in an operating state.

BINARY SEARCH. A method of searching a sequenced table or file. The procedure involves selecting the upper or lower half based upon an examination of its midpoint value. The selected portion is then similarly halved, and so on until the required item is found.

BLOCKING. The combining of two or more records so that they are jointly read or written by one machine instruction.

BUCKET. An area of storage which may contain more than one record and which is referred to as a whole by some addressing technique.

BUFFER. An area of storage which holds data temporarily while it is being received, transmitted, read or written. It is often used to compensate for differences in speed or timing of devices. Buffers are used in terminals, peripheral devices, storage units and in the CPU.

CANONICAL SCHEMA. A model of data which represents the inherent structure of that data and hence is independent of individual applications of the data and also of the software or hardware mechanisms which are employed in representing and using the data.

CATALOG. A directory of all files available to the computer.

CELL. Contiguous storage locations referred to as a group in an addressing or file searching scheme. The cell may be such that it does not cross mechanical boundaries in the storage unit; for example it could be a track or cylinder.

CELLULAR CHAINS. Chains which are not permitted to cross cell boundaries.

CELLULAR MULTILIST. A form of multilist organization (q. v.) in which the chains cannot extend across cell boundaries.

CELLULAR SPLITTING. A technique for handling records added to a file. The records are organized into cells and a cell is split into two cells when it becomes full.

CHAIN. An organization in which records or other items of data are strung together by means of pointers.

CHANNEL. A subsystem for input to and output from the computer. Data from storage units, for example, flows into the computer via a channel.

CHECKPOINT/RESTART. A means of restarting a program at some point other than the beginning, used after a failure or interruption has occurred. Checkpoints may be used at intervals throughout an application program; at these points records are written giving enough information about the status of the program to permit its being restarted at that point.

CIRCULAR FILE. An organization for a file of high volatility, in which new records being added replace the oldest records.

CODASYL. Conference of Data Description Languages. The organization that specified the programming language COBOL. It has now specified a set of manufacturer-independent, application-independent languages designed to form the basis of data-base management.

COMPACTION. A technique for reducing the number of bits in data without destroying any information content.

COMPILER. A computer program which in addition to performing the functions of an assembler has the following characteristics: (1) it makes use of information on the overall logical structure of the program to improve the efficiency of the resulting machine program; (2) its language does not parallel the actual form of the machine language, but is rather oriented toward convenient problem or procedure statement; (3) it usually generates more than one machine instruction for each symbolic instruction.

CONCATENATE. To link together. A *concatenated data set* is a collection of logically connected data sets. A *concatenated key* is composed of more than one field.

CONCEPTUAL MODEL. Conceptual schema (q.v.).

CONCEPTUAL SCHEMA. The overall logical structure of a data base. Schema (q.v.).

CORE STORAGE. A high-speed random-access memory consisting of many ferro-magnetic toroids (cores) strung on wires in matrix arrays. The term is now used loosely to mean the main memory of a computer even though that computer may employ a more advanced memory technology than magnetic cores.

CYLINDER. A concept of storage: that area of storage which can be read without the movement of an access mechanism. The term originated with disk files, in which a cylinder consisted of one track on each disk surface such that each of these tracks could have a read/write head positioned over it simultaneously.

DASD. Direct-Access Storage Device.

DATA ADMINISTRATOR. An individual with an overview of an organization's data.

DATA AGGREGATE (CODASYL definition). A named collection of data-items within a record. There are two types: vectors and repeating groups. A vector is a one-dimensional, ordered collection of data-items, all of which have identical characteristics. A repeating group is a collection of data that occurs an arbitrary number of times within a record occurrence. The collection may consist of data-items, vectors, and repeating groups.

DATA BANK. A collection of data relating to a given set of subjects.

DATA BASE.
(1) A collecton of interrelated data stored together with controlled redundancy to serve one or more applications; the data are stored so that they are independent of programs which use the data; a common and controlled approach is used in adding new data and in modifying and retrieving existing data within a data base. A system is said to contain a collection of data bases if they are disjoint in structure.
(2) CODASYL definition: A DATA BASE consists of all the record occurrences, set occurrences and areas which are controlled by a specific schema. If an installation has multiple data bases, there must be a separate schema for each data base. Furthermore, the content of different data bases is assumed to be disjoint.

DATA-BASE ADMINISTRATOR. An individual with an overview of one or more data bases, who controls the design and use of these data bases.

DATA-BASE MANAGEMENT SYSTEM. The collection of software required for using a data base.

DATA DESCRIPTION LANGUAGE. A language for describing data (in some software for describing the logical, not the physical, data; in other software for both).

DATA DICTIONARY. A catalogue of all data types giving their names and structures.

DATA DIVISION *(COBOL)*. That division of a COBOL program which consists of entries used to define the nature and characteristics of the data to be processed by the object program.

DATA ELEMENT. Synonymous with DATA ITEM (q.v.) or FIELD.

DATA INDEPENDENCE. The property of being able to change the overall logical or physical structure of the data without changing the application program's view of the data.

DATA INDEPENDENCE, LOGICAL. The property of being able to change the overall logical structure of the data base (schema) without changing the application program's view of the data.

DATA INDEPENDENCE, PHYSICAL. The property of being able to change the physical structure of the data without changing the logical structure.

DATA ITEM. The smallest unit of data that has meaning in describing information; the smallest unit of named data. Synonymous with DATA ELEMENT or FIELD.

DATA MANAGEMENT. A general term that collectively describes those functions of the system that provide creation of and access to stored data, enforce data storage conventions, and regulate the use of input/output devices.

DATA MANIPULATION LANGUAGE. The language which the programmer uses to cause data to be transferred between his program and the data base.

    The data manipulation language is not a complete language by itself. It relies on a host programming language to provide a framework for it and to provide the procedural capabilities required to manipulate data.

DATA SET. A named collection of logically related data items, arranged in a prescribed manner, and described by control information to which the programming system has access.

DBDC. Data base/data communications.

DEMAND STAGING. Blocks of data are moved from one storage device to another device with a shorter access time, when programs request them and they are not already in the faster-access storage. Contrast with ANTICIPATORY STAGING (q.v.).

DEVICE/MEDIA CONTROL LANGUAGE. A language for specifying the physical layout and organization of data.

DIALOGUE. A generic word for a preplanned man-machine interaction; it encompasses formal programming languages, languages for interrogating data bases, and innumerable non-formal conversational interchanges, many of which are designed for one specific application.

DICTIONARY. See DATA DICTIONARY.

DIRECT ACCESS. Retrieval or storage of data by a reference to its location on a volume, rather than relative to the previously retrieved or stored data.

DIRECT-ACCESS STORAGE DEVICE (DASD). A data storage unit on which data can be accessed directly at random without having to progress through a serial file such as tape. A disk unit is a direct-access storage device.

DIRECTORY. A table giving the relationships between items of data. Sometimes a table (index) giving the addresses of data.

DISTRIBUTED FREE SPACE. Space left empty at intervals in a data layout to permit the possible insertion of new data.

DL/I. IBM's Data Language/I, for describing logical and physical data structures.

DOMAIN. The collection of data items (fields) of the same type, in a relation (flat file).

DYNAMIC STORAGE ALLOCATION. The allocation of storage space to a procedure based on the instantaneous or actual demand for storage space by that procedure, rather than allocating storage space to a procedure based on its anticipated or predicted demand.

EMBEDDED POINTERS. Pointers in the data records rather than in a directory.

ENTITY. Something about which data is recorded.

ENTITY IDENTIFIER. A key which uniquely identifies an entity or data concerning that entity.

EXTENT. A contiguous area of data storage.

EXTERNAL SCHEMA. A user's or programmer's view of the data. Subschema (q.v.).

FIELD. See DATA ITEM.

FILE. A set of similarly constructed records.

FLAT FILE. A 2-dimensional array of data items.

FUNCTIONAL DEPENDENCE. Attribute B of a relation R is functionally dependent on attribute A or R if, at every instant in time, each value of A has no more than one value of B associated with it in relation R. (Equivalent to saying that A identifies B).

An attribute or collection of attributes, B, of a relation, R, is said to be *fully functionally dependent* on another collection of attributes, A, of R, if B is functionally dependent on the whole of A but not on any subset of A.

HASH TOTAL. A meaningless total of the values of a certain field in a file, maintained for control purposes to ensure that no items are lost or changed invalidly.

HASHING. A direct addressing technique in which the key is converted to a pseudo-random number from which the required address is derived.

HEADER RECORD OR HEADER TABLE. A record containing common, constant, or identifying, information for a group of records which follows.

HEURISTIC. Pertaining to trial-and-error methods of obtaining solutions to problems.

HIERARCHICAL FILE. A file in which some records are subordinate to others in a tree structure.

HIERARCHICAL STORAGE. Storage units linked together to form a storage subsystem, in which some are fast but small and others are large but slow. Blocks of data are moved from the large slow levels to the small fast levels when required.

HIT RATE. A measure of the number of records in a file which are expected to be accessed in a given run. Usually expressed as a percentage:

$$\frac{Number\ of\ input\ transactions \times 100\%}{Number\ of\ records\ in\ the\ file}$$

HOME ADDRESS. (1) A storage location (e.g., a home bucket) into which a data record is logically assigned; as opposed to overflow address. (2) A field that contains the physical address of a track, recorded at the beginning of a track.

HUFFMAN CODE. A code for data compaction in which frequently used characters are encoded with a smaller number of bits than infrequently used characters.

INDEPENDENCE, DATA. See DATA INDEPENDENCE.

INDEPENDENCE, DEVICE. Data organization which is independent of the device on which the data is stored.

INDEX. A table used to determine the location of a record.

INDEX CHAINS. Chains within an index.

INDEX POINT. A hardware reference mark on a disk or drum; used for timing purposes.

INDEX, SECONDARY. See SECONDARY INDEX.

INDEXED-SEQUENTIAL STORAGE. A file structure in which records are stored in ascending sequence by key. Indices showing the highest key on a cylinder/track/ bucket, etc., are used for the selected retrieval of records.

INDICATIVE DATA. Data that identifies or describes; e.g., in a stock file, the product number, description, pack size. Normally, indicative data does not change on a regular, frequent basis during processing (as in, for example, an account balance).

INDIRECT ADDRESSING. Any method of specifying or locating a storage location whereby the key (of itself or through calculation) does not represent an address. For example, locating an address through indices.

INFORMATION SYSTEM. Contrasted with OPERATING SYSTEM, to mean a system in which the data stored will be used in spontaneous ways which are not fully predictable in advance for obtaining information.

INTERNAL SCHEMA. The physical structure of the data.

INTERPRETIVE ROUTINE. A routine which decodes instructions written as pseudo-codes and immediately executes those instructions, as contrasted with a compiler which decodes the pseudo-codes and produces a machine-language routine to be executed at a later time.

INTERSECTION DATA. Data which is associated with the conjunction of two segments (or other data groupings) but which has no meaning if associated with only one of the two segments.

INVERTED FILE. A file structure which permits fast spontaneous searching for previous unspecified information. Independent lists or indices are maintained in records keys which are accessible according to the values of specific fields.

INVERTED LIST. A list organized by a secondary key (q.v.) not a primary key.

ISAM. Index sequential access method (IBM).

KEY. A data item used to identify or locate a record (or other data grouping).

KEY COMPRESSION. A technique for reducing the number of bits in keys; used in making indices occupy less space.

KEY, PRIMARY. A key which uniquely identifies a record (or other data grouping).

KEY, SECONDARY. A key which does not uniquely identify a record, i.e., more than one record can have the same key value. A key which contains the value of an attribute (data item) other than the unique identifier.

LABEL. A set of symbols used to identify or describe an item, record, message, or file. Occasionally it may be the same as the address in storage.

LATENCY. The time taken for a storage location to reach the read/write heads on a rotating surface. For general timing purposes, average latency is used; this is the time taken by one half-revolution of the surface.

LFU. Least frequently used. A replacement algorithm in which when new data has to replace existing data in an area of storage, the least frequently used items are replaced.

LIBRARY.
(1) The room in which volumes (tapes and diskpacks) are stored.
(2) An organized collection of programs, source statements, or object modules, maintained on a direct-access device accessible by the operating system.

LIST. An ordered set of data items. A chain.

LOGICAL. An adjective describing the form of data organization, hardware, or system that is perceived by an application program, programmer, or user; it may be different to the real (physical) form.

LOGICAL DATA BASE. A data base as perceived by its users; it may be structured differently from the physical data-base structure. In IBM's Data Language/I, a logical data base is a tree-structured collection of segments derived from one or more physical data bases by means of pointer linkages.

LOGICAL DATA-BASE DESCRIPTION. A schema. A description of the overall data-base structure as perceived for the users, which is employed by the data-base management software.

LOGICAL FILE. A file as perceived by an application program; it may be in a completely different form from that in which it is stored on the storage units.

LRU. Least recently used. A replacement algorithm in which when new data has to replace existing data in an area of storage, the least recently used items are replaced.

LVIEW. A user's view of data. Subschema (q.v.).

MACHINE-INDEPENDENT. An adjective used to indicate that a procedure or a program is conceived, organized, or oriented without specific reference to the system. Use of this adjective usually implies that the procedure or program is oriented or organized in terms of the logical nature of the problem or processing, rather than in terms of the characteristics of the machine used in handling it.

MACROINSTRUCTION. One line of source program code which generates a program routine rather than one program instruction.

MAINTENANCE OF A FILE. Periodic re-organization of a file to better accommodate items that have been added or deleted.

MANAGEMENT, DATA BASE. See DATA BASE MANAGEMENT SYSTEM.

MAPPING. A definition of the way records are associated with one another.

MIGRATION. Frequently used items of data are moved to areas of storage where they are more rapidly accessible; infrequently used items are moved to areas which are less rapidly accessible and possibly less expensive.

MODEL. The logical structure of the data. Schema (q.v.).

MODULE. The section of storage hardware which holds one volume, such as one spindle of disks.

MULTILIST ORGANIZATION. A chained file organization in which the chains are divided into fragments in each fragment indexed, to permit faster searching.

MULTIPLE-KEY RETRIEVAL. Retrieval which requires searches of data based on the values of several key fields (some or all of which are secondary keys).

NETWORK STRUCTURE. See PLEX STRUCTURE.

NORMAL FORM, FIRST. Data in flat file form.

NORMAL FORM, SECOND. A relation R is in second normal form if it is in first normal form and every nonprime attribute of R is fully functionally dependent (q.v.) on each candidate key of R (E. F. Codd's definition).

NORMAL FORM, THIRD. A relation R is in third normal form if it is in second normal form and every nonprime attribute of R is nontransitively dependent on each candidate key of R (E. F. Codd's definition).

NORMALIZATION. The decomposition of more complex data structures into flat files (relations). This forms the basis of relational data bases.

ON-LINE. An on-line system is one in which the input data enter the computer directly from their point of origin and/or output data are transmitted directly to where they are used. The intermediate stages such as punching data, writing tape, loading disks, or off-line printing are avoided.

ON-LINE STORAGE. Storage devices, and especially the storage media which they contain, under the direct control of a computing system, not off-line or in a volume library.

OPERATING SYSTEM. Software which enables a computer to supervise its own operations, automatically calling in programs, routines, language, and data, as needed for continuous throughput of different types of jobs.

OVERFLOW. The condition when a record (or segment) cannot be stored in its *home address*; i.e., the storage location logically assigned to it on loading. It may be stored in a special OVERFLOW LOCATION, or in the home address of other records.

PAGE FAULT. A program interruption that occurs when a page which is referred to is not in main memory and has to be read in.

PAGING. In virtual storage systems, the technique of making memory appear larger than it is by transferring blocks (pages) of data or programs into that memory from external storage when they are needed.

PARALLEL DATA ORGANIZATIONS. Organizations which permit multiple access arms to search, read, or write, data simultaneously.

PHYSICAL. An adjective, contrasted with LOGICAL (q.v.), which refers to the form in which data or systems exist in reality. Data is often converted by software from the form in which it is *physically* stored to a form in which a user or programmer perceives it.

PHYSICAL DATA BASE. A data base in the form in which it is stored on the storage media, including pointers or other means of interconnecting it. Multiple logical data bases may be derived from one or more physical data bases.

PHYSICAL RECORD. A collection of bits that are physically recorded on the storage medium and which are read or written by one machine input/output instruction.

PLEX STRUCTURE. A relationship between records (or other groupings) in which a child record can have more than one parent record. Also called NETWORK STRUCTURE.

POINTER. The address of a record (or other data groupings) contained in another record so that a program may access the former record when it has retrieved the latter record. The address can be absolute, relative, or symbolic, and hence the pointer is referred to as absolute, relative, or symbolic.

PRIMARY KEY. See KEY, PRIMARY.

PROGRESSIVE OVERFLOW. A method of handling overflow in a randomly stored file which does not require the use of pointers. An overflow record is stored in the first available space and is retrieved by a forward serial search from the home address.

PURGE DATE. The date on or after which a storage area is available to be overwritten. Used in conjunction with a file label, it is a means of protecting file data until an agreed release date is reached.

RANDOM ACCESS. To obtain data directly from any storage location regardless of its position with respect to the previously referenced information. Also called DIRECT ACCESS.

RANDOM ACCESS STORAGE. A storage technique in which the time required to obtain information is independent of the location of the information most recently obtained. This strict definition must be qualified by the observation that we usually mean relatively random. Thus, magnetic drums are relatively non-random access when compared to magnetic cores for main memory, but relatively random access when compared to magnetic tapes for file storage.

RANDOMIZING. An old word for HASHING (q.v.).

REAL TIME.
(1) Pertaining to actual time during which a physical process transpires.
(2) Pertaining to the performance of a computation during the actual time that the related physical process transpires in order that results of the computation can be used in guiding the physical process.
(3) Pertaining to an application in which response to input is fast enough to effect subsequent input, as when conducting the dialogues that take place at terminals on interactive systems.

RECORD.
(1) A group of related fields of information treated as a unit by an application program.

(2) CODASYL definition: A named collection of zero, one or more data-items or data-aggregates. There may be an arbitrary number of occurrences in the data base of each record type specified in the schema for that data base. For example, there would be one occurrence of the record type PAYROLL-RECORD for each employee. This distinction between the actual occurrences of a record and the type of the record is an important one.

(3) IBM's DL/I terminology: A logical data-base record consists of a named hierarchy (tree) of related segments. There may be one or more segment types, each of which may have a different length and format.

RELATION. A flat file. A two-dimensional array of data elements. A file in normalized form.

RELATIONAL ALGEBRA. A language providing a set of operators for manipulating relations.

RELATIONAL CALCULUS. A language in which the user states the results he requires from manipulating a relational data base.

RELATIONAL DATA BASE. A data base made up of relations (as defined above). Its data-base management system has the capability to recombine the data elements to form different relations thus giving great flexibility in the usage of data.

RING STRUCTURE. Data organized with chains such that the end of the chain points to its beginning, thus forming a ring.

ROOT. The base node of a tree structure. Data in the tree may be accessed starting at its root.

SCHEMA.
(1) A map of the overall logical structure of a data base.
(2) CODASYL definition: A SCHEMA consists of DDL (Data Description Language) entries and is a complete description of all of the area, set occurrences, record occurrences and associated data-items and data-aggregates as they exist in the data base.

SCHEMA LANGUAGE. Logical data-base description language.

SEARCH. To examine a series of items for any that have a desired property or properties.

SECONDARY INDEX. An index composed of secondary keys rather than primary keys.

SECONDARY KEY. See KEY, SECONDARY.

SECONDARY STORAGE. Storage facilities forming not an integral part of the computer but directly linked to and controlled by the computer, e.g., disks, magnetic tapes, etc.

SECTOR. The smallest address portion of storage on some disk and drum storage units.

SEEK. To position the access mechanism of a direct-access storage device at a specified location.

SEEK TIME. The time taken to execute a SEEK operation.

SEGMENT. A named fixed-format quantum of data containing one or more fields. A segment is the basic quantum of data which is passed to and from the application programs when IBM Data Language/I is used.

SENSITIVITY. A programmer may view only certain of the data in a logical data base. His program is said to be *sensitized* to that data.

SEQUENCE SET INDEX. The lowest level in a tree-structured index. The entries in this level are in sequence. Searches and other operations may be carried out in the sequence set index; those are called SEQUENCE SET OPERATIONS.

SEQUENTIAL PROCESSING. Accessing records in ascending sequence by key; the next record accessed will have the next higher key, irrespective of its physical position in the file.

SERIAL-ACCESS STORAGE. Storage in which records must be read serially one after the other, e.g. tape.

SERIAL PROCESSING. Accessing records in their physical sequence. The next record accessed will be the record in the next physical-position/location in the field.

SET (CODASYL definition). A SET is a named collection of record types. As such, it establishes the characteristics of an arbitrary number of occurrences of the named set. Each set type specified in the schema must have one record type declared as its OWNER and one or more record types declared as its MEMBER records. Each occurrence of a set must contain one occurrence of its owner record and may contain an arbitrary number of occurrences of each of its member record types.

SET, SINGULAR. A CODASYL set without owner records; the owner is declared to be "SYSTEM." A singular set is used to provide simple nonhierarchical files such as a file of customer records.

SKIP-SEARCHED CHAIN. A chain having pointers which permit it to be searched by skipping, not examining every link in the chain.

SORT. Arrange a file in sequence by a specified key.

STAGING. Blocks of data are moved from one storage device to another with a shorter access time, either before or at the time they are needed.

STORAGE HIERARCHY. Storage units linked together to form a storage subsystem, in which some are fast but small and others are large but slow. Blocks of data are moved (STAGED) from the large slow levels to the small fast levels as required.

SUBMODEL. A user's or programmer's views of the data. Subschema (q.v.).

SUBSCHEMA. A map of a programmer's view of the data he uses. It is derived from the global logical view of the data—the schema. Also called LVIEW, and external schema.

TABLE. A collection of data suitable for quick reference, each item being uniquely identified either by a label or by its relative position.

TERABIT STORAGE. Storage which can hold 10^{12} bits of data.

THIRD NORMAL FORM. A record, segment, or tuple which is normalized (i.e., contains no repeating groups) and in which every nonprime data item is nontransitively dependent and fully dependent on each candidate key.

In other words: the *entire* primary key or candidate key is needed to identify each other data item in the tuple and no data item is identified by a data item which is not in the primary key or candidate key.

TRACK. The circular recording surface transcribed by a read/write head on a drum, disk, or other rotating mechanism.

TRANSACTION. An input record applied to an established file. The input record describes some "event" that will either cause a new file record to be generated, an existing record to be changed, or an existing record to be deleted.

TRANSFER RATE. A measure of the speed with which data is moved between a direct-access device and the central processor. Usually expressed as thousands of characters per second or thousands of bytes per second).

TRANSPARENT DATA. Complexities in the data structure are hidden from the programmers or users (made transparent to them) by the software.

TREE INDEX. An index in the form of a tree structure.

TREE STRUCTURE. A hierarchy of groups of data such that
1. the highest level in the hierarchy has only one group, called a *root*;
2. all groups except the root are related to one and only one group on a higher level than themselves.

A simple master/detail file is a two-level tree. Also called a HIERARCHICAL structure.

TUPLE. A group of related fields. *N* related fields are called an *N*-tuple.

VIRTUAL. Conceptual or appearing to be, rather than actually being. An adjective which implies that data, structures, or hardware, appear to the application programmer or user to be different to what they are in reality, the conversion being performed by software.

VIRTUAL MEMORY. Memory which can appear to the programs to be larger than it really is because blocks of data or program are rapidly moved to or from secondary storage when needed.

VOLATILE FILE. A file with a high rate of additions and deletions.

VOLATILE STORAGE. Storage which loses its contents when the power supply is cut off. Solid-state (LSI) storage is volatile; magnetic storage is not.

VOLUME. Demountable tapes, disks, and cartridges are referred to as *volumes*. The word also refers to a nondemountable disk or other storage medium. It has been defined as "that portion of a single unit of storage medium which is accessible to a single read/write mechanism"; however, some devices exist in which a volume is accessible with two or more read/write mechanisms.

VOLUME TABLE OF CONTENTS (VTOC). A table associated with a volume which describes each file or data set on the volume.

VSAM. Virtual sequential access method, an IBM volume independent indexed sequential access method.

VTOC. See Volume Table of Contents.

WORKING STORAGE. A portion of storage, usually computer main memory, reserved for the temporary results of operations.

WRITE. To record information on a storage device.

REFERENCES

1. The CODASYL Committee is attempting to provide industry-wide machine-independent data-base definitions and languages, with the intention that they become an industry standard. *DBTG Data Description Language* and *DBTG Data Manipulation Language*, reports of the CODASYL Data Base Task Group, May, 1973, published by the ACM, New York, and IFIP Data Processing Group, Amsterdam.

2. From an internal IBM description of its common manufacturing information system.

3. For a discussion of the desirability and usefulness of different response times, see J. Martin, *Design of Man-Computer Dialogues*, Prentice-Hall, Inc., 1973, Englewood Cliffs, N. J., Chapter 18.

4. Richard L. Nolan, "Computer Data Bases: The Future is Now," *Harvard Business Review* (Sept–Oct. 1973).

5. From a systems study for the state of Arkansas prepared by the Information Systems Planning Staff of the Office of the Information Systems Executive Committee, State of Arkansas, 1974.

6. This comment is clarified in the discussion of physical data structures in J. Martin, *Computer Data-Base Organization*, Prentice-Hall, Inc., Englewood Cliffs, N. J., 1975.

7. This example is taken from a systems study for a local government property data base conducted by ISCOL at the University of Lancaster, England, 1973.

8. E. F. Codd, "A Relational Model of Data for Large Shared Data Banks," *Comm. ACM.* 13 (June 6, 1970), 377–387.

9. E. F. Codd, "Further Normalization of the Data Base Relational Model," *Courant Computer Science Symposia*, 6, "Data Base Systems," New York University, published by Prentice-Hall, Inc., Englewood Cliffs, N. J., 1972.

10. E. F. Codd, "Relational Completeness of Data Base Sublanguages," Courant Computer Science Symposia, 6, "Data Base Systems," New York University, published by Prentice-Hall, Inc., Englewood Cliffs, N. J., 1972.

11. E. F. Codd, "A Data Base Sublanguage Founded on the Relational Calculus," *Proc. 1971 ACM-SIGFIDET Workshop on Data Description, Access and Control*, available from ACM Headquarters, New York, 1972.

12. J. Martin, *Computer Data-Base Organization*, Prentice-Hall, Inc., Englewood Cliffs, N. J., 1975, Chapter 36.

13. *Ibid.*, Chapter 26–30.

14. *Guide Michelin, France* (red guide), published each year by Pneu Michelin, Services de Tourisme, 97 Boulevard Pereine, Paris 17^e.

15. J. Martin, *Design of Man-Computer Dialogues*, Prentice-Hall, Inc., Englewood Cliffs, N. J., 1973.

16. Five papers describing the ARPA network appear in the *Proceedings of the Spring Joint Computer Conference, 1970*, AFIPS Press, Montvale, N. J., 1970:

    (a) L. Roberts, "Computer Network Development to Achieve Resource Sharing."

    (b) F. Heart, R. Kahn, S. Ornstein, W. Crowther, and D. Walden, "The Interface Message Processor for the ARPA Computer Network."

    (c) L. Kleinrock "Analytic and Simulation Methods in Computer Network Design."

    (d) H. Frank, I. Frisch, and W. Chou, "Topological Considerations in the Design of the ARPA Network."

    (e) S. Carr, S. Crocker, and V. Cerf, "HOST–HOST Communication Protocol in the ARPA Network."

17. National Bureau of Standards Handbook 113, *CODASYL Data Description Language Journal of Development*. U. S. Department of Commerce, National Bureau of Standards, Washington, D. C., 1974.

18. R. W. Engles, "An Analysis of the April 1971 Data Base Task Group Report," *Proc. ACM SIGFIDET Workshop on Data Description, Access and Control, 1971.*

19. *Data Language/I—System/370 DOS/VS, General Information Manual GH20–1246*, IBM, White Plains, N. Y., 1974.

20. *Information Management System Virtual Storage (IMS/VS) General Information Manual GH20–1260*, IBM, White Plains, N. Y., 1974.

21. *Information Management System/360, Version 2, Application Programming Reference Manual SH20–0912*, IBM, White Plains, N. Y., 1974.

22. *Information Management System/360, Version 2, System Programming Reference Manual SH20–0911*, IBM, White Plains, N. Y., 1974.

23. *Interactive Query Facility (IQF) for IMS/360 Version 2, General Information Manual GH20–1074*, IBM, White Plains, N. Y., 1974.

24. Manuals and information on the MARK IV File Management System are available from Informatics Inc., MARK IV Systems Company, 21050 Vanowen St., Canoga Park, Calif. 91303.

25. GIS and IQF manuals are available from IBM Corp., 1133 Westchester Ave., White Plains, N. Y. 10604.

26. *IQF General Information Manual, GH20–1074* IBM Corp., White Plains, N. Y.

27. This example is taken from an IBM slide presentation on GIS/VS, *No. GV20–0480*, Nov. 1973.

28. J. Martin, *Design of Man-Computer Dialogues*, Prentice-Hall, Englewood Cliffs, N. J., 1973.

29. *IMS Dictionary System*, IBM manuals LB21–1257 and SB21–1256, IBM Corp., Field Developed Programs, 11141 Georgia Avenue, Wheaton, Md. 20902.

30. Oscar Niemeyer, the chief architect of Brazilia, writing in *Brazil*, Thames and Hudson, London, 1971.

31. R. C. Canning, "The Cautious Path to a Data Base," *EDP Analyzer*, II, No. 6 (June 1973).

32. Richard L. Nolan, "Computer Data Bases: The Future is Now," *Harvard Business Review*, p. 101 (Sept.–Oct. 1973). (The rest of Mr. Nolan's article is excellent!)

33. *Ibid.*, p. 105.

34. *The Data Base Administrator*, a report prepared by members of the Data Base Administration Project of the Information Management Group of GUIDE, Nov. 1972.

35. *Establishment of a Data Base Administration Function*, SHARE document SSD #246, 1974, SHARE Inc., 25 Broadway, Suits 750, New York, N. Y. 10004 .

36. *The Data Administrator: Catalyst for Corporate Change*, prepared by members of the Data Administration Project, GUIDE International, New York, 1975.

37. J. Martin, *Security, Accuracy and Privacy in Computer Systems*, Prentice-Hall, Inc., Englewood Cliffs, N. J., 1973, Section II.

38. *Ibid.*, Chapter 7.

39. Colonel T. B. Mancinelli, "Management Information Systems: The Trouble With Them," *Computers and Automation* (July 1972).

40. J. Dearden, "Myth of Real-Time Management Information," *Harvard Business Review* (May–June 1966).

41. J. Dearden, "MIS is a Mirage," *Harvard Business Review* (Jan.–Feb. 1972).

42. M. K. Evans and L. R. Hague, "Master Plan for Information Systems," *Harvard Business Review* (Jan.–Feb. 1962).

43. A. Jay, *Management and Machiavelli*, Holt, Rinehart and Winston, Inc., New York, 1968.

44. C. Argyris, "Resistance to Rational Management Systems," *Innovation* (Feb. 1970).

INDEX